D1563182

THE AGE OF SATURN

Frontispiece   A melancholic Saturn as an old king, with spade and sceptre,
in his zodiacal houses of Capricorn and Aquarius.

THE AGE OF SATURN

Literature and History
in the *Canterbury Tales*

Peter Brown
Andrew Butcher

BASIL BLACKWELL

First published 1991

Basil Blackwell Ltd
108 Cowley Road, Oxford, OX4 1 JF, UK

Basil Blackwell, Inc.
3 Cambridge Center
Cambridge, Massachusetts 02142, USA

British Library Cataloguing in Publication Data
A CIP catalogue record for this book is available from the British Library.

Library of Congress Cataloging in Publication Data
Brown, Peter, 1948–
    The age of Saturn: literature and history in the Canterbury tales/Peter Brown, Andrew Butcher.
        p.   cm.
    Includes bibliographical references and index.
    ISBN 0-631-15351-9 (hardback)
    1. Chaucer, Geoffrey, d. 1400. Canterbury tales. 2. Chaucer, Geoffrey, d. 1400 – Political and social views. 3. Chaucer, Geoffrey, d. 1400 – Knowledge – Occultism. 4. Literature and society – England – History. 5. Saturn (Planet) in literature. 6. Social history in literature. 7. Zodiac in literature. I. Butcher, Andrew (Andrew F.) II. Title.
PR1875. S63B76   1991
821′. 1 – dc20
                                                                    90-39268
                                                                          CIP

Typeset in 11 on 13 pt Garamond 156
by Graphicraft Typesetters Ltd., Hong Kong
Printed in Great Britain by T. J. Press Ltd, Padstow, Cornwall

Contents

Note on the Illustrations

The illustrations in this book have two key functions: each is used, in the conventional way, to amplify a point made in our argument; but they also constitute an argument in their own right about the pervasiveness in the *Canterbury Tales* of a range of imagery which influenced deeply Chaucer's perceptions of contemporary crisis.

The majority of the illustrations feature Saturn and his effects. As such they exemplify a type of astrological picture well known in the later Middle Ages, 'the planet and his children'. Each planet is represented as a human figure with distinguishing emblems, together with the zodiac signs in which that planet is particularly powerful. Below, the human activities over which the god has dominion are shown in a series of 'vignettes' juxtaposed in a more or less complex way. Other illustrations depict Saturn with zodiac signs but without the 'children', or other aspects of Saturn's history or qualities. The one illustration outside of Saturnian iconography is that of the fool.

Saturnine images occur with greatest frequency in the Knight's Tale, but all of the works under discussion (with the possible exception of the Wife of Bath's Prologue and Tale) locate part of their meaning in an image directly connected with Saturn's rule. There would therefore appear to be, on Chaucer's part, an attempt to use the images of Saturn and his children as a system designed to explain a range of disturbing events such as imprisonment, revolt, sudden death, and certain psychological states, particularly that of melancholy. The extent to which Chaucer represented contemporary experience by this means justifies its name as 'the age of Saturn'.

List of Illustrations

Acknowledgements

Without the stimulus of teaching the *Canterbury Tales*, and of discussing our ideas with students and colleagues, this book could not have been written: to them and to others who have taken a close interest in its development, particularly Stephan Chambers at Blackwell and Derek Pearsall at Harvard University, we are especially grateful. Staff at the British Library and Bodleian Library have been unfailingly helpful, as have the staff at the University of Kent Library, whose courtesies extend beyond the call of duty. The Colyer-Fergusson Charitable Trust, administered by the Faculty of Humanities at the University of Kent, made a generous contribution towards the cost of the illustrations. Gill Hogarth and Sue Macdonald, typists extraordinaire, have displayed exceptional skill, patience and discretion in dealing with two beleaguered authors. Finally, Helen and Mary have done more than they realize to realize this book.

For Matthew, who asked
the right questions.

Abbreviations

Apoc.   Apocalypse
Ecclus   Ecclesiasticus
EETS es   Early English Text Society, original series
EETS os   Early English Text Society, extra series
FrankT   Franklin's Tale
GP   General Prologue
HF   *House of Fame*
MED   *Middle English Dictionary* (ed. Kurath, Kuhn et al. 1954–)
OED   *Oxford English Dictionary*
PardT   Pardoner's Tale
ParsT   Parson's Tale
PMLA   *Publications of the Modern Language Association of America*
Ret.   Chaucer's Retraction
TC   *Troilus and Criseyde*

Introduction

This book is intended as a contribution to an enterprise which has been under way for many years, one which has gathered momentum during the 1980s: the reintegration of Chaucer's writings with the social and political life of the later fourteenth century.

TRADITIONAL APPROACHES

To read the *Canterbury Tales* is to confront the distant past. Simply to hold a printed copy of Chaucer's work is to testify to the differences between a print culture, in which the authoritative edition is widely available, and a manuscript culture, in which different versions were known, often orally, to relatively small audiences. The very extensiveness of the glossary, from *abaissen* to *yore*, is an indication of the gap which separates us from the terms and ideas current 600 years ago. Or again, 'that dry and intolerable chitinous murmur of footnotes' (Jameson 1981: 34) is a persistent reminder that other, non-literary, forms of life inhabit the text.

What kind of response is appropriate to the work of a poet whose culture is at best half familiar and half alien, whose society is both a direct ancestor of our own and so radically different? Clearly, to read Chaucer with the intention of attaining the fullest possible understanding is self-consciously to enter into the nature of historical contexts and the processes of change. But what are these contexts and processes?

The traditional apparatus of scholarship, of the sort exemplified in the standard edition, presumes that the historical processes which impinge on the *Canterbury Tales* are, by their nature, diachronic, positivist, evolutionist and determinist. In these respects such scholarship bears the mark of its origins in a later eighteenth-century romanticism for which the collecting, identifying and legitimizing of literary texts was part of a nationalist project (Aarsleff 1985; Patterson 1987: ix), and of its subsequent need to win institutional respectability. According to the conventions, the scholar's persona is that of an objective, impersonal and unemotional collector of data which are then interpreted according to pseudo-scientific laws. Thus the definition of a word is arrived at by tracing it to its origins in Latin or Old French, and by providing examples of usage chronologically arranged (usually from literary sources). If the text should refer to events or people for which there is separate documentation, then this information, or 'external evidence', is provided in subsidiary form in the introduction or annotation. Arcane ideas and customs are dealt with in similar ways, with appropriate references to the work of other scholars. The validity of the text itself is established according to a genetic arrangement of the known manuscripts, which are examined according to the ancillary disciplines of palaeography, codicology, dialectology, orthography and the like.

Although the text, created by an editor, hedged with variant readings and fringed with introduction, notes and glossary, is the paradigm of traditional literary scholarship, the same historical attitudes are evident in critical work as well. Literary history of the orthodox type arranges its material in chronological sequence, itemizes and quantifies the output of the writers concerned, provides some evaluation of relative merit, and plots the influence of one writer on another. The realist fiction thus created is of a discrete world of literary events, peopled by writers of greater or lesser stature, under the control of an omniscient scholar-author. A refined and particular version of such narratives is the literary biography. Source study might also be cited as a critical practice which endorses similar principles. In all such endeavours the work, or its author, is the central phenomenon, rather like the prize exhibit in a museum, with other related specimens identified in neighbouring cabinets. One such cabinet might bear the title 'historical background' and would iterate the main events and themes of the period covered by the author's life – famine, plague, revolt, war, dynasties – with perfunctory reference to his works.

At its worst the traditional approach to Chaucer through history is antiquarian, accumulating information for its curiosity value, and stifling in its suggestion that the text can only be properly understood with the benefit of a vast and specialized extraneous knowledge. Yet for all its pretence of historicizing literature the underlying assumptions are that history and literature are separate categories; that literature is a suitable case for treatment according to the unquestioned terms of positivist enquiry; and that a literary text is satisfactorily explained when such a process is complete.

However unsatisfactory the received approach may seem, to dismiss it out of hand as redundant in the light of modern strategies is arrogant and pointless, hypocritical and plain wrong-headed. Arrogant and pointless, because traditional scholarship has provided the very tools without which most present-day students of Chaucer could not proceed. Anyone writing on Chaucer today owes an enormous debt to the painstaking and dedicated labours represented, for example, by the Chaucer *Concordance* (Tatlock and Kennedy 1927), the *Chaucer Life-Records* (ed. Crow and Olson 1966), Robinson's edition of Chaucer's *Works* (ed. Benson et al. 1987), the *Sources and Analogues* (ed. Bryan and Dempster 1941), the *Middle English Dictionary* (ed. Kurath, Kuhn, et al. 1954–) and the *Chaucer Variorum* (ed. Ruggiers and Baker 1979–). Hypocritical, not only because of one's unavoidable dependence on such pillars of scholarship, but also because critical discourse itself, in order to remain intelligible, and as the present introduction illustrates, cannot avoid a structure and a voice which bear the hallmarks of its inheritance: the material is ordered in temporal sequence; that sequence is linked according to certain assumptions about influence, cause and effect; and an appeal is made to the reader's rational faculties by presenting and evaluating evidence in a way that avoids the appearance of subjectivity.

It is wrong-headed, because traditional scholarship continues to form the foundation upon which innovative approaches to the historical nature of Chaucer's writing are built. *The Allegory of Love* (Lewis

1936) is a classic instance of how the orthodox 'background' approach can be developed into a contextual study of a medieval system of ideas and feelings which (however much one might dispute the existence of 'courtly love') is thoroughly integrated with an interpretation of Chaucer's poetry. *Chaucer and the Imagery of Narrative* (Kolve 1984) is a more recent example of an excursion into the history of ideas and into iconographic representation which, when brought to bear on Chaucer's poetry, yields some challenging new interpretations both of meaning and of methods of composition. The author of *Chaucer's Language and the Philosopher's Tradition* considers in great detail the usage of just a few words, and invokes the principle of 'contemporary language architecture' (Burnley 1979: 3) to refine the possibilities of meaning (and hence of modern interpretation) available to Chaucer and his audience at a particular time. Even the Chaucer canon itself is not a settled issue: differences continue to be aired about the authenticity of the Canon's Yeoman's Prologue and Tale (ed. Blake 1980: 3–13) and of *The Equatorie of the Planets* (North 1988: 169–81). Needless to say, opposing scholars deploy the full arsenal of linguistic, palaeographic and codicological armaments.

NEW APPROACHES

Traditional scholarship, then, is a going concern. It flourishes and, whatever the drawbacks of its methods, it remains an indispensable historical approach to the study of Chaucer. In view of its past achievements and persistent success in promoting new interpretations its continued existence ought to be a source of celebration rather than despair. But it is only of limited use in promoting a closer relationship between the *Canterbury Tales* and its milieu, as early attempts demonstrated. Daiches (1938), concerned with identifying a practical and useful function for literature within the social machine, was flummoxed by Chaucer. In his view Chaucer, being a literary genius, dispensed with the particularities of social life in order to universalize human experience. Unlike Langland he was not directly responsive to contemporary social forces, and instead adopted the posture of a 'tolerant ironist', standing apart to look at the failings of humanity 'half sad, half amused' (p. 63).

Writing two years later, Loomis took issue with the prevailing view of 'Chaucer's bland unconcern with the great issues of his day' (R. Loomis 1940: 131) and argued instead that, adept though Chaucer may have been at not taking sides, the historical evidence indicates that he could hardly have avoided being *au fait* with the controversies which surrounded such topics as Lollardy, war and social revolt. Schlauch (1956) had a more sophisticated model than that of Daiches, but again took refuge in irony. The ironic attitude surfaces, for Schlauch, in Chaucer's representation – at once affectionate and compassionate – of individuals (the Monk, the Prioress) caught in authority structures which chafe. Chaucer was no revolutionary, but his perceptions were so penetrating as to raise, perhaps unintentionally, questions about the very institutions which he himself served. In this he reflected the spirit of the expanding and advancing mercantile class from which he came (pp. 229–76).

There have, of course, been extreme reactions against traditional literary scholarship, notably by the New Critics. It is not the purpose of this introduction to provide a detailed account of that phase of Chaucer studies, which has in any case recently been discussed at length elsewhere (Pearsall 1986: 134–7; Patterson 1987: 18–26), but rather to indicate its understanding of the historical process. That understanding was deliberately minimal, with the exception of lexical history (Empson 1961: 80–90). For the New Critic the text lived, if it lived at all, through its emotional and aesthetic effects on the reader. As a strategy for interpretation it therefore stressed not the determining quality of the past but the validity of present experience. In turning inwards to the text and the self, and in reading with a sharply focused attention and intellectual intensity it paid tribute to ambiguity, irony, paradox, stylistic variation, complexity and character, defined as the antithesis of such external factors as society.

Chaucer emerged from the New Critical massage and sauna several pounds lighter but considerably more supple, sinewy and open to ingenious approaches. This phase of Chaucer criticism discovered the Chaucerian narrator, subtly different from his real-life counterpart

5

(Donaldson 1954), and irony and stylistic juxtaposition as the hall-mark of Chaucer's distinctively Gothic style (Muscatine 1957). The impression was of a Chaucer rather like the professional academics who had created him: someone who perforce lived with a certain value-system but who at the same time escaped the contingencies of his historical circumstances through a detached and relativistic attitude to the cultural norms and events of his time, whether they were those of patronage, professional life, religion or social revolt (Muscatine 1972: 32). The sense of tension evident in his work as low style replaced high style, or as one voice challenged the world view of another, was held to be a feature of Gothic style in general, evidenced both in architecture and in the visual arts. Thus in avoiding positivism the New Critics encountered another kind of history: feelings and attitudes became legitimate subjects of critical enquiry, ones which surfaced in certain aesthetic formations.

The New Critics in turn provoked a counter-reaction, of which the leading figure remains D. W. Robertson, Jr. He advocated a return to an extreme form of positivism. Post-romantic critical treatments of Chaucer's poetry were stigmatized as anachronistic, sentimental and solipsistic (Robertson 1951, 1962). Instead, the only historical questions which a scholar might legitimately consider were those directly related to the medieval period. In particular, the Bible and patristic commentary, the classics and their Christian glosses, were held to be the keys to unlock authentic systems of meaning in a medieval text. The essential meaning underlying all others was the Augustinian doctrine of charity: that was what Chaucer's writing ultimately promoted. Unlike Muscatine's Chaucer, Robertson's was a devout man who accepted unquestioningly the hierarchical ideals of medieval thought and society.

It is true that so-called 'Historical Criticism' identified important sources of reference and imagery, and ones which continue to be profitably mined for their application to Chaucer's work. But it is also true – as medievalists continue to emphasize – that the Robertson approach is actually ahistorical, not to say reductive (Utley 1965; Pearsall 1986: 138–9; Patterson 1987: 26–39). It collapses the culture of the best part of a millennium into a relatively homogeneous and stable religious creed; it accentuates therein one (admittedly important) feature of a single theologian; and it postulates a determinist relationship between that creed and the meaning of Chaucer's poetry. It cannot be denied that exegetical interpretation was practised in the later fourteenth century, nor that there were those who, like Chaucer's Parson, would direct its methods at the secular world. What does not follow is that it is the only valid and authentic reading response.

Lately, Robertson's writings indicate that his conception of medieval culture has considerably widened, however much he reiterates his earlier views (Robertson 1980b). For example, he advocates a systematic examination of court documents of various kinds to further the attempt to understand more fully the ideas and images which peopled the world of Chaucer and his audience. Although Robertson may be somewhat disingenuous in his undertaking – finding, for example, corroboration in a will of the idea of human life as the pilgrimage of an exile, or in historical 'evidence' confirmation of his preconceived view of the Wife of Bath (Robertson 1981: 16 and 26) – it is difficult to quarrel with the stated principle of his project if only because, conscientiously carried out, it may well help to elaborate and undermine Robertson's hitherto monolithic view of the Chaucerian moment. In a recent article (Robertson 1986) he devotes most of his space to a descriptive analysis of the plague and its economic and social consequences. There follows a fairly routine account of the pilgrim portraits, set against this rather sophisticated background, which sorts the pilgrims loosely and predictably into those who have remained steadfast in adversity and those who have temporized. The moralized interpretation carries no conviction. It is as if Robertson has discovered, without yet being able to admit it, the apparent disjunction between what we can discover of late fourteenth-century life and Chaucer's response to it. There are no easy answers: the nature of the relationship with history remains obscure.

Ironically, Robertson is in this respect close to Muscatine. In his *Poetry and Crisis in the Age of Chaucer* (1972) Muscatine anatomized those features of later fourteenth-century English society which justify its description as a period of unparalleled crisis: extended war, relentless heavy taxation, famine, depopulation, plague, social revolt, heresy. He went on to argue that Chaucer's response to the particular predicaments of his age was to develop a style characterized by

7

structural and tonal irony and by pathos. This is an attractive hypothesis because it suggests that the historical context is deeply embedded in Chaucer's modes of composition and is therefore susceptible to literary analysis. But it is a hypothesis of a peculiarly literary kind, proposing in effect an 'influence' study according to which the findings of medieval historians can be identified in Chaucer's poetic transformations. Crucially, it neglects the process by which particular elements in the crisis are given literary form. Literature and history, though suggestively juxtaposed, remain separate, and Muscatine's central question, 'how do they connect?', remains unanswered.

When the problem is tackled from the point of view of a political historian the answer can be no more satisfactory. Coleman (1981) doubts neither the seriousness of the social upheavals of 1350 to 1400, nor the directness with which literature responded. For her, complaint is the representative genre of the period, focusing the fears and aspirations of an increasingly literate middle class. Certain lyrics, or *Piers Plowman*, or above all the writings of John Gower, are used to demonstrate the ways in which writers with a variety of political views addressed pressing issues. But since Chaucer seldom mentions topical matters, let alone voices an opinion on them, he slips through the net. There is no extended discussion of the *Canterbury Tales*, and although Coleman is alive to the dangers of using literature to illustrate historical themes (p. 46), she does in practice use Chaucer in this way, as when the Friar's Tale is cited as evidence of the activities of an ecclesiastical court (p. 68).

Among the most conscientious and effective attempts to track the connections between Chaucer's writings and history have been those of David Aers (Aers 1980; 1986; 1988). Although a literary scholar, he has made strenuous efforts to understand and incorporate in his work historical analyses of the period. Rejecting the underlying principles of positivism, the New Critics, and the Robertsonians, he has systematically identified specific topics which, when pursued into a medieval and Chaucerian setting, have demonstrated (with some exceptions) how deeply Chaucer was implicated in the ideological structures of his time. That Aers's topics – reflexivity, the female, community, class, gender – have a modern ring is no accident. While committed to revealing the otherness of the past he does so in order to demonstrate its relationship with the present. The critic, no less than Chaucer, is caught in the historical process.

It was against such a background (or should it be 'within such a context'?) that *The Age of Saturn* was written. It is now perhaps appropriate to sketch the academic careers and teaching experiences which also contributed to the book's development. In our view *The Age of Saturn* would have been impossible without the willingness of each of us to go beyond the prescribed boundaries of our individual disciplines, and without a kind of collaboration which focused the research techniques of both literary and historical studies on a common subject. Our disciplinary attitudes and co-operation in turn reflect the influence of earlier educational experiences.

Andrew Butcher was born in Canterbury and attended school there. Under the tutelage of the city and cathedral archivist, William Urry (Urry 1988) he began a lifelong study of the extensive documentary sources for the medieval and Tudor history of the city of Canterbury and its cathedral. He read History at Oxford, where his interests tended towards the economic and social history of the later Middle Ages. Since becoming a member of the History Board at Kent he has developed approaches to his field through anthropology, biography and the study of *mentalité*. Peter Brown received his schooling in Stoke-on-Trent and then read English in the School of European Studies at the University of Sussex. Interdisciplinary elements of his course included the study of philosophy and history and a year's residence in France. Medieval literature did not form a substantial part of the Sussex curriculum, and it was largely thanks to the enthusiasms of two Sussex dons, Stephen Medcalf and Gabriel Josipovici, that his interest in Chaucer began in earnest. At the Centre for Medieval Studies, University of York, he researched and later wrote a doctoral thesis arguing for the influence of medieval optical science on Chaucer's descriptive habits, using analogies from the visual arts. At Kent his teaching, though centred on the Middle Ages, has covered most periods of English literature.

Institutional and pedagogic history has also left its mark on this book through the ethos and organization of the Faculty of Humanities at the University of Kent. In spite of a relatively hostile economic environment the Faculty continues to foster enterprises which cross traditional disciplinary boundaries. Thus the present authors have enjoyed the privilege of being co-teachers for a number of years and in a range of courses: for an international graduate summer school on the medieval world, as contributors to an occasional seminar within a Faculty-wide option in medieval narrative literature, as co-lecturers at various sixth-form gatherings, as the initiators and seminar leaders of a special option, 'Crisis, Text and Image 1350–1400', and most recently as devisers and teachers (with others) of an MA in medieval and Tudor studies.

The Age of Saturn began and developed through the experience of co-teaching and the rapport (personal and intellectual) which that promoted. As we taught, it became increasingly clear that, under pressure of the joint approach, the *Canterbury Tales* in particular (which inevitably formed a central part of the syllabus) spoke in ways that were for us new and exciting. As the book took shape, and as our interpretations became more sharply defined, we tested them on our students, particularly in the special option (Brown and Butcher 1987). Thus teaching and research benefited each other, and this account of classroom experiences would be incomplete without a tribute to the many students who questioned our hypotheses and who resisted our readings.

When the prospect of writing a book began to be attractive the selection of tales was determined by our sense of which were the most extensively studied and by which responded best to the kind of approach we were developing. Although we were each relatively familiar with the chosen texts, when the time came to begin a chapter in earnest we used a method which undoubtedly led to interpretations which we had not anticipated. Having discussed in a general way the kinds of topic which we might profitably study in relation to a given tale, we then subjected the entire text to an extremely detailed close reading. In practice this often meant annotating the poem line by line, noticing verbal patterns, recurrent images, special terminology, matters for which we often had no immediate explanation. (Why *is*

January 'hastif'?) We then exchanged notes and at our second meeting arrived at a revised agenda of topics, one which was often considerably different from the first, and which is now reflected in the sub-headings of each chapter. At that point we divided up the work, allocating topics to each other so that we were not necessarily left with ones biased towards our own discipline. Once the topics were drafted we again exchanged copy and discussed alterations. The whole chapter was then typed out and revised once more when the book was complete. One other procedure helped, we believe, to refresh the writing: at the outset we deliberately avoided secondary literature unless absolutely essential. Relying on our own knowledge of other scholars' interpretations and approaches we wanted our encounter with the text to be, for the purpose of the exercise, as direct as possible. Only when a chapter was typed did we systematically read in the secondary literature, and then make any necessary adjustments and acknowledgements.

We began work on *The Age of Saturn* all too aware that many others had attempted without success to establish the connections between Chaucer's writings and the history of his time. The central problem faced by them, and the one faced by us, was the same as the problem posed by Muscatine in the case of Chaucer: how do history and literature connect? On the one hand there is a writer who favours indirection and irony, on the other a man (also called Chaucer!) who was at the centre of court and diplomatic life, with all its litany of crises. Chaucer's involvement in a world which by its nature was sensitive to all these ups and downs is amply documented, as is the context of crisis itself. On the other hand, there is the poetry, which is not, like that of Gower and Langland, a direct consideration of besetting social and political problems.

We began *The Age of Saturn* on the assumption that the connections between literature and history existed, and were waiting to be discovered. We were encouraged by previous attempts and partial successes, and aware of the difficulties and traps, especially the trap of allegorizing the text to make it fit historical data. It gradually became clear that to solve the problem of apparent discontinuity between text and history we had first to recognize the varieties of history which the writing evoked. For in the *Canterbury Tales*, Chaucer (so we came to realize) deals with social and political matters at different levels, and for each level a different kind of history is made to speak. At the general level, it might be the position of women in urban society after the demographic changes caused by the Black Death. At a more particular level it might be a political crisis at court caused by an ailing king in his dotage and the machinations of a powerful mistress. In another sphere it might concern religious controversy centring on the activities of John Wyclif. We also realized that, while it was vital to register the different historical levels to which the poetry points, it was equally important to be receptive to the different kinds of evidence within the text. In one instance, the diction itself may point to a type of discourse which is historically locatable; in another the play of styles may indicate a concern with, for example, social status; or manipulations of genre could signal an evaluative treatment of the protagonists; elsewhere iconographic detail may be relevant.

Broadly speaking, within each chapter we undertook two kinds of investigatory process. The first began with the text and moved outwards to consider such matters as its relations with source and genre, or its treatment of, say, sexuality; the second proposed and described a context, such as social mobility, in order to work inwards towards the detail of Chaucer's work. It will be seen that these processes have common aims. They are intended to free the poetry from a purely literary existence, in which the subjects treated by Chaucer are referred only to the text in which they occur, deriving meaning from it alone; and they are designed to rescue 'context', be it literary or historical, from a subsidiary status as background to the literary work. The result is not a belittling of Chaucer's poetry as the product of various influences and movements. On the contrary, the importance of his writing is increased the more it is seen not as self-sufficient poetry, but as a literature powerful in its ability to deal with issues which, while having a continuing relevance and interest, had particular and important application at the time of writing.

In the course of our endeavours we were occasionally rewarded with a sense of discovery and breakthrough. (No doubt the reviewers will tell us whether or not that was merely the self-induced result of an over-sophisticated approach.) In our opening chapter, on the Wife of Bath, we take issue – as others have done – with the received interpretation of her character as a masterpiece of realist representation. Instead, we attempt to reveal the artifice by which Chaucer created her from antifeminist and antimatrimonial materials. That allows us to proceed to an examination of her function as an articulator not of well-worn clichés but of vigorous, female alternatives to male authority structures, particularly through the power of speech, sexuality, astrology and faery. Such genuine challenges to the status quo square with the unusually potent position of women in society after the extraordinary changes in population patterns caused by plague. Thus the discussion of marriage which the Wife rehearses is not only about personal relations but also about the ordering of society.

Marriage as a microcosm of larger social and political relationships is also a feature of the Franklin's Tale. Here, the social disturbance underlying the narrative is that of those who, like the Franklin, like Arveragus, like Chaucer, find that their actual position in society is not easily accommodated by traditional roles and stratification. Within the tale, and in the Squire's Tale, styles of discourse are particularly effective in revealing the limitations of aristocratic life, its assumptions and ideals.

The politics of religion forms a framework for the Pardoner's Tale, and particularly the collaboration of Gaunt, Sudbury and Wyclif in forming a policy on papal taxation. The particular nature of their activities is placed by Chaucer within a broad moral framework which points to the consequences of reneging on basic Christian doctrine. The voice of Lollardy is heard, unexpectedly, through the rhetoric of the Pardoner, which also identifies him as a God-denying fool.

Discourse is again of great significance for the Merchant's Tale, with its vituperative attack on certain forms of sexuality. It is an attack echoed elsewhere when writers deal with the relationship between a senile Edward III and his mistress Alice Perrers. The political crisis which that provoked finds many echoes in Chaucer's poem, not least in the discordant use of competing genres.

With the Knight's Tale Chaucer attempts an overarching analysis of governance and its political ideology and social manifestations. Although Theseus is a wise and strong ruler who practises the precepts of chivalry to the best of his ability, he is subject to a higher power. That is not the benevolence of Jupiter but the malevolence of Saturn. The influence of Saturn is evident iconographically from an early stage of the narrative, and particularly through the life and death of Arcite. In retrospect the kinds of power which Saturn claims identify him not merely as the evil genius of the Knight's Tale but also as an 'explanation' of the turmoil which beset the age of Chaucer.

IN THEORY...

Even this brief synopsis will have revealed the extent to which our findings are dependent on a variety of different approaches to literature and history. In theory it would be possible to pin our colours to the mast by saying what we accept, what reject, from critical theory past and present. We might deny the determination of positivism, but want to maintain, as others have recently done (Askins 1985), that Chaucer's poetry *can* be a response to a particular event or occasion, however much critics tend to fight shy of such a possibility (Howard 1972). We might endorse with New Critics like Muscatine the study of style as expressive of value, but reject the notion that it is 'independent of historical association' (Muscatine 1957: 2). We would certainly question the centrality of character and instead opt for a deconstructionist attitude designed to dismantle and penetrate the illusion of character, to see the techniques which bring it into existence as functions (among others) of the author's intention (Martin 1986: 122). At the same time we would stop short of the deconstructionist hell of relativity (Culler 1983: 259–60) and identify a radically Christian Chaucer for whom there were limits to what might be re-evaluated. That in turn would set us against the exegetical school, for whom Chaucer is a conservative in ideology, but at the same time we would want to endorse the iconographic procedures (if not the findings) of Robertsonian criticism.

Such an attempt to situate our method and theory would run the risk of our being labelled irredeemably untheorized and empiricist, but in present circumstances that is probably unavoidable. As others have acknowledged, researches into Chaucer and history are at such an early stage of development, our knowledge of the workings of medieval culture is still so incomplete, that it would be folly to imagine that any of the single theories so far advanced can accommodate the complexity of interrelationship that is beginning to emerge (Lawton 1977). Indeed, any historical project of enquiry into Chaucer's writings which begins with programmatic assumptions about the nature of the history/literature relationship is likely to end with little more than a reflection of its own preconceptions. A certain degree of pragmatism, and a willingness to test various approaches and theories old and new, using them or discarding them as seems appropriate, is more likely to result in a persuasive synthesis. Interestingly, the two writers who have most recently surveyed historical approaches to Chaucer have, quite independently of each other, come to similar conclusions. Thus Pearsall (1986: 144) urges a return to that most fundamental testing ground: '...it is attention to the language of medieval literature, to the minutest detail of synchronic semantics, for instance, and to the architecture of connotation (e.g. Burnley, 1979), that promises best a way through the babble of theorising, and a securely rooted understanding of the manner in which history is embedded in the language of literature.' And Patterson (1987: 73–4), deploring the reductive tendencies of conservative and left-wing critics alike, argues for the recuperation of a humanist respect for personal difference as a counter-force to historical determinates:

> In literary-historical terms this respect presents itself in the form of intention, an interpretive category that contemporary criticism has largely written off as a vestige of positivism ... But a text is ... a function of specific human intentions, in the sense both of self-consciously maintained purposes and of impulses that may be incapable of articulation but nonetheless issue from a historical intentionality, and it is a large part of our task to understand how these intentions went into its making.

Further afield, it is interesting to observe an author of a book on recent theories of narrative (Martin 1986: 163) advocating: 'Rather than proposing a theory and then showing how it might work in practice, one can use an inductive approach – simply begin reading a text and develop conclusions about the process along the way.' Writing as a historian, E. P. Thompson (1978: 231) has also rejected the primacy of theory (especially of the Stalinist–Althusserian variety) to reassert the necessity of tried procedures: 'The disciplined historical discourse of the proof consists in a dialogue between concept and evidence, a dialogue conducted by successive hypotheses, on the one hand, and empirical research on the other.' But whatever the dangers of premature theorizing, in present conditions any theory about the relations of history and literature, whether based on the medieval period or not, has a vital role to play in corroborating, stimulating and challenging hypotheses evolved in the reading of Chaucer. In this respect the 'New Historicism', now gaining ground in studies of early modern literature, affords some instructive comparisons with the state of play in medieval studies (Goldberg 1982; Greenblatt 1982: 3–6; Norbrook 1984; Martines 1985: 1–17; Dollimore 1985; Howard 1986; Montrose 1986).

We take it as axiomatic if that literature is to speak eloquently of its time then the past must be recovered as completely and with as much complexity as possible. Such a recovery is to be effected both through traditional linguistic routes (McGann 1985a: 12) and through the disciplines of history, anthropology, sociology and philosophy. By these means the past can take on a life, become comprehensible (however different), explicable in its own terms, communicative to the sympathetic and unprejudiced scholar (Bloomfield 1981). In Parry's memorable words, 'I make for myself a picture of great detail' (1936: 411).

Central to the enterprise, as the phenomenon requiring understanding and explanation, is the text (Eagleton 1976: 3), raising questions about its origins, functions and meaning (McGann 1985a: 81; 1985b: 9 and 15–16), in short its historical reception (Jauss 1982). Historical criticism achieves its best results when its focus is relatively narrow and specific (Butler 1985: 44). Close reading is an essential tool and not at all inimical to a study of historicity (McGann 1985a: 5; Olson 1986: 17), but attention must be paid to the synchronic as well as to the diachronic vectors of language, for it is in the use of a living language that the constituent values of the writer's world are revealed (Barthes 1972: 100; Jameson 1972: 6; Aers 1988: 5).

In order to understand the historical referents of language at a given time it is appropriate to study a range of texts beyond those which fall into the literary canon (Butler 1985: 28–9; Frow 1986: 158; Martin 1986: 19). To do so helps to reveal the extent to which a single literary text is a jostling of different languages, or heteroglossia (Bakhtin 1981: 262–3; Martin 1986: 149). The literary work is intertextual in that it uses a variety of linguistic registers associated both with non-literary contemporary discourse and with the inherited discourses of, say, literary source, convention, genre, style and form (Knight 1977; Strohm 1977: 34–9; 1979; Frow 1986: 187), features of a text which have their own historical identities (Butler 1985: 33; Martin 1986: 26 and 71). To represent the text in this way, as part of a network of other texts some of which are non-literary, has the effect of breaking generic boundaries, including the ones between historical and literary writing. Histories, no less than novels, are imaginative inventions (Leitch 1983: 125–9; Frow 1986: 28; Martin 1986: 73), with their own tropes, susceptible therefore to literary analysis (White 1973: 1–11 and 29–38; 1978: 81–134).

How does literature function in relation to the society in which it is grounded? First, it defamiliarizes or makes strange what passes for reality, so encouraging a reassessment of what has become accepted as 'natural' (Jameson 1972: 50–60; Eagleton 1976: 64–7; Martin 1986: 47). Second, it reveals, deliberately or otherwise, a system of ideas (political, religious, economic) within which writer and audience exist and communicate (R. Williams 1960: 276–7; Eagleton 1976: vii and 4–24; 1978: 101 and 178; 1985: 116). Third, as well as manifesting an ideology, the literary text also displays a structure of feeling, attitude and value that is located in the individual, subjective experience of living at a particular time (Thompson 1978: 363; R. Williams 1977: 33; Eagleton 1978: 169–71; 1985: 116).

However effective the attempt to historicize a text, it can never be complete. The alterity of the past can never be overcome, nor can the critic ever know true objectivity (Aarsleff 1985: 93; Aers 1986: 1–2; Patterson 1987: 42–5). Recognition of the inescapable otherness of a text (Jauss 1979: 181–91), the impossibility ever of fully understanding it, and of the inherent subjectivity of critical activity, lead not to a rejection of the drive for a fuller interpretation – which must be conscientiously sustained – but to a keen awareness of the historical factors, including literary tradition, which determine the critic's own existence, activity and mental set (Ferster 1986: 150–1). In attempting to comprehend the historical process linking the text to its time and place the critic is led to perceive the relevance of the historical process linking the present to a particular study of the past (Eagleton 1976: viii; McGann 1985a: 109; 1985b: 12).

HYPOTHETICAL CONCLUSIONS

With such theoretical and procedural considerations in mind, what provisional conclusions have we reached about the historical connections of the *Canterbury Tales*? Their particular context is that of the fifty years or so after the Black Death, of the last years of Edward III and the reign of Richard II. That period incorporates extraordinary demographic change and concomitant alterations in social, economic and political structures. It involves new phases in the Hundred Years' War, a new era in papal relations, and remarkable challenges to the authority of church and crown. It manifests a more widespread literacy and a sophisticated English vernacular literature which at once embodies and subverts traditional modes of discourse. And it is a period in which contemporaries themselves identify a range of crises within social, economic and political institutions and within their associated explanatory systems.

We hope that our studies of six *Canterbury Tales* help to provide an anatomy of the *mentalité* which informs both Chaucer and his audience. The most obvious instance is his use of astrology and particularly the role of Saturn to 'explain' the late fourteenth-century crisis. At all times, Chaucer anchors general features of social upheaval in the experience of individuals, and here it has been fruitful to observe the use made of marriage as a microcosm for larger forms of 'governaunce', whether social, political or religious (Mann 1983). Chaucer also identifies psychological imbalance (as found, say, in January, the Pardoner and Dorigen) as a symptom of 'breakdown' in larger spheres of which the individual is a part (the court, the church, aristocratic society). Associated with the use of psychological imbalance is the use of faery as a mechanism for exploring alternative worlds – worlds which, by being distorted in themselves, offer a means of contrast with reality. Whatever the means of analysis, Chaucer makes use of traditional visual images – of which the garden is the most notable example – which, far from having a purely decorative function, act as keys to the understanding of a tale and its concerns. Thus the garden in the Merchant's Tale, with its various strata of meaning, offers a way of understanding the 'paradise lost' flavour of the mid-1370s at the English court.

The presence of such images is one of the reasons why Chaucer's poetry appears to be indirect, to be dealing with contemporary issues, if at all, at several removes. The indirection, it might be thought, exists to protect Chaucer from retribution and censorship. But if a crisis like that at court in 1376 was so well known to Chaucer's audience they would immediately have been able to read the tale's political content. In that case, Chaucer's indirections serve the altogether different purpose of pointing to the profound moral and spiritual significance of a topical scandal.

Such considerations indicate that the approach we have taken may represent a chapter in Chaucer's intellectual biography. Not only the way in which he responds to particular circumstances, but also the range of his engagement with contemporary issues, is impressive. The nature of that engagement indicates that Chaucer had a much more complex relationship with his benefactors and patrons than is usually thought. Further, it leads to some possible revisions in the dating of the composition of the tales. But perhaps most important of all it enables the *Canterbury Tales* to be read as evidence of crisis as seen by an insider, as the testimony of one articulate man of unusual sensitivity and intelligence placed as he was at the centre of events.

Chaucer had an unusually assimilative, syncretic and integrative imagination, but he lived at a time of disintegrating social and religious forms and values. He is not a poet who chose to 'rise above' such circumstances; rather he wrote works which articulate and analyse, sometimes in coded form, the specific problems which he and his society faced. His tendency was not to offer easy solutions, but to provoke, air and sustain debate, often by adopting the point of view of a Christian radical.

Chaucer's reflexivity was therefore not limited to aesthetic matters. It was one which entailed using the concepts, terminology and images of Christian ideology and morality to present and analyse corruption, abuse and degeneration. In practice, this meant more than rejuvenating narrative sources – it meant making a new synthesis addressed to particular circumstances. His works cannot be read as the product of an exclusively literary frame of mind. The very choice of source and convention, and their novel combinations, were deliberately designed to speak about contemporary issues. If modern readers tend to value Chaucer because, like Shakespeare (Longhurst 1982: 150–4 and 159–60; Drakakis 1985), he 'universalizes' human experience, they are to some extent right. He did attempt to set contemporary abuses *sub specie aeternitatis*. But it was the vitality of his response to a historical moment, as much as his drive to construct it according to a perceived truth, that has made his work durable (Knight 1980a: 16). In savouring the 'eternal' residue modern readers have tended to miss the importance of the specific circumstances which made a return to Christian roots essential as a means of obtaining a steady perspective on a world turned upside-down.

I

The Wife of Bath

This chapter is concerned with Chaucer's discussion of the nature of marriage and the position of women in the Wife of Bath's Prologue and Tale. Our purpose is to explore such issues in the context of their special significance in England in the second half of the fourteenth century. Taking the institution of marriage to be central to any system of medieval values, our exploration argues for wide-ranging implications for the prologue and tale, involving authority and government at all levels of society. Demonstrating the existence of a sustained and balanced argument across prologue and tale, we describe not simply the construction of the rival claims of 'experience' over 'authority' but of a necessary alternative to the received and dominant ideology. In this, we emphasize the importance of a feminine voice in human affairs; the vital role of natural forces, astrology and faery; and the power and influence of networks of gossip and kin, folk tradition and the spoken word. The right resolution of sexual relations within marriage provides a microcosm of political relations in a society in which material values dominate, traditional order has been disturbed, and authority undermined. In establishing a radical Christian solution, Chaucer confronts the problem of authority in fictional composition and challenges the values and presuppositions of his audience. The 'colourful character' of the Wife of Bath emerges as fabricated from the stereotypes of antifeminist and antimatrimonial literature, and the necessary process of social and political reconstruction and reform begins with that realization.

THE WIFE OF BATH'S PROLOGUE AND ITS SOURCES

The untutored and natural response of a modern reader to the Wife of Bath's Prologue is enthusiastic. The Wife of Bath is a colourful character who uses salty expressions, she is rich in experience, she is a feminist before her time. Surely it was Chaucer's intention to make her attractive, provocative and larger than life. But a justifiable enthusiasm for the Wife of Bath needs to be wary of those anachronistic preconceptions which a modern reader might take to fictional characters. It is as well to remember that Chaucer's realism is not solely, or even predominantly, angled towards providing his audience with a slice of contemporary life in the manner of a realist novel (Shumaker 1951: 77–89).

The Wife of Bath is a fabrication, an illusion artificially created through certain literary techniques. In this she is no different from any other character in fiction (Culler 1975: 131–60). Where Chaucer differs from, say, a nineteenth-century novelist, is in the way in which he exposes to view the very materials out of which he has made this beguiling creature. An inspection of the texts on which Chaucer drew in writing the Wife of Bath's Prologue is, in every sense, a disillusioning experience, because in the process the three-dimensional, flesh-and-blood woman who elicits such a warm reaction seems to become little more than an automaton kept alive by the cunning artifice of her inventor. Yet it is necessary to experience this disillusionment if we are to move away from the false sense that the Wife of Bath is merely a woman for our own times, and towards a better understanding of how she is also a response to a fourteenth-century reality (Jordan 1967: 208–26).

An example will illustrate the disillusioning process. In the course of telling the pilgrims about her first three husbands, the Wife of Bath reports at length the type of quarrelling which took place between her and them. One of the complaints customarily made from the male side runs as follows:

'Thou seist that oxen, assess, hors, and houndes,
They been assayed at diverse stoundes;
Bacyns, lavours, er that men hem bye,
Spoones and stooles, and al swich housbondrye,
And so been pottes, clothes, and array;
But folk of wyves maken noon assay,
Til they be wedded...'
                    (ed. Benson et al. 1987: lines 285–91)

At a first encounter these lines, and others like them, are easily swallowed as graphic instances of the arguments which engaged the Wife and her marital partners. The attitude which the man has supposedly expressed represents women as commodities and marriage as a kind of commercial transaction, and so the reader's sympathy is very much with the woman who, in the eyes of the man, has been reduced to the status of an object. At the same time the reader knows that the Wife of Bath is an undependable narrator in such matters: she is quite prepared to put words into the mouth of her husband and to make false accusations if this will allow her to berate, browbeat and dominate him. The passage in which these lines occur begins with an exhortation to 'wise wives' who wish to control their partners:

Thus shulde ye speke and bere hem wrong on honde,
For half so boldely kan ther no man
Swere and lyen, as a womman kan.
                    (226–8)

For all that the Wife of Bath says, within marriage she manipulates the materialism of her partners: the husbands in question are considered 'good' to the extent that they are rich and old, for these qualities allow the Wife to control both their behaviour and their wealth. From such observations the reader is led easily to considerations of the Wife of Bath's character, the openness and honesty of her explanation of the means by which she masters men, her proto-feminism, what she has learnt from experience, and so on. To read her prologue in such a way is to import those preconceptions about character previously discussed. A corrective to the character view of the Wife of Bath is provided by referring to Theophrastus' *Golden Book on Marriage*, for the opinion about women which she credits to her husband is taken by Chaucer from that source (ed. Miller 1977: 412):

> Horses, asses, cattle, even slaves of the smallest worth, clothes, kettles, wooden seats, cups, and earthenware pitchers, are first tried and then bought: a wife is the only thing that is not shown before she is married, for fear she may not give satisfaction.

Immediately, the question of character, and of remembered experience, become problematic. Not only did the Wife's husband never speak the words credited to him, the Wife herself did not invent them either. For that matter, neither did Chaucer – he copied them from Jerome, who copied Theophrastus.

In writing the Wife of Bath's Prologue Chaucer used an exceptionally wide range of sources. In his introduction to the chapter concerning the prologue in Bryan and Dempster's *Sources and Analogues*, the author acknowledges that a complete survey of analogues and originals would be impossible (Whiting 1941: 207). Instead, he presents illustrative excerpts from four works which Chaucer knew: Jerome's *Epistle against Jovinian*, Walter Map's *Courtiers' Trifles*, the *Romance of the Rose* by Jean de Meun and Eustache Deschamps' *Mirror of Marriage*. To these have since been added other works, such as the *Communiloquium* of Gerald of Wales (Pratt 1966: 619–24) and Peter Abelard's *A Story of Misfortunes* (ed. Miller 1977: 447–51). A profusion of other texts and authors is mentioned in the Wife of Bath's Prologue; chief among these is the Bible with, at the other extreme, Ptolemy's *Almagest* and Ovid. Jankyn's 'Book of Wicked Wives', which is representative of a certain kind of clerical compilation, is a storehouse of texts such as Chaucer used (Pratt 1962; Lawler 1985). To a much greater extent than any other work in the *Canterbury Tales*, then, the

Wife of Bath's Prologue may be seen as a compilation of material culled from diverse authors. The texts so gathered have as associated, unifying themes sex and marriage. For these reasons the prologue itself may be seen as a work not dissimilar in its organization and subject matter to Jankyn's book, although the bias of each is different.

The recession of sources exemplified above is troubling. Its effect, combined with that of placing the Wife of Bath's Prologue against the variegated background of texts used by Chaucer, is to reduce the Wife of Bath's character to a confection of fragmentary sources, her experience to ideas derived from written precedents (Matthews 1974: 434–43; Hanning 1985: 16–20; Pearsall 1985: 72–9). At this point, the critical reader is left with an alternative route of interpretation. The first step is to recognize that the Wife's prologue belongs in a tradition of writings which share sexual and matrimonial themes. From such a perspective the Wife's controversial views seem not to have been produced by a fictional, fourteenth-century experience, but to express issues of perennial interest. The second step entails studying the innovations to which Chaucer subjects his inherited source material. From that point of view it is possible to admire Chaucer's artistry, the skill with which he has invested unpromising and inert material with the semblance of similitude.

Such critical steps and their consequences are useful and inviting, but they involve a major limitation, which is that the Wife of Bath's Prologue, by being considered as an aesthetically admirable artifice belonging within a literary tradition, is deprived of a firm location in late fourteenth-century English social life. But this is precisely what the work does have. However, the roots binding poem to society are not to be found by accepting at face value the illusion of character and realistic setting which Chaucer presents, nor just by exploring matters of aesthetics and tradition. There is a further step to be made, and that involves the exploration of attitudes towards sex and marriage, and their metaphorical implications, in the post-Black Death period during which Chaucer wrote. Such an excursus is radical for another reason: it enables us to consider Chaucer's manipulation of source material as being not exclusively conditioned by aesthetic considerations, but equally as being determined by the conditions in which he wrote.

Consequently his skill as a writer, his response to tradition, his choice of source material, his handling of conventions, may be seen as key responses to a historical situation rather than the process by which a literary genius created a timeless masterpiece.

With the above observations in mind, the example used earlier can be taken a little further: its disillusioning effect over, we may now enquire more closely into its function. The husband's sentiments as reported by the Wife of Bath originate in a work of male authorship which, by being associated with the name of Jerome, carry a weight of authority appropriate to a church father (Bornstein 1983: 17–19). As used by Jerome, they are intended to serve as a warning against marriage. Chaucer, as can clearly be seen, wrests the original passage out of context, first by putting it at the disposal of a woman who wishes to browbeat an already married man, thus putting Jerome's words into the mouth of the very sort of woman whom Theophrastus despises; and then by allowing her to ridicule the author's sentiments with verbal abuse of her husband: 'olde dotard shrewe!' (291). The effects, of course, are comic, but they are serious too: behind the laughter which the Wife's marital behaviour provokes lies a serious challenge to accepted and traditional ideas about the role and status of women.

Chaucer perceived in his reading of works on sex and marriage the existence of a female prototype who, in the hands of male authors, was characteristically presented as predatory, deceitful and manipulating. This is the true origin of the Wife of Bath, whom he 'brings to life' in part by inverting the application of texts normally hostile to women. The Wife of Bath's very existence as a fictional figure is a challenge to received ideas about women because she is the embodiment and living exponent of all that male clerical writers most feared. She was created out of the 'bad woman' stereotype by antifeminist and antimatrimonial authorities. It is through them that Chaucer makes possible the Wife of Bath (Patterson 1983: 660–76).

From his sources, Chaucer made particular and deliberate selections. The principles of selection were determined in part by his response to the contemporary condition of women. That condition may be seen as itself affected by the dominant ideology of the church, but it was also governed by the social and economic status of women as generally reflected, say, in courtesy books (Bornstein 1983: 44–53). As we shall see, the lines earlier quoted, though they derive from Jerome, fit into a pattern of meaning whereby Chaucer systematically draws attention to marriage as an economic transaction, a bonding so materialistic in its motives as to be empty of spiritual content.

WOMEN IN URBAN SOCIETY

The organization of fourteenth-century urban society was characterized by clear divisions according to sex. In the sphere of economic activity, and especially as regards production for and regulation of the formal market, women were substantially excluded: they were seldom, if ever, permitted to enjoy the full advantages of the urban franchise (as 'freemen') in buying, selling, or producing, and, in so far as they did participate, did so most frequently by right of their husbands. Female involvement in the informal economy, closely linked to household production and consumption, was more complete, particularly where food and drink were concerned. It seems also that basic processes in cloth manufacture were very often part of the necessary by-employments practised by women. Yet even this greater participation was restricted at law relative to the freedom of action of male burgesses, and women were frequently in the technical position of acting as agents for their husbands. A measure of economic independence on the woman's part, however, could have a divisive effect on the traditionally male-dominated household economy (Howell 1986: 19–21). Unmarried women and widows, among the less prosperous, might scrape a living performing low-paid labour in trade or craft, engaging in by-employments, serving as domestic labour in more prosperous households, or by prostitution. Exceptionally, it was possible for single women to trade, by special licence, as a *femme sole* or *sola mercatrix* (Bornstein 1983: 96–101). As portrayed in the General Prologue, therefore – 'Of clooth-makyng she hadde swich an haunt, / She passed hem of Ypres and of Gaunt' (GP 447–8) – the Wife of Bath was an unusual if not a unique figure, working in both town and country (Carruthers 1979: 210; Robertson 1980a: 403–11).

The separation of male and female roles extended also into the realms of ecclesiastical and civic ceremonial and of government. Within the church or in religious procession, in the procession of trade and craft associations or of civic and ward officers, the separation of men and women was the usual practice, the women often joining the ranks of the unenfranchised (whatever their status) as non-participant members of the governed audience witnessing the public demonstration in symbolic terms of the realities of urban political power. Civic officers in the urban courts and urban administration were exclusively male and, with the exception of nunneries and some hospitals, all religious institutions were closed to women; and the officers of ecclesiastical courts were all male. The domestic government of the household may have given some latitude to female control, especially in the management of servants and apprentices, but the final authority rested with the husband. Whatever the real balance of ability or personality, and no matter how forceful a woman might be, she was obliged to work within structures designed to perpetuate male control.

Such a separation, at least within the formal sectors of urban society, encouraged the development of less formal social groupings and networks which arose from neighbourhood connection or kinship, and these relationships permitted the expression of ideas contradictory to or subversive of exclusive male dominance. At their most formal, alternative female social groups might be found in religious associations within parish churches, societies with separate cults and charitable aims of mutual self-help; and less formally they might exist in the attachment to particular saints, altars and lights within a local church. Between neighbours and kin such associations might not necessarily be exclusively female but the existence of men within the alternative groupings did not exclude women from positions of importance.

The place of the married woman within urban social networks is clearly described in the Wife of Bath's Prologue (Pearsall 1985: 79–80). The Wife's world is one of neighbour, 'gossib' and 'freend', of 'novice' and 'chamberere', of 'my fadres folk and his allyes', of the apprentice and the 'nece' and of other worthy wives. It is a world whose connections and influence her husband seeks to control and even destroy. She complains that

'... if I have a gossib or a freend,
Withouten gilt, thou chidest as a feend,
If that I walke or pleye unto his hous!'
(243–5)

Free to associate with female neighbours and domestic servants the husband exercises a double standard in attempting to restrict his wife's relationships with other men, whether neighbours or kin. Any respect which he shows to her personal domestic servants, her nurse and maid, is a sham and, perhaps more significant, so is any honour he might do to her 'fadres folk and his allyes' (301). Bearing in mind that servants might often be supplied from the households of kin as well as of neighbours, then, in his scant regard for his wife's family and its connections, the husband denies the importance of relationships in the female line. Exclusively female associations were more difficult to control. The Wife of Bath's Prologue provides a glimpse of the intimate alliances of the separate female domain of worthy wives and 'neces', with the female *gossib* at its most intense centre. Such networks of alliances constituted important institutions of social control within the community as a whole and might be particularly subversive of male authority, inviting official disapproval of the scold or 'jangleresse'. As portrayed by the Wife of Bath, and suggested elsewhere, the relationship with the *gossib*, a relationship of fictive kinship, was of great importance, parallel to and challenging the relationship with the priest or confessor.

THE WRITTEN AND SPOKEN WORD

In matters of verbal expression, the Wife of Bath has views which rival those of orthodox male authority. Here, it is important to note that the word 'authority', as used in her prologue, has two distinct but related meanings (Davis et al. 1979). The first meaning relates to the power which dominant individuals or social groups are able to exert (*MED* 1–3); the second meaning applies to written texts, that is to the products of 'authors' held in general esteem (*MED* 4).

Various forms of the written word exert a strong influence on the Wife of Bath and she feels obliged to take issue with them. First, there are the writings by biblical commentators and scholars who are hostile to women or to marriage. Their activities are described by the Wife as 'glossing' up and down, which literally means writing explanatory comments in the margin of a text, but which is also capable of conveying sexual insult: Dame Alice describes Jankyn's love-making as 'glossing' (509). She combats what she sees as misrepresentation by accusing the commentators of bias. They are male clerics (supposedly celibate), who cannot possibly speak well of a woman unless she be a saint (688–90). She also appeals to common sense, for instance by ridiculing the clerkly notion that the genitals were only made for 'purgacioun / Of uryne' and to tell the difference between the sexes (119–24). Again, like the good critic she is, she herself offers rival interpretations of the Bible to justify her own attitudes, as when she uses the example of Solomon's many wives as a precedent for her five husbands (35–8).

Second, there is a type of writing of a more substantial kind, not textual commentary but what might loosely be called writing in the antifeminist and antimatrimonial tradition. The authors are both Christian and pre-Christian. They include Ovid as well as Jerome, though the tradition as a whole carries the approval of Christian theology. The line of influence is represented by the words Chaucer puts, via the Wife of Bath, into the mouths of her earlier husbands, and by Jankyn's 'Book of Wicked Wives', a compilation in which hostile attitudes towards women are given theological sanction through the story of Adam and Eve:

> Upon a nyght Jankyn, that was oure sire,
> Redde on his book, as he sat by the fire,
> Of Eva first, that for hir wikkednesse
> Was al mankynde broght to wrecchednesse,
> For which that Jhesu Crist hymself was slayn,
> That boghte us with his herte blood agayn.
> Lo, heere expres of womman may ye fynde
> That womman was the los of al mankynde.
> *(713–20)*

The Wife of Bath deals with this particular object by destroying it. Her disdain for book learning is elsewhere in evidence:

> *'After thy text, ne after thy rubriche,*
> *I wol nat wirche as muchel as a gnat.'*
> *(346–7)*

But it would be misleading to suggest that she has no respect at all for the written word. She is certainly far from illiterate, for she can beat biblical expositors at their own game. In practice, Dame Alice stops short of attacking the Bible itself. Her target is men's partial interpretation of holy writ. When the Bible appears to favour her own views it is a 'gentil text' (29), a book that speaks directly: 'Right thus the Apostel tolde it unto me' (160).

Third, the Wife of Bath also refers to Ptolemy's *Almagest* as a source of proverbs to support some parts of her argument (180–2 and 323–5). Ptolemy is referred to as an astrologer (324) and, as we shall see, it is appropriate to ask why the Wife should be interested in that aspect of his work. The fact that proverbs form the only kind of written authority (apart from the Bible) with which she attempts to counteract an entire library of hostile literature is in itself interesting. For proverbs circulate orally as well as in written form; they express 'some truth ascertained by experience or observation and familiar to all' (*OED*; Whiting with Whiting 1968: x–xvii). Now the Wife of Bath's husband also uses proverbs, from a store which enshrines antifeminist 'wisdom'. Proverbs have the peculiar quality of abstracting general and sententious thought from the particularities of experience, from which they divert attention. The Wife of Bath is engaged in countering views of women which, by becoming proverbial, have ceased to correspond to the complexity of female life. In attacking male proverbs about women she is trying to fracture an ossified discourse which expresses *idées fixes*. She thus chooses from Ptolemy and elsewhere proverbs of her own, running counter to received male wisdom, which demonstrate that the aura of universal sapience surrounding proverbs is not to be taken as an indication that the views they express transcend

31

others, but that it is in the nature of proverbs to produce such an aura. Proverbs are the common currency with which she and Jankyn exchange in speech conflicting points of view (Whiting 1934: 92–100).

There is another type of spoken authority, apart from the proverbs of Jankyn, to which Dame Alice reacts – the sermon. In springtime she enjoys sermons for the entertainment they provide (557), and a considerable amount of what she knows derives from listening to such authoritative utterances:

> ... me was toold, certeyn, nat longe agoon is,
> That sith that Crist ne wente nevere but onis
> To weddyng, in the Cane of Galilee ...
>
> (9–11)

She also has to endure sermons from her husbands (247 and 641). In response, the Wife of Bath delivers in her prologue a sermon in her own right, a practice which that other consummate preacher and glosser, the Pardoner, recognizes in a voice full of irony: 'Ye been a noble prechour in this cas' (165).

The Wife also counters written and spoken authority with straightforward verbal abuse. The opinions which she puts into the mouths of her first three husbands are culled from fairly standard written material on women. The husbands are made the mouthpieces of male, bookish, authority hostile to women. The Wife of Bath torpedoes their rhetoric with plainspeaking insults:

> 'Thow seyst we wyves wol oure vices hide
> Til we be fast, and thanne we wol hem shewe –
> Wel may that be a proverbe of a shrewe!
> . . . .
> Thus seistow, olde barel-ful of lyes!'
>
> (282–4 and 302)

Chiding (223), grouching, murmuring (406) and answering word for word (422) form a major part of the Wife's strategy in mastering her husbands, using her skill as a 'verray jangleresse' when necessary to hide her own misdemeanours (638).

There is one further way in which the Wife of Bath uses the spoken word as a means of escaping from the male-dominated authority of the written word – through gossip. Dame Alice has a companion, a friend, to whom she tells everything, and who is described as a *gossib*. Her husband views this person as a threat (243–5) since she in turn reports to Dame Alice every small deed that he has committed, which leads to some embarrassment:

> For hadde myn housbonde pissed on a wal,
> Or doon a thyng that sholde han cost his lyf,
> To hire, and to another worthy wyf,
> And to my nece, which that I loved weel,
> I wolde han toold his conseil every deel.
> And so I dide ful often, God it woot,
> That made his face often reed and hoot
> For verray shame, and blamed hymself for he
> Had toold to me so greet a pryvetee.
>
> *(534–42)*

Thus the written word and some forms of the spoken word carry an authority which the Wife of Bath recognizes as containing a strong male bias and hostility towards women. She appeals to the text of the Bible as being in some ways neutral and offers her own interpretations of it in order to combat antifeminist and antimatrimonial glosses. But it is chiefly by speaking that she, as a woman, is able to counteract male control of words: through proverbs, through offering a rival sermon, through abuse and grumbling and through gossip. In the process she develops and establishes a specifically subversive form of discourse (Patterson 1983: 676–84).

SEASON, ASTROLOGY AND ECCLESIASTICAL CALENDAR

Within the consciousness of Chaucer and his contemporaries the determining forces of nature and season, astrological influence, and the ecclesiastical calendar, were woven together. They provided a loosely integrated system of explanation which depended upon a sense of temporal auspiciousness and magical or quasi-magical effects. Although in popular practice such a system might permit the loose combination of its explanatory elements, in the process of understanding there was also a real tension between them. The uncontrollable forces of nature were, arguably, determined and directed by religious and astrological forces. Religion and astrology stood in the fourteenth century as, theoretically, the only two systematic schemes which pretended to a total explanation of human behaviour, and thus might appear to be rival authorities. Certainly, the church attacked the teaching of astral determination, fully recognizing the power of a coherent, comprehensive and flexible system of thought which seems to have been most influential in intellectual and court circles. The system, however, possessed a widely recognized symbolism, often overlaying that of Christian symbolism itself, and found throughout fourteenth-century society.

The importance of all three of these forces is recognized in the Wife of Bath's Prologue. Significantly, the Wife becomes identified with nature and astrology and, implicitly, opposed to the calendrical influence of the church. The view of marriage expressed through her in the prologue and within the tale is once more to be seen as a view which contradicts the opinions of contemporary, late fourteenth-century, established authority and looks to other forms of explanation and understanding. Lent is the chosen time for the central episode in the Wife of Bath's Prologue, in which the relationship with Jankyn is established. Within the ecclesiastical calendar Lent is a time of sobriety and chastity, when marriage is proscribed except under exceptional circumstances, a time of intense piety and contemplation of one of the most significant events of the Christian year. The Wife of Bath celebrates the season of March, April and May (and perhaps especially May, the month of the Virgin) in such a way as to affront ecclesiastical authority. She goes not to her priest for confession but to her *gossib*, walking 'Fro hous to hous, to heere sundry talys', 'gay' when she should be sober (544–7). She searches for grace in making her 'visitaciouns' (a parody, perhaps, of ecclesiastical visitations), going

> *To vigilies and to processiouns,*
> *To prechyng eek, and to thise pilgrimages,*
> *To pleyes of myracles, and to mariages ...*
> *(556–8)*

She goes, however, not especially for the religious content of this ceremonial and ritual or to take part in demonstrations of political and social order and control, but rather to see and to be seen, to engage in a social intercourse of lusty self-expression. It is as though she celebrates the season in just the way condemned by the reforming ecclesiastics of the thirteenth and fourteenth centuries (e.g. Robert Grosseteste, bishop of Lincoln, in edicts produced *c*.1236–44) or, indeed, by Lollard commentators. Hers is the assertion of the alternative society of folk tradition, especially to be witnessed in May-time celebrations, fundamentally celebrations of nature in springtime.

The force of nature in folk tradition is reinforced by astrology. Born under the sign of Taurus, the latest sign in Lent, and influenced by Venus and Mars, the Wife of Bath is an embodiment of the season of the year in which she becomes betrothed to Jankyn, and an embodiment of the argument she is conducting against the determination of gender and marital relations by male-dominated and ecclesiastical authorities. Developing the argument further she claims that 'it is an impossible / That any clerk wol speke good of wyves' (688–9). Amplified in astrological terms the issues become polarized between the male and celibate sphere of 'wysdam and science' under Mercury, and the female and non-celibate sphere of 'ryot and dispence' under Venus (699–700). What is more, she argues that under Pisces, the earliest sign of Lent, Mercury and Venus are opposed and their properties are irreconcilable (Hamlin 1974: 153–6).

For the Wife of Bath it is the force of nature and temporal auspiciousness which should determine the character of marriage, and not
the teaching of the church in her day. To take the argument one stage
further, she may be seen to be arguing for the importance of alternative structures of authority, of nature and astrology, of the old ways of
folk tradition and the teachings of science, in coping with contemporary problems.

FAERY

The opening lines of the Wife of Bath's Tale (857–81) again set two
systems of authority in satiric juxtaposition. Conventionally the world
of faery is described as belonging to the past, a past superseded by the
church and its agents, the friars. It is the friars

> *That serchen every lond and every streem,*
> *As thikke as motes in the sonne-beem,*
> *Blessynge halles, chambres, kichenes, boures,*
> *Citees, burghes, castels, hye toures,*
> *Thropes, bernes, shipnes, dayeryes –*
> *This maketh that ther ben no fayeryes.*
>
> *(867–72)*

Formerly, then, it was the faeries that, like present-day friars, were to
be found everywhere. But how effective had the work of the friars
been? The ironic tone of the passage may suggest what seems, indeed,
to be the social reality: that despite the endeavours of the church, the
world of faery was very much alive in the popular imagination. It was
a world peopled by all kinds of creature: 'goblins, elves, and fairies
were part of that great army of good and bad spirits with which the
world was thought to be infested' (Thomas 1971: 606). Though there
seems to have been little specialization of function among these
creatures, the queen of the faeries was recognized as a source of
knowledge and wisdom; and the social function of faery seems to have
been corrective, responsible for inflicting small punishments upon

humans for their transgression of social norms, and observable in the incidence of setbacks and disappointments. At the level of mental processes the belief in the power of faery might constrain action in the manner of conscience, while faery hallucinations might be associated with mental disturbance.

Within the argument of the Wife of Bath's Prologue and Tale the power of faery may be seen to represent an alternative authority, of greater authority than the church, whose female ruler conveys to the knight the essential nature of marriage in order to redeem him from the crime of rape which he had committed. Aspects of faery are used, significantly, at points of psychological crisis in the Wife's tale. Having searched for a solution to the question ' "What thyng is it that wommen moost desiren" ' (905) the knight is at the end of his allotted time and in despair at his inability to find an answer: 'Withinne his brest ful sorweful was the goost' (986). At that point he sees or imagines a faery dance, and at its vanishing confronts the 'olde wyf' (1000) who is to save his life. Looking at the climax of the tale, when the knight kisses the old woman, the magical power of faery is used to convey physical and psychological transformation as the old woman is made young and beautiful (at least in the eyes of the knight). In part, at least, the discovery of the nature of marriage is a victory for the female, faery authority (Blanch 1985: 41–7; Fradenburg 1986: 47).

SEXUALITY AND GENDER

Sexuality, one of the preoccupations of the Wife of Bath's Prologue and Tale, is treated as a varied and complex subject. At one extreme is the attitude of the church, which prizes virginity, though allowing sexuality its place within marriage as a procreative force. At the other extreme is the opinion of the Wife of Bath, who sees sexuality as a natural force, God-given, and to be used 'as frely as my Makere hath it sent' (150). But it is simplistic to see the question of male and female sexuality, as explored by Chaucer, resolved into an antithesis between, say, promiscuity and chastity. In her opening speech on marriage and virginity, the Wife of Bath is making a claim for the sexual urge to be considered not as a necessary but rather unpleasant bodily

function, such as 'purgacioun of uryne' might be, but as the fundamental bond between men and women, without which the world
could not be peopled by those Christian idealists who opt for
virginity.

The treatment of gender relations in the prologue and tale is best
approached by considering the topic as an aspect of a rather larger
subject concerning the relations between male and female bodies. For
it is through physical exertions of the body that the tussle for authority between the sexes is in part played out. When it is a question of
physical force, men tend to get the upper hand. In the domestic brawl
which breaks out at the end of the prologue, Jankyn is the victor
physically, if not in other ways. The Wife of Bath tears three pages
from the provocative 'Book of Wicked Wives'. She hits her husband
on the cheek so that he falls backwards into the fire. In return, Jankyn
strikes his wife on the head. She is felled as if dead. Dame Alice
pretends that she is dying, murdered by a violent husband. Jankyn
moves closer to apologize for his actions, and no sooner has he done
so than Dame Alice strikes him again. Eventually, she does manage to
make him submit and so she wins the conflict, but by talk and not by
more force. As retribution for wife-beating, she persuades him to give
her 'the governance of hous and lond, / And of his tonge, and of
his hond also' (814–15). She also makes Jankyn burn his book of
antifeminist stories, stories designed to justify the control of women
by men. In fact, it is precisely by behaving like one such wicked wife
in using deceit (the stratagem of pretending to die) that the Wife of
Bath has been able to turn the tables on her husband. When over-
mastered by physical force, she resorts to other tactics.

For all that, a fight with the Wife of Bath would have been a serious
matter. Jankyn may be stronger but he does not escape without being
heavily bruised about the face. As a woman in a man's world, Alice is
unusually strong, tough and mannish, qualities which she refers to as
her 'sturdy hardynesse' (612). Chaucer alludes to this aspect of her
outlook when he describes, in the General Prologue portrait, her bold,
red face, her spurs, and her hat shaped like a shield as if the wearer is
ready for battle. It is as if Chaucer is suggesting that to survive and
succeed in a man's world, a woman like the Wife of Bath must assume
some of the attributes normally associated with the opposite sex.

In her previous four marriages, the Wife of Bath had less muscular husbands and had less recourse to physical force. On the other hand, she has consistently used deceit, and claims that false swearing and lying are generally better practised by women than men (227–8 and 404–6). However, the means whereby she has got her own way through an authority of the *body* is by the manipulation of sexual power. With the first three husbands she has used her body as an object of male desire with which to taunt, provoke and control the man, his wealth and possessions. She attributes the impatience and complaining of her husbands not – as is actually the case – to their simmering resentment at her success in mastering them, but to sexual frustration. Then, in a fit of sham generosity, she promises sexual favours, a tactic which diverts attention away from the real cause of the man's discontent, and from the fact that she is probably far from being the faithful wife:

> '*What eyleth yow to grucche thus and grone?*
> *Is it for ye wolde have my queynte allone?*
> *Wy, taak it al! Lo, have it every deel!*
> *Peter! I shrewe yow, but ye love it weel;*
> *For if I wolde selle my bele chose,*
> *I koude walke as fressh as is a rose;*
> *But I wol kepe it for youre owene tooth.*
> *Ye be to blame, by God! I sey yow sooth.'*
> *(443–50)*

The Wife of Bath is also prepared to use sex in return for a husband's wealth or property. She promises him a miserable time in bed until he has surrendered some kind of material possession. Then she pretends sexual pleasure in order to keep her side of the bargain:

> *For wynnyng wolde I al his lust endure,*
> *And make me a feyned appetit ...*
> *(416–17)*

Through her policy of sexual control, the Wife of Bath escapes from being regarded as a chattel by her husband (313–14) and instead makes sex the desirable possession which her husband craves.

The Wife's attitude towards sexuality changes in the case of her fifth husband, Jankyn, when the sexual impulse itself masters her. It is not just that she admires the legs and feet of this young man as he carries the bier of her fourth husband, but also that Jankyn behaves with confidence and authority when he takes his wife to bed:

> But in oure bed he was so fressh and gay,
> And therwithal so wel koude he me glose,
> Whan that he wolde han my bele chose;
> That thogh he hadde me bete on every bon,
> He koude wynne agayn my love anon.
>
> (508–12)

Here is a marital experience which Dame Alice has probably not previously enjoyed with any of her first three husbands, who were old, or with the fourth, who had a mistress. There is something involuntary about the Wife's yielding of sexual control to Jankyn. Nor is he self-consciously attempting to control her by this means. Sexuality here emerges as a natural, independent force which may sometimes escape the constraints and manipulations of human devising.

Thus, in her prologue, the authority of man's body affects the Wife of Bath chiefly through physical force. She attempts to counter such authority sometimes by using limited physical force on her own account, or by deceit, or through the manipulation of her own sexual appeal. Occasionally, the force and unpredictability of sexual urges surprise even her. Chaucer presents a similar picture of sexual relations in the tale itself. The rape is an act of male aggression made possible by superior physical strength: 'By verray force, he rafte hire may-denhed' (888). At this early stage of the narrative, the knight's attitude towards women is predatory, presuming dominance. By being placed within the power of a female court, however, he enters a female world where the sense of justice is altogether different from the summary and violent male variety practised by King Arthur. He is obliged to undergo an educative process whereby he recognizes the legitimate equality of the male and female principles. The threshold of his entry into the world where the female principle holds sway is marked by the faery dance. At this point of the narrative he moves from despair to a hope of deliverance, and he begins a sexual quest (which is also spiritual) such as is often heralded by dancing in medieval literature.

The female world which he has entered is one in which social obligations must be kept, not violated, especially in so far as they concern relations and obligations between women and men. His body is now at women's command as completely as his female victim was at his (911–12), and however much he may resent the control of female power (1061) he cannot escape it without forfeiting his integrity. So it is that, in return for the knowledge which saves his life – what women most desire is sovereignty – he must marry the hag. The limitation and hypocrisy of his sexual attitudes now lie exposed. He cannot tolerate the thought of marriage to an ugly old woman, though he supposedly possesses the quality of *gentillesse*, which should enable him to overlook surface imperfections in order to treat all women with equal courtesy. Ironically, what he was all too ready to do with the young maiden he is unable to do with the hag. She is troubled by his lack of sexual interest, and by the attitude of the male community in general:

> '*Fareth every knyght thus with his wyf as ye?*
> *Is this the lawe of kyng Arthures hous?*
> *Is every knyght of his so dangerous?*'
> *(1088–90)*

It is only when the knight accepts the truth which the hag has enabled him to discover, and then puts it into practice by allowing her the sovereignty in taking the crucial decision, that he is able to enter a state of matrimony undreamt of by traditional male authorities. The hag changes into a beautiful young woman who undertakes to be faithful and subservient to her lord's wishes.

The most important point about the woman's faithful subservience is that it is adopted of her own free will, not 'By verray force ... rafte' (888). There is a true equality between male and female at the end of the tale such as also occurs in the aftermath of the fight between Dame Alice and Jankyn (Pearsall 1985: 86–91). Both clerk and knight abandon their customary male stance of dominance, admit the legitimacy of the female principle, and in so doing achieve a rare moment of sexual-cum-marital harmony and integration. Interestingly, the moments of equilibrium, brief though they are, are marked by a sudden cessation of frenzied bodily movements. In the prologue the fisticuffs between Jankyn and the Wife of Bath subsides; in the tale there is peace after the knight's tendency to 'walwe and wynde' (1102) in bed. Emotional and psychological unity are reflected in bodily equanimity.

MARRIAGE: RITUAL

'Marriage, which is necessarily overt, public, ceremonious, surrounded by special words and deeds, is at the center of any system of values, at the junction between the material and the spiritual' (Duby 1984: 19). Its central importance as an institution, and its social context as a *rite de passage*, made marriage an occasion for elaborate ritual, both secular and ecclesiastical. The Wife of Bath's Prologue and Tale incorporate this ritual and employ it descriptively and structurally. In the prologue the episode in which Jankyn, Dame Alice and her *gossib* go into the fields (543–84) may be best understood as a ritual of secular betrothal, however immoral and comic the circumstances, with the *gossib* acting, in place of the priest, as the all-important witness. The description of the false dream in which 'blood bitokeneth gold' (581) may also refer to the giving of coin as a marriage token by the man, an act which may symbolize the purchase of female sexuality or, as in this case ironically, virginity. And if this episode does draw upon the non-ecclesiastical ceremonial and the tricks of 'my dames loor' (583) then the marriage to Jankyn may be seen to have its origins not in the world of ecclesiastically regulated property relations, but in the realm of the natural values of an alternative society in which body and spirit are more at one. The customary summary rituals of weeping and mourning for the fourth husband, arising from a relationship of false values, are only observed outwardly. Rather there is the assertion of love and appetite against the unnatural teaching of the church and male authority.

Within the tale an appreciation of the significance of marriage ritual is essential to an understanding of the development of the argument as to the nature of marriage. Four elements of marriage ritual are drawn upon, each being used symbolically in the process of analysis. The first element is that of hand-fasting in the plighting of the troth (1009), an action which represents the making of the contract, a social and economic promise (but no more), though the old woman indicates a wider importance when she concludes ' "I dar me wel avante / Thy lyf is sauf" ' (1014–15). The second, vital element of witnessing has yet to come, and when it does the circumstances are unusual. Before a representative court of women, 'Ful many a noble wyf, and many a mayde, / And many a wydwe' (1026–7), the knight gives the correct solution to the question posed by the queen and he is given his (new) life. This life, however, is conditional upon the public recognition and witnessing before the female assembly of the knight's former betrothal. The reluctance of the knight to fulfil his promise brings him to a point of crisis, symbolized in the description of the making of the marriage itself. The appropriate ritual of joy and array at the feast, in public celebration, is absent:

> *I seye ther nas no joye ne feeste at al;*
> *Ther nas but hevynesse and muche sorwe.*
> *For prively he wedded hire on morwe ...*
> *(1078–80)*

At the resolution of the crisis the final element of the marriage ritual is employed. Persuaded by the arguments of the old woman, the knight kisses her. Body and spirit are now brought together, and a physical and psychological transformation takes place as the true nature of marriage is realized. Hand-fasting, witnessing, feasting and kissing, drawn from the secular rites of marriage, are thus imbued with a

powerful symbolic value, the rituals themselves immediately recognizable and their implied meaning a challenge to contemporary
ideology.

MARRIAGE: CHANGE

The extraordinarily wide-ranging discussion of marriage which is conducted in the Wife of Bath's Prologue and Tale needs to be read not
only with an awareness of secular and ecclesiastical forms and debate
in medieval society as a whole, but within the special context of late
fourteenth-century England. If ever there was a period in which the
issues surrounding marriage, family and kin became of paramount
importance then it would be in the era of unparalleled demographic
destruction ushered in by the Black Death. 'Through marriage,
societies try to maintain and perpetuate their own structures, seen in
terms of a set of symbols and of the image they have of their own ideal
perfection' (Duby 1984: 18). It follows that when repeated epidemics
produced crisis mortalities, distorted age and sex ratios, broke up
traditional patterns of community self-replication and family and kin
connections, brought about considerable geographical and rural
mobility, and stimulated significant redistributions of wealth, then the
nature of marriage became a matter not only of immediate practical
concern but an issue central to an understanding of society as a whole
and of the ways in which contemporaries adapted to a profound social
crisis. At the level of description and metaphor, of practice and ideology, the Wife of Bath's Prologue and Tale engage their author and its
late fourteenth-century audience in an argument which concerns the
survival of society as they knew it.

Nowhere were the consequences of plague mortality more keenly
experienced than in urban society, where death rates were probably at
their highest and no community escaped. Violent discontinuities were
normal and traditional order and authority, both lay and ecclesiastical,
received a succession of shocks. Demographic disruption provided a
considerable stimulus to the marriage and remarriage market and conventional attitudes to age and sex were severely tested. In this respect
the five-times-married Wife of Bath is not so very unusual, nor is the

speed of her remarriage to Jankyn 'at the monthes ende' (ed. Dupaquier et al. 1981), but the extraordinary social and economic circumstances of the late fourteenth century do confront traditional teaching just as the Wife confronts both authority and her audience. And, inevitably, if the nature of marriage, age and sex is under reconsideration, then so is the position of women – nowhere more so than as regards the widow, who emerges at such a time as the structural focus of the demographic crisis as, by extension, does the whole issue of the independence and authority of women of all kinds. What is more, if the symbols and rituals of marriage are not to appear empty and irrelevant, and the society which they embody is not to become devalued, then they must be re-examined and revitalized. If the true nature of marriage can be restored then so can the true nature of society.

MARRIAGE: MATTER AND SPIRIT

Chaucer was concerned to show that sexuality, rather than being condemned to the status of a divisive force, belonged within marriage. At the same time he attempted to demonstrate that marriage is a spiritual as well as a material bond. Medieval marriage was a commodity market, and no more so than in the second half of the fourteenth century. Chaucer exploits the profession of the Wife of Bath to provide a vivid impression of how the condition of marriage was affected and corrupted by an excess of material values (Delany 1975: 104–9; David 1976: 143–6; Carruthers 1979: 209–15).The rediscovery of the spiritual nature of marriage is made through a return to fundamental Christian beliefs which run counter to the church's ideology of male dominance.

Mann notes that only one mention occurs of the Wife's 'cloothmakyng' (GP 447): 'The fact ... strongly suggests that the only reason for introducing it here is to emphasise her estate function' (Mann 1973: 122). There may be no other direct reference to the Wife's occupation, but her prologue (and the General Prologue portrait) are riddled with details which show that her commercial activities are far from forgotten (Robertson 1981: 23–4). Bath was associated with clothmaking, and the allusion to Ypres and Ghent (GP 448) is also topical: they were centres for the Flemish wool trade, and Flemish weavers had emigrated to England during the fourteenth century. Furthermore, the references to the Wife of Bath's clothes are made in such a way that we are asked to look both at the item of clothing and the stuff of which they are made, their texture and quality: 'her coverchiefs ful fyne weren of ground', her stockings are 'of fyn scarlet reed' (GP 453–6). She dresses in a striking, showy, even flashy way, almost as if she is a living advertisement for her own industry. The loud clothes are also an indication of pride, signified when she insists in being first to go to the offering (GP 449–52); and she dresses showily to attract men (the red of her stockings is a colour tradition-ally used for such a purpose).

The Wife of Bath's professional experience colours her whole out-look. As well as being a clothmaker she is, by virtue of that activity, a buyer of wool, a seller of cloth, a trader, merchant and saleswoman. Her dealings with men are conditioned and minutely affected by her professional instincts. Her first three husbands were rich and old – ideal commodities to a woman with an eye for a bargain and a quick profit. The Wife recounts with gaiety their failing sexual prowess and the effort which they put into love-making (201–3). 'I tolde of it no stoor' is a revealing comment, since *tolde* means 'to reckon' in the sense of reckoning accounts and *stoor* means 'store' or stock in the shopkeeper's sense. In other words, the Wife of Bath did not evaluate her husbands' sexual capabilities very highly, and she thinks of those capabilities in commercial terms. She is quite ready to write off the 'loss' because on the other side of the account she can show a con-siderable profit: 'They had me yeven hir lond and hir tresoor' (204). Once the Wife of Bath has acquired the land and riches of these men she has supremacy, or the controlling interest in the partnership. Then, it is no longer necessary to elicit her husbands' love. For the Wife of Bath, money and property are the bonds which tie men to women; and her ability to arouse love is no more than a lure with which to entice men to her control, a window-display.

Once she has established control, the relationship which develops is very much that of an employer and a worker, with the worker/ husband as a dispensable or replaceable item. The Wife's first three

husbands have to work hard to satisfy her. Their night shifts in the
Wife's bed leave them exhausted and complaining:

> *But sith I hadde hem hoolly in myn hond,*
> *And sith they hadde me yeven al hir lond,*
> *What sholde I taken keep hem for to plese,*
> *But it were for my profit and myn ese?*
> *I sette hem so a-werke, by my fey,*
> *That many a nyght they songen 'Weilawey!'*
> *(211–16)*

In order to win her good humour and favour they must make payment verging on bribes:

> *I governed hem so wel, after my lawe,*
> *That ech of hem ful blisful was and fawe*
> *To brynge me gaye thynges fro the fayre.*
> *They were ful glad whan I spak to hem faire;*
> *For, God it woot, I chidde hem spitously.*
> *(219–23)*

Sexual favours also depend on payment. The expression 'to pay the
marriage debt' occurs in Corinthians 3–4; there, it means that wife and
husband should recognize their sexual obligations towards each other.
As usual, the Wife of Bath changes the application of the text. In the
first place, she denies her husband his sexual rights. In the second
place, she demands actual payment from him in return for sex:

> *I wolde no lenger in the bed abyde,*
> *If that I felte his arm over my syde,*
> *Til he had maad his raunson unto me;*
> *Thanne wolde I suffre hym do his nycetee.*

And therfore every man this tale I telle,
Wynne whoso may, for al is for to selle;
With empty hand men may none haukes lure.
For wynnyng wolde I al his lust endure,
And make me a feyned appetit …
(409–17)

It is not entirely clear whether the Wife of Bath is referring to the 'wynnyng' of all of her husband's wealth and property, or to particular payments for each sexual act. In either case, her attitude towards sex seems mercenary. Sex, at least with these men, is a commodity.

The Wife's market-place ethics are again in evidence when she describes the process of courting her fifth husband, Jankyn. He, unlike his predecessors, is young, poor and sexually potent. The Wife of Bath says she loved him best because he was 'daungerous' (514) – standoffish or feigning lack of interest in her advances. This behaviour only made him more desirable in her eyes, for whatever is forbidden or difficult becomes more intensely attractive. The Wife describes their courtship in terms of buying and selling. When, at market, there is a lack of buyers, wise women put all their wares on display; if there are a lot of customers, traders put up their prices; if something is cheap and easy to obtain, it is not valued:

With daunger oute we al oure chaffare;
Greet prees at market maketh deere ware,
And to greet cheep is holde at litel prys:
This knoweth every womman that is wys.
(521–4)

In other ways, too, the Wife of Bath pursues her desired possession with all her professional skill. Like the wise merchant or careful spender, she makes provision for a secure future by always keeping an eye to a future husband:

For certeinly – I sey for no bobance –
Yet was I nevere withouten purveiance
Of mariage, n'of othere thynges eek.
I holde a mouses herte nat worth a leek
That hath but oon hole for to sterte to,
And if that faille, thanne is al ydo.
                    (569–74)

In practice, the marriage with Jankyn is different in kind from that with the previous four husbands. The Wife of Bath has nothing to gain materially from their union, since the clerk is poor; and unlike the first three husbands, he is young and virile. Jankyn's sexual attractiveness, the sight of his legs 'clene and faire' (598), is what draws the Wife to him. At first, though, it seems that their marriage is going the same way as all the others. If anything, the positions and attitudes of man and woman are more extreme, for Jankyn, through his calling and through the misogynist anthology in his possession, represents the very tradition of male hostility towards women against which the Wife's energies are directed. Jankyn attempts to control her gregarious instincts, and her gossiping, by quoting chapter and verse from the 'Book of Wicked Wives' (637–46). The Wife will have none of it and the book becomes a bone of contention between husband and wife.

The fight in which their 'debaat' culminates is a realization in dramatic terms of the conflict between male and female authority which is the dynamic of the prologue. Only when the book is burned, and the noxious influence of church-sanctioned authority removed, can man and wife enter into a state which is truly a marriage between equal individuals, in which freedom, not restraint, is the predominant atmosphere. For although the Wife of Bath wins nominal mastery over Jankyn when he cedes 'governance of hous and lond / And of his tonge, and of his hond also' (814–15), she does not then take advantage of her victory to make his life a misery. On the contrary, 'debaat' ceases, and

God helpe me so, I was to hym as kynde
As any wyf from Denmark unto Ynde,
And also trewe, and so was he to me.
(823–5)

Consideration, fidelity, and trust are not countenanced in the anti-matrimonial tradition, but in this instance they are offered as answers to the reductive stereotypes proffered by church authorities. There is a sense of discovery, of a genuine breakthrough, at this point in the prologue. The Wife, the reader, and not least Jankyn, who has renounced his position of dominance and put himself under female control, have arrived at an important moment of realization. He denies male mastery and so liberates them both. Words of aggression have turned to words of tenderness:

'... Myne owene trewe wyf,
Do as thee lust the terme of al thy lyf;
Keep thyn honour, and keep eek myn estaat ...'
(819–21)

There is a second reinforcing moment of realization and resolution (the points of equanimity already discussed), at a similiar place in the tale itself. Again, the hag is not interested in the material side of marriage. In an attempt to be rid of her, the knight offers wealth: ' "Taak al my good and lat my body go" ' (1061). But the hag has other interests. She wants love and sexual fulfilment through marriage, by which she sets great value:

'For thogh that I be foul, and oold, and poore
I nolde for al the metal, ne for oore
That under erthe is grave or lith above,
But if thy wyf I were, and eek thy love.'
(1063–6)

The dilemma in which the hag places her newly wedded husband – whether to have her young, beautiful and unfaithful, or old, ugly and faithful – invites him to choose between female stereotypes and so perpetuate the traditional male attitude towards women. Instead, he sidesteps his quandary, after much heart-searching, by calling on the wife to make the decision. Thus he cedes mastery and freedom to his wife, admitting the key female desire which it has been the object of his quest to discover:

> 'Thanne have I gete of yow maistrie,' quod she,
> 'Syn I may chese and governe as me lest?'
> 'Ye, certes, wyf,' quod he, 'I holde it best.'
>
> (1236–8)

As a consequence of giving his wife freedom of choice and self-government, the knight enters a genuinely blissful state of matrimony in which the lady becomes transformed into an ideal beyond male stereotypes, one hardly imaginable outside the bounds of faery. Yet this perfect female creature – the young and beautiful wife who is also faithful – is not *only* possible in a never-never world. She has been brought into existence through the knight's realistic acceptance of what it is that women most want. Finally, the tale does not suggest that such women as the transformed hag can exist only within the realms of fiction, but that the world of faery of which she is a part is, as much as anything, a psycholgical and emotional state which can actually be entered and enjoyed by those men able to admit the female principle into their marriages (Patterson 1983: 679–81; Blanch 1985: 47–8).

In referring the crucial decision to his wife, the knight ensures marital peace and harmony instead of conflict, a true marriage instead of an unhappy one and, in return for the voluntary renunciation of his mastery, the voluntary submission of hers:

> And she obeyed hym in every thyng
> That myghte doon hym plesance or likyng.
>
> (1255–6)

The marriage thus instituted is more fundamentally Christian than the views of marriage presented by many medieval church authorities, with which it is in conflict. Chaucer's return to the church's basic teaching is radical in relation to the church's practice. That Chaucer requires his readership to return to fundamentals in the matter of marriage in an attempt to recover what it should be, and can be, is clear from the hag's sermon on *gentillesse*, in which the clichés of the knight's thinking on marriage (a wife should not be ugly, old or of unequal social status) are exposed as sham in the light of Christ's example. *Gentillesse*, which a knight should practise, is not to be confused with the accidental material contingencies of birth, wealth and beauty. It is a moral and spiritual quality independent of them and deriving from one with whom all can claim kinship:

> *'Crist wole we clayme of hym oure gentillesse,*
> *Nat of oure eldres for hire old richesse.'*
> *(1117–18)*

Gentillesse derives from God's grace and cannot be inherited at birth (1163–4). It entails the practice of virtue and the avoidance of sin (1175–6), and is therefore a principle too wide to be the prerogative of a single social class. The possession and practice of *gentillesse* is not at all hindered by poverty, since God himself '"In wilful poverte chees to lyve his lyf"' (1179). This is an immensely powerful and searching speech which persuades the knight to abandon his preconceptions about women and marriage, and to choose spiritual essence instead of material emptiness.

THE WIFE OF BATH'S TALE AND ITS GENRE

There is a fine logic to the confrontation between the Wife of Bath and the authorities who 'invented' her. A similar logic exists in Chaucer's choice of a hag as the central female figure of the Wife of Bath's Tale. For if, as Jerome and other writers suggested, a young and beautiful wife will be unfaithful, then it is sensible for men to marry old and ugly ones. Yet men, like the knight of Arthur's court, prefer young and beautiful women. Such are the self-contradictory male attitudes so clearly exposed in the tale.

It will be clear from these remarks that we view prologue and tale as thoroughly integrated works, and mutually dependent. On first impression, though, the tale seems an unlikely and unexpected narrative from the colloquial mouth of the Wife of Bath. From the vivid domestic brawl between Dame Alice and Jankyn, the reader is catapulted into the seemingly distant never-never land of faery. One way of sidestepping the problem of discontinuity between prologue and tale has been by reference to the Shipman's Tale, which Chaucer may at one time have intended for the Wife of Bath: there a female narrator is implied; the setting is mercantile; the sexual relations between Don John and the merchant's wife are conducted as commodity transactions; the language is loaded with *double entendres* (Silverman 1953: 329–36; Aers 1983: 342–4). All of these factors would make the tale square with the Wife of Bath's marital experiences – up to a point. Although the Shipman's Tale would form a fitting sequel to the Wife's first three or four marriages, and would seem to perpetuate the fabliau spirit in which the prologue ends, it does little to reflect the relationship with Jankyn, which *is* accurately mirrored, especially at the end, in the Wife of Bath's Tale. Perhaps it is possible to see here Chaucer's developing conception of the Wife of Bath, as she moved form being a figure conjured out of antifeminist writing into a creation altogether more complex (Pratt 1961: 47–9).

The shift which occurs between prologue and tale may be deliberate, a change of register which is meant to convey a sense of entry into a realm of ideas which, having been announced in the prologue, are now taken more seriously and subjected to a much more searching enquiry at a higher level of discourse. The sense of change and entry is effected through the juxtaposition of different genres. The domestic brawl with which the prologue ends raises the expectation that the tale proper will include similar episodes, and so be a fabliau like the Miller's Tale, Reeve's Tale or Shipman's Tale, concerned with the tribulations of married life. The theme is certainly there, but it is presented in the surprising context of an Arthurian romance.

The sudden transformation in genre is thought-provoking, and that may be part of Chaucer's purpose: he wanted his audience to puzzle out the likenesses in apparently unlike compositions. In fact there are extensive connections between the two parts of this single work. One type of connection is formal and concerns the placing of descriptive narrative specificity within prologue and tale (Patterson 1983: 678–9). The prolgoue begins with a general treatment of the subject of marriage; proceeds to an account of the narrator's first four marriages in which the first three husbands are lumped together, the fourth being given special attention; and then concludes with a closely textured recounting of the courting of Jankyn and his behaviour in marriage. With the transition from general to particular comes an acceleration in pace until the climax of sequential activity in the brawl with Jankyn. In the tale itself there occurs a reverse process of winding down: the pace is fastest at the beginning with the pointed remarks about friars, the rape, and the trial; it then slows during the knight's quest for an answer to the question posed by the queen; and the tale ends in a measured manner as the hag holds forth on *gentillesse*. Descriptively, the procedure is again the reverse of what occurs in the prologue, for there is a movement form the detailed to the general. Thus prologue and tale are balanced.

Another kind of balancing or matching exists in the nature of the material used by Chaucer in writing the Wife of Bath's Tale, for on close inspection it reveals a variety similar to that found in the prologue. There exist narrative analogues in John Gower's *Tale of Florent* and two anonymous works, the *Marriage of Sir Gawaine* and the *Weddynge of Sir Gawen and Dame Ragnell*. But there are several incursions into the received romance plot: the opening aside on friars, Ovid's story of Midas from the *Metamorphoses*, an excerpt from Dante's *Convivio* on the nature of nobility, and from Jean de Meun's *Romance of the Rose* on *gentillesse*. The Wife of Bath's Tale, no less than her prologue, should be seen as a compilation, though one which makes greater use of a single narrative as a means of organizing the material.

The genre of the tale itself may be less unsuitable for expressing the Wife of Bath's ideas than at first appears. In the first place it may be thought of as a black romance in which certain conventions of the genre are inverted and expectations confounded as if the narrator is questioning another type of female stereotype, that purveyed through chivalric literature. The hero dose not, initially, behave in a courteous manner when he rapes on sight a young woman; he does not succeed in his quest until aided by a woman; the heroine is not, for most of the story, a beauty; their marriage is not an occasion for glorious celebrations at the court of King Arthur; their first night is not to be imagined, as is for example the love-making of Troilus and Criseyde, as a lovely and lyrical experience:

> *Now wolden som men seye, paraventure,*
> *That for my necligence I do not cure*
> *To tellen yow the joye and al th'array*
> *That at the feeste was that ilke day.*
> *To which thyng shortly answeren I shal:*
> *I seye ther nas no joye ne feeste at al;*
> *Ther nas but hevynesse and muche sorwe.*
> *For prively he wedded hire on morwe,*
> *And al day after hidde hym as an owle,*
> *So wo was hym, his wyf looked so foule.*
>   *Greet was the wo the knyght hadde in his thoght,*
> *Whan he was with his wyf abedde ybroght;*
> *He walweth and he turneth to and fro.*
>
>   *(1073–85)*

The negative and upside-down world of the Wife of Bath's Tale is not put to rights until the end of the story, when a fairy-tale union between young knight and beautiful woman becomes a 'reality'.

The Wife of Bath's Tale has been discussed as part of an extremely capacious category of medieval story-telling, the romance, a genre which in Chaucer's work includes narratives with such diverse effects as those found in Thopas and the Knight's Tale. It is more strictly accurate to designate the Wife of Bath's Tale as a sub-species of romance, the Breton lay (Hoepffner 1959), a genre which became naturalized in England (Beston 1974; Johnston 1974). Although the tale is not normally included among the surviving Middle English

Breton lays, it conforms to the narrative pattern of the genre more strictly than the Franklin's Tale, which is often cited as the one example of a Chaucerian lay (Smithers 1953; Johnston 1972). There are a number of distinctive features about the lay which suggest that, far from its being an extraordinary choice of genre for the Wife of Bath, it is in fact highly appropriate. First, as the prologue to the Franklin's Tale makes clear, this kind of romance was considered to be a distinctively oral form of story-telling, at least as it originally existed among the 'British' (Donovan 1969: 44–6; Yoder 1977: 74–7; Clifford 1982: 11–12):

> *This olde gentil Britouns in his dayes*
> *Of diverse aventures maden layes,*
> *Rymeyed in hir firste Briton tonge,*
> *Whiche layes with hir instrumentz they songe*
> *Or elles redden hem for hir plesaunce;*
> *And oon of hem have I in remembraunce,*
> *Which I shal seyn with good wyl as I kan.*
>
> *(FrankT 709–15)*

A more elaborate statement of this view of the lay may be found in the opening lines of *Lay le Freine* (ed. Sands 1966: 234–5), a work found together with other Middle English lays in the Auchinleck manuscript, a book with which Chaucer may have been acquainted (L. Loomis 1941). The reputation of the lay as an oral form of poetry makes it a particularly suitable choice for a narrator who wields the spoken word to such great effect. Second, as the surviving collection of lays by Marie de France indicates, the genre in one of its incarnations was associated with female authorship, which again makes it a fitting choice for the Wife of Bath (Everett 1929: 120–1; Eisner 1937: 14–15 and 136). Third, the content of the lays of Marie de France indicates that the genre was capable of being used for a kind of inversion of romance values whereby the point of view of female character within sexual relations is stressed, a reversal in which supernatural forces, including faeries, have an important function (Hanning and Ferrante 1978: 1–27; Clifford 1982: 56–60; Burgess 1987: 101–33). The suitability of this feature of the lay to the Wife of Bath needs no stressing. Her attitudes, values and polemical intentions are well served by the narrative vehicle chosen for her by Chaucer.

There is a general point to be made about the profuse range of genres employed by Chaucer in the Wife of Bath's Prologue and Tale. The opening reminds the reader of debate literature; her examples and biblical quotations read like a sermon; the tale of Jankyn is worthy of a fabliau; there is an eruption of a four-cornered debate between Wife, Friar, Summoner and Host once the tale is ended; the tale itself begins in a fabliau mood only to be transposed to a romance; and within the romance is a 'sermon' on *gentillesse*. The profusion of genres provides prologue and tale with a sense of vitality, but it would be mistaken to say that this impression is created just to provide the Wife of Bath's character with vivacity. In her command of genre she is, as in other aspects of her existence, all-embracing. But the consequence of moving back and forth rapidly from one kind of discourse to another is to relate the issues with which she is concerned to different kinds of audience. For as genres change, so do the targets of address. The debate on marriage and the sermonizing of the prologue imply a clerical audience; the account of her marriages is also appealing to those with mercantile values; while the lay raises issues of concern to the nobility.

It is possible to draw three conclusions from this multi-levelled appeal of prologue and tale. The first is that the issues which the Wife of Bath broaches concerning sex and marriage are of concern to the whole of society, that clerics no less than nobles are involved in an ideology which typecasts women and which underpins the actual male control of women in fourteenth-century society (Zacher 1976: 104–6). The question of sovereignty, in particular, raises the larger questions of power and domination in the possession of land and property (Knight 1980b: 13–14), and in some analogues of the tale the question of sexual mastery is explicitly linked to national sovereignty (Eisner 1937: 17–44 and 129). The second is that a woman's mentality is capable of being peculiarly all-inclusive, able to undergo treatment as an inferior, while perceiving the false suppositions on which male dominance is based, and endeavouring to avoid the worst effects of that dominance by evolving an alternative, distinctively female cultural network. The third is that Chaucer intends to address the entire problem of sex and marriage and has found a vehicle for doing so.

The range of genres in the Wife of Bath's Prologue and Tale, their multi-layered audience appeal, and the dynamic effect of the Wife's contribution on her pilgrim audience, make that contribution a small-scale model of the *Canterbury Tales* as a whole. It is therefore legitimate to propose that, through the Wife of Bath, Chaucer is questioning the function of his own art and its relation to his audience. The sense that narrative art itself is in question is reinforced by the disproportionate lengths of prologue and tale. The Wife of Bath announces in response to the Pardoner's interruption that her tale is 'Of tribulacion in mariage' (173). Yet at this stage she has still to complete the bulk of her preamble. There is a constant deferring of expectation as, the stories of her husbands turn out not to be her tale, and the tale itself not what the prologue leads the reader to expect. The question 'Which *is* the Wife of Bath's tale?' is not ridiculous, for the title 'Of tribulacion in mariage' applies equally well to the tale of five husbands as to the Arthurian lay. The question probably cannot be answered, and perhaps that is its point. For the dilemma experienced by the reader is germane to one of the central themes of prologue and tale, as indeed of the *Canterbury Tales* themselves: that the crucial function of narrative art in its relation to audience is not to be found in the appreciation which would simply respond to lovable characters, nor in the literary historicism which would go no further than identifying sources, genres, tradition and innovation; it is to be found in the process of interpretation, in 'glossing', in discovering that there is a wisdom to be found in the old forms which can make of literature a live issue, speaking both to its time and place, and beyond.

2

The Franklin

If the comedy of the Wife of Bath's Prologue and Tale arises from the conflict of authorities, that of the Squire's Tale and the Franklin's Tale comes from the conflict between social orders and from social pretension, touching closely the social position of the author himself. In this chapter we examine Chaucer's concern with social status, social mobility, and social and political morality, through his arguments in the Squire's Tale and the Franklin's Tale. The two tales are complementary, pursuing the same matter from subtly different social positions, possessing many parallels, yet developing a progressive argument about social and political relations within a society involved with chivalric ideals. Both examine the dangerous contradictions within such a society and ultimately suggest the need and means for reform. This discussion arises directly from a concern with such problems which was widely acknowledged in England in the second half of the fourteenth century.

Just as Chaucer's consideration of authority led to an examination of the whole process of fictional composition which challenged the perceptions of his audience, so in the Squire's Tale and the Franklin's Tale he undertakes an evaluation of language, rhetoric and genre inextricably involved with the maintenance and reinforcement of aristocratic values at a time when those values are encountering searching criticism. Once again his treatment is deeply subversive of prevailing modes of discourse, deliberately disconcerting his audience, encouraging ambiguity and debate, and searching for means of expression to act as correlatives of the fundamental Christian values he seeks to reassert.

CHAUCER, THE SQUIRE AND THE FRANKLIN

The relationship between Chaucer, the Squire and the Franklin is one which deserves special attention. In order to appreciate the subtle nuances of the satire employed in the General Prologue and in the Squire's Tale, Franklin's Prologue and Franklin's Tale, a precise description of Chaucer's own position is worth searching for. The Squire was described in the General Prologue as the Knight's son, a young man, proved overseas in *chevauchée*, the epitome of young and fashionable chivalry – the kind of figure, perhaps, to whom the commons so frequently objected in the court of Richard II. He is a man who has inherited his status, who has proved himself worthy in arms and who will, in due course, become a knight. The Franklin, however, as described in the General Prologue, completely lacks a chivalric dimension and has no inherited status. It has recently been confirmed that the reference to him as 'a worthy vavasour' (GP 360) in all probability derives from a French literary tradition in which the vavasour has an ambiguous position on the fringes of aristocratic life (Pearcy 1973: 33–59; Carruthers 1981: 290–2), but which has no contemporary social significance (Coss 1983: 109–50). He does, however, seem to perform many of the administrative and political functions formerly associated with knighthood (Robertson 1974: 277), and indeed to have had his real-life counterparts (Manly 1926: 162–8; Wood-Legh 1928: 145–51; Specht 1981: 132–41; Turville-Petre 1982: 334–5; Saul 1983: 10–11):

> *At sessiouns ther was he lord and sire;*
> *Ful ofte tyme he was knyght of the shire.*
> . . . .
> *A shirreve hadde he been, and a contour.*
> *(GP 355–6 and 359)*

As such, it has been argued, Chaucer's Franklin is atypical. The description in the General Prologue 'puts him firmly among the country gentry, among that majority who did not bother to assume the expense of knighthood' (Hilton 1975: 25). The franklins and petty franklins recorded in the 1379 Poll Tax returns for southern and eastern Warwickshire lacked such stature though their assessments might be equated with those of lesser squires (Hilton 1975: 26). Yet, however sure some writers have been of the Franklin's *gentil* status (Gerould 1926: 262–79; Carruthers 1981: 283–90; Specht 1981: *passim*), the ambiguity as regards it may be precisely his significance. Absent from traditional estates satire (Mann 1973: 152), he represents a social stratum in the upper reaches of the peasantry which, in the peculiar conditions of the fourteenth century, and especially those after the Black Death, began to take on some of the political and administrative functions of a declining chivalric group, the knights, while never acquiring a heritable nobility or gentility (Saul 1983: 12–18).

Where then did Chaucer stand in relation to Squire and Franklin? If the Franklin occupied an ambiguous social position in the upper stratum of the peasantry then Chaucer might be said to occupy an ambiguous social position in the upper stratum of townsmen, that stratum which sought to enhance its position by the acquisition of offices under the crown and by investment in land. One way of investigating Chaucer's own social standing is by an analysis of the network of his acquaintances, and much has been done on these lines in the attempt to determine Chaucer's circle (Strohm 1977). Another way to consider the problem is by analysis of the language of social status as it applied to Chaucer. As the son of a wine merchant his involvement in aristocratic and royal households and his diplomatic, justicial and administrative activity under the crown enhanced his status. In the period for which evidence survives for his career between 1366 and 1400 he is variously described as 'vallet', 'vallectus', 'scutifer', 'armiger', 'esquier', 'escuier' and, in receipt of mourning liveries in 1369, as one of the 'esquiers de meindre degree' (ed. Crow and Olson 1966: *passim*). The problem of determining social status in the late fourteenth century is made more difficult by

61

the co-existence of three languages of social description. Throughout his career, however, Chaucer is known, in English and French, as an esquire. Between 1372 and 1381 he is simultaneously known as 'vallectus', 'scutifer' and 'armiger', and although after 1381 he is most commonly called 'armiger' or 'esquire', the term 'scutifer' is also applied to him. In reinforcement of his armigerous standing is the evidence of his own deposition in the Scrope-Grosvenor case of 1386 where he claimed to be 'esquier del age de xl ans et plus armeez par xxvii ans' (ed. Crow and Olson 1966: 370), and the testimony to the existence of his armorial seal, revealed in 1409 (ed. Crow and Olson 1966: 542). Chaucer was then an armigerous esquire, but the significance of such a description is far from clear in a period when the language of social status contained many ambiguities, the product of an unprecedented social mobility.

At the end of the thirteenth century the language of social demarcation did little to recognize the stratification of landed society below the rank of knight. In the course of the fourteenth century, however, the dwindling number of knights, reduced by economic difficulties, were joined by groups of lesser status clearly designated in a new social terminology as 'scutifers', those of sufficient wealth to enter the ranks of the knights; 'armigers', men-at-arms who had not acquired knighthood; 'valets', who in the early fourteenth century were those just below the rank of knight yet of sufficient wealth to maintain such status, often retained in the service of a magnate; and 'esquires', descriptive of a fairly broad social group ranging from potential knights and younger sons of knights returned from war in France, to those with little or no lands, rents or chattels, but only military experience or service in a noble household (Postan 1942: 11–12). Gradually, under the pressure of a quickening social mobility, sharp lines of social distinction became blurred, further social categories were designated, and attempts were made to prevent the erosion of status. Interestingly, the control of the descriptive language of status became an aspect of the defensive attitude of those in power in the face of rapid social change.

In the years following the Black Death, and particularly after the second major pandemic of 1361–2, changed demographic and economic conditions favoured the advancement of smaller landowners.

Now the social hierarchy below the level of knights was peopled not only by 'esquires', 'valets', 'scutifers' and 'armigers', but also by 'sergeants', 'firmarii', 'yeomen' and 'franklins'. What is more, realignments within the terminological hierarchy saw a loss of status for the 'valet' and the social enhancement of the 'esquire', a term which became virtually identical with the 'armiger'. In seeking to control the wearing of garments denoting social status, the Commons' Petition of 1363 had already acknowledged this linguistic shift, indicating that 'valletz' were then wearing the clothing of 'esquires' and 'esquires' the clothing of 'knights'. John Trevisa, in his translation of Higden's *Polychronicon*, expressed the same ideas a little more systematically: 'þherefore hit is,' he wrote, 'þat a ȝeman arraieþ hym as a squyer, a squyer as a knyȝt, a kniȝt as a duke [and] a duke as a kyng' (ed. Babington and Lomby 1869: II. 171). Progressively, moreover, it seems that the esquire came to possess something of the chivalric aura of knighthood, acquiring a respectability and gentility, adopting heraldic devices and entering the ranks of the armigerous, attaining a distinction which might be conferred, like knighthood, by the crown. In so far as they came to be recognized as of noble or *gentil* blood they became divided from other newly emerging ranks in the late fourteenth century, though in practice they might perform similar administrative and political functions. Among these ranks there were those whose life as a group deserving distinctive linguistic description was only short. Such were the 'firmarii' and the franklins – they might be free but they were never *gentil* – and, while their designation lasted, they remained the social inferior of knight and esquire whose duties they frequently fulfilled (Coleman 1981: 58–9).

In the light of such developments Chaucer's own social position is, perhaps, a little clearer. He was a beneficiary of those social and economic changes in the fourteenth century which produced a considerable complexity and ambiguity in *gentil* society, especially in the years after the Black Death as social distinctions multiplied in the upper ranks of the peasantry and the lower ranks of the nobility. Like the Franklin, with whom he shared administrative and judicial offices (Blenner-Hassett 1953: 791), and the Squire, he was caught up in a movement of upward social mobility which produced considerable tension between social groups (Brewer 1968: 303–5). That mobility severely tested traditional ideologies, especially those which were the product of the chivalric society emerging in Europe in the twelfth and thirteenth centuries. The existence of such social tension helps to explain the relations between Chaucer's Franklin and Squire and their conflicting modes of discourse, and it helps to explain why the concept of *gentillesse* should be of central concern.

What is more, when the Franklin concludes his tale with

Lordynges, this question, thanne, wol I aske now,
Which was the mooste fre, as thynketh yow?
(1621–2)

he is asking a question at the heart of the conflict (both open and concealed) between aspiring social groups, over power and authority in a Christian society. Such conflict, in this period, was by no means confined to social groups in the upper ranks of society: it was to be found more generally in town and countryside, and perhaps increasingly in the 1360s and 1370s. The question of freedom was central to the demands of the rebels in 1381 and many of those in authority, and perhaps some of the more extreme among the rebels, may have believed with Higden (*Polychronicon*) that the purpose of the revolt 'was to have sleyne alle the noble blood in Ynglonde of eiþer kynde, and the kynge at the laste also, and so to have disposede the realme at theire pleasure' (ed. Babington and Lumby 1882: VIII. 456). Certainly, in the apocalyptic language of the time, the whole process of rapid social mobility might signify more than the passing discomfort of social realignment (Coleman 1981: 62). Trevisa's Higden, discussing clothing and status, begins 'Yit som gooth a boute to alle manere staate and beeth in noon astaat, for they that note take everiche degree beeth of non degre', before moving to the passage quoted above describing the new aspirations of yeomen, squires, knights and dukes. Most significantly, however, he concludes this passage with reference to the prophecy of 'an holy anker to Kyng Egilred' in which it was predicted that 'than the worlde schal be so unstable and so dyvers and variable that the unstabilnesse of thoughtes schal be bytokened by many manere dyversite of clothinge'. Social and political adaptation has become interpreted in terms of a threat to both civil and religious order and the outward manifestations of that adaptation are taken to be signs of impending catastrophe or apocalypse. Not that disaster was necessarily considered inevitable; rather that the language of disaster was invoked in an attempt to control and prevent. The tales of the Franklin and the Squire are concerned with central contemporary issues immediate to Chaucer's own experience but capable of projection and articulation in terms of cosmic order. In exploring these issues through an examination of the complex moral and social significance of *gentillesse* (Burnley 1979: 151–70) and freedom, Chaucer seeks to supply a radical Christian solution to problems of social and political disorder.

THE SQUIRE'S TALE

Because the Squire's Tale is curtailed it is tempting to regard it as unfinished and in some way inferior, a discarded fragment, less worthy of attention than the completed tales for which Chaucer found a convenient use. It seems likely, however, that such an attitude seriously underestimates the importance of the fragment. Arguably, and against the tendency of some recent studies (Lawton 1985: 106–29; Seaman 1986: 12–18), the Squire's Tale is no fragment at all but an integral part of a unit embracing Squire's Tale and Franklin's Tale (Kee 1975: 4–6). Verbal and thematic parallels and similarities, concern with rhetoric, and an inclusive contemporary context of a profound concern with matters of social mobility and social order, draw the two tales together. It may be that the Squire's Tale should be regarded as a complete section in a pair of explorations of similar arguments taken from subtly different social positions across the divide of gentility.

The comedy of the Squire's Tale derives from social pretensions and, taken at its most profound in the examination of the nature of *gentillesse*, this is the subject matter of the two tales. The most obvious location of the social pretension is in the Squire's rhetorical practice and, if it were not already obvious, the Franklin's interruption directs the audience ironically to the Squire's eloquence. Both in narrative

organization and in modes of expression and description the inadequacy of the *gentil* squire is made abundantly clear (Pearsall 1964).
But his tale works at another level too. The substance and significance
of his narrative may be poorly, and even at times preposterously,
expressed but there is a serious purpose which exists in curious
tension with the inadequacy of rhetorical presentation, adding to the
comedy but also giving an extra dimension to the social and political
questions at the heart of the discussion.

Both Franklin and Squire are concerned with rhetoric and both
recognize it to be an important aspect of social demarcation. In their
use of language, Squire and Franklin emphasize the social distance
between them. Speaking of the beauty of King Cambyuskan's daughter, Canacee, the Squire says:

> But for to telle yow al hir beautee,
> It lyth nat in my tonge, n'yn my konnyng;
> I dar nat undertake so heigh a thyng.
> Myn Englissh eek is insufficient.
> It moste been a rethor excellent
> That koude his colours longynge for that art,
> If he sholde hire discryven every part.
> I am noon swich, I moot speke as I kan.
>
> *(34–41)*

If this speech is compared with that made by the Franklin in the
prologue to his tale – 'But, sires, by cause I am a burel man ... My
spirit feeleth noght of swich mateere' (716–27) – then marked differences emerge. Clearly the Franklin knows *about* rhetoric (Harrison
1935), and perhaps feels the social need to demonstrate this, while
acknowledging that his expertise was not acquired as part of a gentle
upbringing or education. The Franklin's language is more direct and
economical both in this passage and in his tale. In terms of narrative
skill, indeed, he shows himself to be the Squire's superior.

The passage spoken by the Squire is occupied with a particular rhetorical device and has no need to demonstrate that its author knows

about rhetoric: his knowledge has been internalized, it is part of his gentility. Here, as elsewhere in his tale, almost obsessively, the Squire employs the device of inexpressibility. His language is careful and even precious, lacking for the most part the urgency and richness of the Franklin's. As the Squire's Tale unfolds it often seems more concerned with its own mode of expression as a *gentil* manifestation than with narrative development. Circumlocution, repetition and variation, and self-deprecation, become ends in themselves. Despite a calculated modesty of tone, however, the Squire is not beyond a condescension or even arrogance which emphasizes the social distance between the *gentil* and the lewd and, by implication, between the *gentils* and all other social groups. If anything, his calculated self-effacement implies a superiority. His whole tale and its attitude to narrative promote an uneasy relationship with his audience of fellow-pilgrims as well as with a wider audience, and this contributes to the necessity for interruption.

In discussing the speculation which arises over the nature of the magic horse given to Cambyuskan by the strange knight the Squire remarks:

> *Of sondry doutes thus they jangle and trete,*
> *As lewed peple demeth comunly*
> *Of thynges that been maad moore subtilly*
> *Than they kan in hir lewednesse comprehende;*
> *They demen gladly to the badder ende.*
>
> *(220–4)*

The effect of this passage is complex. There is a kind of sneering superiority about it which is the other side of the modesty conveyed through the inexpressibility topos. But it also serves to curtail the narrative and the developing interest of the audience; and the manner of the curtailment casts a shadow forward over subsequent narrative development, creating an unease about involvement or interest in the tale, suggesting the social inferiority of curiosity, and alienating audience and fellow-pilgrims.

67

Again, in describing interest in the gift of the mirror, the Squire comments:

> *And somme of hem wondred on the mirour,*
> *That born was up into the maister-tour,*
> *Hou men myghte in it swiche thynges se.*
> *Another answerde and seyde it myghte wel be*
> *Naturelly, by composiciouns*
> *Of anglis and of slye reflexiouns,*
> *And seyde that in Rome was swich oon,*
> *They speken of Alocen, and Vitulon,*
> *And Aristotle, that writen in hir lyves*
> *Of queynte mirours and of perspectives,*
> *As knowen they that han hir bookes herd.*
>
> *(225–35)*

Since such wonder is lewd incomprehension, to pursue such matters is somehow socially demeaning (Kahrl 1973: 203). The consequence of such an attitude is to emasculate the narrative, to make it two-dimensional. Not only is development within the story curtailed but so too is imagination; the metaphorical power of ideas is denied and what remains is rhetoric and arid scholarship, both being demonstrations of a *gentil* education. The superior tone which the Squire adopts in referring to his sources for information about mirrors becomes an end in itself.

Speaking of the magic ring given to Canacee the Squire is drawn again to comment on such wondering:

> *But nathelees somme seiden that it was*
> *Wonder to maken of fern-asshen glas,*
> *And yet nys glas nat lyk asshen of fern;*
> *But, for they han yknowen it so fern,*
> *Therfore cesseth hir janglyng and hir wonder.*
> *As soore wondren somme on cause of thonder,*
> *On ebbe, on flood, on gossomer, and on myst,*

And alle thyng, til that the cause is wyst.
Thus jangle they, and demen, and devyse
Til that the kyng gan fro the bord aryse.
(253–62)

Because the discussion is seen as a worthless interlude before the departure of the king, and because the objects of discussion are contemptuously presented without revealing the substance of discussion, the feelings aroused are those of sterility and frustration. The deliberate superficiality of the Squire becomes exasperating.

If the Squire uses rhetoric and book-learning as weapons of social status it is also apparent, and part of Chaucer's comic intention, that despite his learning he is a poor practitioner as a story-teller. He is fully aware of the constituent elements of *gentil* story-telling: he seeks to embellish his narrative with appropriate colours; he introduces astrological, calendrical and seasonal detail; he displays a knowledge of the science of humours; he demonstrates an extensive knowledge of written authorities; but his tale is unduly circumlocutory, digressive and repetitive, and narrative development, when it is not slow, is curtailed at the moment of growing interest. In other words, if the Squire's intention is to impress by his command of *gentil* discourse then the opposite is the case. His social pretension is condemned by his manifest inadequacy.

At one point it seems that the Squire has begun to recognize some of the frustration of his audience when he says:

The knotte why that every tale is toold,
If it be taried til that lust be coold
Of hem that han it after herkned yoore,
The savour passeth ever lenger the moore,
For fulsomnesse of his prolixitee;
And by the same resoun, thynketh me,
I sholde to the knotte condescende,
And maken of hir walkyng soone an ende.
(401–8)

69

Although he then moves to what may conceivably be the centre-piece of the 'unfinished' tale he is still far from reaching a dénouement. His audience's sighs of relief quickly turn to groans when it becomes clear that all the Squire is doing is bringing to an end his description of Canacee's early morning walk prior to an extended treatment of the outcome of that walk. Finally, when he reveals the full, elaborate and bewildering scope of his tale, and that what has passed so far is only a small part of the proposed work, the Franklin intervenes on behalf of the audience. The Squire's rehearsal of forthcoming events is, however, designed by Chaucer to prove a breaking-point. The prospect of further episodes of sterile rhetorical description concerned with 'aventures and of batailles' (659) is too much to take.

But the satirical treatment of the Squire's discourse and the deliberate intention that it should be rejected should not lead to a rejection of the themes which the Squire's Tale articulates. Contained within the structure of the feast, the arrival of the strange knight and his gifts, the sleep and the dream, and the story of the falcon and the tercelet, is matter which explores ideas developed more successfully in the Franklin's Tale. The arrival of the strange knight on the auspicious day of the king's nativity sets in motion events which culminate (within the tale) in a story of chivalric betrayal – not, perhaps, the story which would have been expected from the Squire.

A suggestion of menace and danger is introduced soon after the knight's dramatic entry. The comparison of the stranger with Gawayn and the mention of the realm of 'fairye' sensitize the audience to Arthurian themes and to a possible retribution. In describing the properties of the magic mirror we are told that it

'Hath swich a myght that men may in it see
Whan ther shal fallen any adversitee
Unto youre regne or to youreself also,
'And openly who is youre freend or foo.
And over al this, if any lady bright
Hath set hire herte on any maner wight,
If he be fals, she shal his tresoun see ...'
(133–9)

The dramatic implication of introducing such an object and so describing its properties would seem to be that adversity and treason are to be found in the ensuing story. Imminent danger is suggested by the magic, Excalibur-like sword, with its contradictory powers of destruction and healing. And the projected need for healing arises again from the description of the properties of the magic ring:

> '*And every gras that groweth upon roote*
> *She shal eek knowe, and whom it wol do boote,*
> *Al be his woundes never so depe and wyde.*'
> *(153–5)*

In discussion of the magic horse there is a return to the theme of treason. The lewd speculation about the origins and purpose of the horse (voicing the speculation of the tale's audience) comes first to the somewhat menacing conclusion that 'It was a fairye' and then to a comparison with the Trojan horse:

> '*Myn herte,*' quod oon, '*is everemoore in drede;*
> *I trowe som men of armes been therinne,*
> *That shapen hem this citee for to wynne.*'
> *(212–14)*

Returning to Arthurian themes, and maintaining the suggestion of danger and betrayal, the Squire makes reference to Lancelot in describing (or *not* describing) the scene when the strange knight and Canacee dance together:

> *Swich subtil lookyng and dissymulynges*
> *For drede of jalouse mennes aperceyvynges?*
> *(285–6)*

With the feast at an end, and the assembly departed for bed,

> *Ful were hire heddes of fumositee,*
> *That causeth dreem of which ther nys no charge.*
> *(358–9)*

The Squire, characteristically, supplies no detail of the dreams but we do learn that Canacee is excited by the gifts of ring and mirror:

> *And in hire sleep, right for impressioun*
> *Of hire mirour, she hadde a visioun.*
> *(371–2)*

As a consequence of the vision Canacee wakes early, determines to go for a walk, and comes upon the falcon – the story of the falcon and the tercelet deriving from the dream vision produced by the magic gifts of the strange, Gawayn-like knight. The image of the falcon in the tree, blood pouring down its dried, white trunk, is the most powerful of the whole tale. It invites symbolic interpretation – the proud chivalric bird bleeding to death:

> *Ybeten hadde she hirself so pitously*
> *With bothe hir wynges, til the rede blood*
> *Ran endelong the tree ther-as she stood.*
> *(414–16)*

The reference to blood recalls the earlier injunction of Cambyuskan, made in a different context, to '"Cherisseth blood, natures freend"' (353), and anticipates the falcon's final condemnation of the tercelet:

'No gentillesse of blood ne may hem bynde.
'So ferde this tercelet, allas the day!
Though he were gentil born, and fressh and gay,
And goodlich for to seen, and humble and free,
He saugh upon a tyme a kyte flee,
And sodeynly he loved this kyte so
That al his love is clene fro me ago,
And hath his trouthe falsed in this wyse.'
(620–7)

Seduced by 'newefangelnesse', the tercelet betrays the falcon for the lower-ranking kite. The betrayal, and even destruction, of gentility seems to be the danger threatened earlier (Haller 1965: 291–3; Davenport 1988: 47–9). If so, then the nature of that gentility is conveyed by the falcon in respect of her own honour. The falcon makes clear that in respect of the tercelet she

Graunted hym love, upon this condicioun,
That everemoore myn honour and renoun
Were saved, bothe privee and apert ...
(529–31)

Set against *gentillesse* is the tercelet's '"treson and falsnesse"' (506). The falcon praises the *gentil* virtues of '"trouthe"' (508), of innocence and '"seuertee"' (528), of '"devout humblesse"' (544) and '"plesance"' (509), and the merit of giving love freely – and of performing the appropriate '"cerymonyes and obeisaunces, / And ... observaunces"' (515–16). The tercelet, however, is represented as a lying hypocrite, crowned with malice, '"ful of doublenesse"' (543), a serpent hidden under flowers, a tiger and, returning to Trojan imagery, as worse than '"Jason ne Parys of Troye"'(548). And, in a striking image which might be projected on to chivalric society itself,

'As in a toumbe is al the faire above,
And under is the corps, swich as ye woot,
Swich was this ypocrite ...'
(518–20)

Taken together, the themes introduced by the Squire are very much those of contemporary moral and political criticism. Notably, the falcon believes that there is no way in which she can be saved, but in Canacee the Squire's Tale would seem to possess an agent of redemption, chosen to restore the falcon. The gift of healing powers bestowed upon her by the strange knight are now to be used. Rescued and comforted by Canacee, the falcon declares, 'Right in hir haukes ledene':

'That pitee renneth soone in gentil herte,
Feelynge his similitude in peynes smerte,
Is preved alday, as men may it see,
As wel by werk as by auctoritee;
For gentil herte kitheth gentillesse.
I se wel that ye han of my distresse
Compassion, my faire Canacee,
Of verray wommanly benignytee
That Nature in youre principles hath set.'
(479–87)

Making a pen for the falcon at her bedside, Canacee 'covered it with veluettes blewe, / In signe of trouthe that is in wommen sene' (644–5). What the Squire's Tale seems to suggest is that the female principle in society, with its natural gentility, is capable of healing the wounds of chivalric betrayal. For the Squire, perhaps wishfully, the added suggestion is that *gentil* society is capable of healing itself, since Canacee is the king's daughter. It seems, moreover, in the synopsis of the 'uncompleted' portion of the tale, that the Squire envisages the king's son playing an important part in restoring society to its former order.

RHETORIC: THE POWER OF WORDS

One of the effects of the Squire's ornate style, unmodulated as it is by the variety of different kinds of diction, has been to reduce his tale to something merely decorative, more remarkable for the ingenuity of its verbal elaborations than for its content. Following his remarks the Franklin suddenly praises the Squire for acquitting himself '"gentilly"', with wit and, considering his youth, '"feelyngly"' (673–6). He says that his eloquence is unlikely to be equalled by any other pilgrim and confesses to taking great delight in the young man's discourse. These remarks are ironic, disparaging, but there lies behind them the hint of a desire to be able to emulate the Squire's fine words. That hint is communicated through the association of eloquence with *gentil* birth. In other words, the Franklin recognizes that a particular kind of utterance, and especially that which expresses a 'lordly' conception of experience, is the prerogative of the aristocracy. The Squire's diction exudes the unquestioning confidence of that aristocracy, his style reflecting social position and power. No wonder the Franklin intervenes, even if he does not interrupt (Pearsall 1964: 90–1). For, as it now emerges, and as many have argued, he aspires to that very rank from which, by birth, he is excluded (Lumiansky 1955: 180–93; Burlin 1974: 184–7; Saul 1983: 21–3). He has a son who is a wastrel, and wishes that he were capable of the 'discrecioun' (685) demonstrated by the Squire. Material wealth – the basis of the Franklin's social and political power – counts for nothing unless it be accompanied by the manner, the style, the ethos of the court:

'... Fy on possessioun,
But if a man be vertuous withal!
. . . .
'... he hath levere talken with a page
Than to comune with any gentil wight
Where he myghte lerne gentillesse aright.'
(686–7 and 692–4)

A grasp of the intimate connections between social rank and style of speech is fundamental to an understanding of the meaning of rhetoric within the Franklin's Tale (Fyler 1987: 330–2). For if style reflects status, choice of diction is crucial and problematic to a man who, although coming from a lower social stratum itself critical of the aristocracy, nevertheless envies the position, privilege and power of the nobility. It is this order of problem which lies behind the Franklin's self-conscious speech on rhetoric and behind his more general self-consciousness about rhetorical utterance (Middleton 1980: 15–24). In the event, his utterance succeeds in maintaining a fascinating ambivalence. While denying his ability to utter anything but 'rude speche', he nevertheless frames his denial in an elegant enough form not unworthy of the rhetorical arts of which he claims to be ignorant (Burlin 1974: 189–92). There is here a second, complementary ambivalence towards the social implications of another kind of discourse. In claiming to be a 'burel' man, the Franklin is identifying himself as both socially inferior and unlettered. It is in his attitude towards learning and towards clerks and their speech (expressing intellectual power) that the Franklin reveals, again, both scorn and admiration. There will be other examples, but the prologue speech on rhetoric captures this second kind of doubleness: the Franklin claims never to have learned rhetoric, yet he is familiar with the name of Cicero, one of the masters of the art, and with the existence of rhetorical devices which give colour to plain speech.

Before passing on to consider the ways in which the Franklin's ambivalent attitudes are expressed in the tale, it would be as well to form a sharper sense of what 'rhetoric' means in this context. In its broadest terms it is an art of persuasion whereby the narrator attempts to entertain, instruct, and perhaps question. It is also an art of composition, whereby old tales are renewed, elaborated, and given fresh significance. The Franklin indicates his source material at the beginning of the prologue when he refers to the Breton lay (709–16) from which his story supposedly derives (Knight 1980b: 17–20), and there are further reminders that the Franklin is 'composing' from received sources. For example, when Aurelius and the magician arrive in Brittany it is December, 'as thise bookes me remembre' (1243). To be successful, rhetoric as an art of composition must achieve a balanced blend of what we might call the plagiarism of a plot, its amplification, and the pointing of its significance. Rhetoric is therefore an art of narrative control. All too easily, a narrative can escape the control of the teller and threaten to become without form and direction, as happens with the Squire. The Franklin appears to be rather more aware of the need to maintain order over his material: 'What sholde I make a lenger tale of this?' (1165, and see 1550). Finally, rhetoric concerns diction, ornament and style. The choice of words, of figures of speech, can cause style to be elevated, plain, or a combination of these. And style, as we have already seen, has a meaning all of its own.

Within the Franklin's Tale, the highest, most ornate style of rhetorical utterance is put into the mouths of the two major aristocratic protagonists, Dorigen and Aurelius (Knight 1980b: 20–1). At the same time, this style of discourse is represented in a critical light, so that we are obliged to question both the nature of the language and the attitudes of the speaker (Pearsall 1985: 148–50 and 155–6). On one occasion, the narrator himself points to the unnecessary artificiality of the high style by himself slipping into a kind of expression more to be expected from the mouth of the Squire; but he soon corrects himself:

> ... the brighte sonne loste his hewe;
> For th'orisonte hath reft the sonne his lyght –
> This is as muche to seye as it was nyght –
> (1016–18)

A more biting instance of the same satirical technique occurs at the end of Dorigen's long catalogue of women, derived from Jerome's *Epistle against Jovinian* (Dempster 1937: 16–23), who committed suicide rather than submit themselves to dishonour, or who remained steadfastly faithful to their husbands. In plain language, the Franklin comments: 'Thus pleyned Dorigen a day or tweye' (1457), thus deflating her oratory, however effective it might be considered as a free-standing speech (Sledd 1947; Morgan 1977: 77–92). Dorigen's attitude to her crisis is as exaggerated as her verbal response (Burlin

77

1974: 195–6), for although 'Purposynge evere that she wolde deye' (1458) she actually does nothing and instead confesses to Arveragus.

The complaint spoken by Dorigen on this occasion is a characteristic kind of speech. Her other set piece, as she gazes at the black rocks, is also a complaint (1354). Aurelius is another master of plaintive rhetoric, as his courting of Dorigen (943–50 and 991) and his 'orisoun' to Apollo, which is also a 'pleynt' (1024–30), reveal. The coincidence of bravura pieces in the high style, as declaimed by Dorigen and Aurelius, with the genre of complaint, has a point. For the declamatory, self-posturing nature of their speeches, the artificiality of their diction, to which the Franklin has alerted us, help to indicate that these supposed *cris de coeur* have perhaps been brought about by personal crises as contrived as the language which gives them vent. The complaints of Dorigen and Aurelius do indeed function, in Chaucer's subtle hands, as a kind of 'instrument of moral and emotional exploration', but one which exposes moral and emotional superficiality and display of an 'operatic' kind, not depth (Davenport 1988: 8, 179 and 190–3). For if their complaints have a common denominator, it is that, aided by vacuous language, they are directed towards the non-existent, towards projections of the self born from a deluded sense of reality. The complaints are, in fact, nothing but empty breath, fanciful attempts to conjure a desired end result out of nothing but the power of words. Thus Dorigen wishes for the disappearance of the rocks and imagines herself dead in a manner which reveals what one critic has called her 'hyperbolic' character (Knight 1969: 20–2); Aurelius also prays for the rocks to disappear, and implores Dorigen to be his mistress. But the rocks remain, in spite of appearances to the contrary, Dorigen does not commit suicide, and she has no desire to, and does not, become the lover of Aurelius.

One further way in which the words given to Aurelius and Dorigen do not ring true concerns what may be called aristocratic role-playing (Green 1980: 115–18). The amour which begins to develop between Dorigen and Aurelius is conducted in terms which read like so many clichés collected from other courtly romances. It is as if they are doomed to assume the roles which a certain kind of vocabulary defines. Aurelius' appeal to his mistress in the garden is a classic instance. We seem to have heard such speeches so many times before:

'For wel I woot my servyce is in vayn;
My gerdon is but brestyng of myn herte.
Madame, reweth upon my peynes smerte;
For with a word ye may me sleen or save.
Heere at youre feet God wolde that I were grave!
I ne have as now no leyser moore to seye;
Have mercy, sweete, or ye wol do me deye!'
                                        (972-8)

These lines and others like them are almost laughable in their formulaic predictability (Knight 1969: 23–7), and in terms of Chaucer's own poetic development instance a return to the amorous complaint which, earlier in his literary career, he learnt from French sources (Davenport 1988: 10–23 and 180). It may be objected that Aurelius' attitude towards Dorigen is no different from that of Arveragus during his courtship. But there are important differences. Arveragus is a man of action, who undertakes 'many a labour, many a greet emprise' (732) before Dorigen is won, and he resorts to verbal courtship only reluctantly (736–7) for his deeds are eloquent enough – an attitude the Franklin sorely admires. True, Aurelius undertakes the removal of the rocks, but only after much languishing, and with help of his brother and the deceptions of a magician. The received rhetoric of courtship encourages Aurelius and Dorigen to assume false identities, to take on 'speaking parts' with many precedents in courtly literature of which the most extreme example is Aurelius' imitation of 'Ekko' (951). Unfortunately for Dorigen, she responds to Aurelius' cue by making the kind of promise which might be expected of any romance heroine, but which is at odds with her earlier commitment to Arveragus.

There is a further occasion on which Dorigen is lured into adopting a new role. Once Aurelius has appeared to remove the rocks, she must accept the consequence: that, according to her promise, she must now become his mistress. The possibility of an escape opens up, of an alternative. Significantly, the lure takes the form of narratives, or rather 'examples' of other women who chose death rather than shame, stories that 'beren witnesse / ... as the bookes telle' (1367 and 1378). The conclusion seems inescapable:

'I wol conclude that it is bet for me
To sleen myself than been defouled thus.'
(1422–3)

And yet, as we have seen, Dorigen does not follow these precedents, she does not opt for any of the roles or interpretations of her experience which these narratives define (Ferster 1986: 160). Instead, after three days of intending to die, of sorrow and weeping, she confesses to Arveragus (Knight 1980b: 26–7). With this action, she breaks the persuasive spell of the 'examples', the role which their rhetoric offers. At the same time, she breaks free of the role of romance heroine, for which she has never been well suited, and is obliged to face the consequences of remaining true to Arveragus, paradoxical though they at first seem, and not at all in keeping with the model suggested by one kind of exemplum – that of the faithful wife (Baker 1961: 61–3).

Just as the Franklin exposes the role-playing and speechifying of refined, aristocratic life as a sham, so he exposes, through an attack on its esoteric language, the world of learning. As in the case of courtly rhetoric, there is more than a hint of the admiration for that intellectual power which the command of a technical terminology is supposed to reveal. In the course of Dorigen's meditation on the rocks, 'clerkes' are recognized as being the guardians of an orthodoxy whereby all things are held to exist 'for the beste' (884–5). The thought is of little comfort to Dorigen, who continues to view the rocks with great misgiving. She cannot square their existence with the existence of a fair, stable and reasonable universe, and leaves the dilemma to men of learning, whose job it is to debate such matters:

'To clerkes lete I al disputison.
But wolde God that alle thise rokkes blake
Were sonken into helle for his sake!
Thise rokkes sleen myn herte for the feere.'
(890–3)

Thus the academic world of 'clerkes' is represented as divorced from the realities of human emotions. The portrayal of the suave clerk of 'Orliens' takes this implication further (Davenport 1988: 195–6). He creates illusions through his bookish knowledge (1198–208), but these arts are represented as suspect and worthless. For the clerk is not, after all, able to make the rocks disappear. Instead, he discovers by consulting his books the time when there will be a tide high and enduring enough to convince people that the rocks have gone (North 1988: 424–9). The idea that he possesses genuine magic power is a deception reinforced by impressive jargon (Eade 1982: 58–69):

> ... *nyght and day he spedde hym that he kan*
> *To wayten a tyme of his conclusioun;*
> *This is to seye, to maken illusioun,*
> *By swich an apparence or jogelrye –*
> *I ne kan no termes of astrologye ...*
>
> *(1262–6)*

And yet, as we have come to expect by now, the Franklin is very well acquainted with the words of that rhetoric whose power he discounts. Although he continues to cast aspersions on the clerk's 'japes and his wrecchednesse / Of swich a supersticious cursednesse' (1271–2), he nevertheless goes on to use those very terms of astrology of which he denies knowledge. The account of 'tables Tolletanes ... / Ful wel corrected' (1273–4) and other astrological gear, and the calculation which follows, are no doubt designed to draw attention to the means whereby the clerk convinces others of his magical powers – through a rhetoric of mystifying terms – for it is all at last dismissed as 'illusiouns and swiche meschaunces / As hethen folk useden in thilke dayes' (1292–3). The Franklin's disavowal of knowledge concerning astrology is as unconvincing as his earlier profession of ignorance about rhetoric. He is actually quite well informed about both subjects and has acquired those 'languages' of the aristocrat and intellectual which he both disdains and admires.

If the Franklin is so critical of courtly and intellectual rhetoric, its excesses, and the power it implies, what does he offer as an alternative? The answer lies in his representation of Arveragus, who is a hero after the Franklin's own heart. For, as various critics have noticed, and in contrast with his counterpart in Boccaccio, Arveragus is the social inferior of Dorigen (and Aurelius) much as the Franklin is the social inferior of the Squire (Peck 1967: 261; Hieatt 1975: 63 and 71–2; Aers 1980: 160–9). Dorigen, it will be remembered, is of such high birth that Arveragus hardly dare confess his love. She was

> ... *comen of so heigh kynrede*
> *That wel unnethes dorste this knyght, for drede,*
> *Telle hire his wo, his peyne, and his distresse.*
> *(735–7)*

He, for his part, possesses 'worthynesse' (738), a term denoting adequate if not superior material and social status as well as moral value. The sovereignty which he maintains over Dorigen is a kind of shield which hides his actual inferiority (751–2): 'the name of soveraynetee, / That wolde he have for shame of his degree' (Fyler 1987: 321–3). The winning of 'worshipe and honour' (811), in which Arveragus soon engages, may therefore be a practical necessity if he is to advance his status so that it might be on a par with his wife's. Now in offering an alternative to the excesses and implications of courtly and intellectual rhetoric the Franklin is, first, an advocate of plain speaking which, by the side of elevated discourse, or 'vanities of the courtly style' (Middleton 1978: 95–6), can often make it seem absurd. The language espoused by Arveragus in the course of Dorigen's confession, for example, is of this unadorned kind. To his wife's admission of having promised to become the mistress of Aurelius, and in the aftermath of her anguish about suicide, however self-induced that might be, Arveragus asks simply, 'with glad chiere, in freendly wyse / ... "Is ther oght elles, Dorigen, but this?"' (1467 and 1469). His words express sympathy and love and demonstrate that speech may act as a channel of these human qualities rather than as a barrier between individuals or orders.

The expression of sympathy here, and the consequent discharge of Dorigen's sense of anguish and isolation, recalls an earlier occasion, on which her friends attempted, through words and other means, to console her during Arveragus' long absence:

> Hire freendes, whiche that knewe hir hevy thoght,
> Conforten hire in al that ever they may.
> They prechen hire, they telle hire nyght and day
> That causelees she sleeth hirself, allas!
>
> (822–5)

Gradually, Dorigen begins to adjust to loneliness, but it is a slow process, like the process of engraving stone:

> By proces, as ye knowen everichoon,
> Men may so longe graven in a stoon
> Til som figure therinne emprented be.
> So longe han they conforted hire til she
> Receyved hath, by hope and by resoun,
> The emprentyng of hire consolacioun,
> Thurgh which hir grete sorwe gan aswage ...
>
> (829–35)

The use of this rhetorical device, an analogy which gives force to the metaphor 'emprentyng' in the penultimate line, reveals that there is after all a rhetoric which, used purposefully and with restraint, is neither artificial nor overweening, but genuinely clarifying and persuasive. The example chosen here has a force beyond its immediate context because it introduces the idea, before Dorigen ever sees the rocks, that there is something obdurate about her own emotions, an affinity between her and them, deriving less from the 'immutability' of her love (Owen 1953: 295), more from her paralysing anxiety. As she later laments: '"Thise rokkes sleen myn herte for the feere"' (893); and she is then 'astoned' (1339) at news that the rocks have disappeared.

Arveragus' expression of plain-speaking, friendly sympathy is followed by a further demonstration of what unadorned language can
achieve. For the first time he exerts his authority, by instructing her
both to keep her word to Aurelius, and not to tell anyone else of the
'aventure' (1474–86). The source of Arveragus' authority is not to be
found in the words themselves, as has been the case with the courtly
and clerkly 'languages', but in himself. Having proved himself the
social equal and moral superior of his wife, authority comes naturally
to him. His decisive words are more truly effective in achieving a
resolution of the story's dilemmas than the complaints of Dorigen and
Aurelius or the mumbo-jumbo of the clerk of Orleans.

It is also true that Arveragus' words spring from genuine emotions,
as his sudden weeping demonstrates. This also distinguishes his kind
of utterance from the complaint with its contrived emotions, predictable postures and forced tears (1078–9). The notion of 'true rhetoric' – the heartfelt utterance which seeks to persuade urgently and
effectively – has been present from the beginning of the tale. Even
Dorigen herself, in attempting to repulse Aurelius, can muster plain
words which express 'deep simplicity of truth and loyalty' (Pearsall
1985: 153–4):

> 'Ne shal I nevere been untrewe wyf
> In word ne werk, as fer as I have wit;
> I wol been his to whom that I am knyt.'
> *(984–6)*

The Franklin praises the Squire, if ironically, for speaking
'"feelyngly"', and although he denies that he has any sensitivity about
the colours of rhetoric – '"My spirit feeleth noght of swich mateere"'
(727) – his very denial asks us to consider what the Franklin does, actually, 'speak feelingly' about. It emerges that he is a man with strong
feelings about those groupings of powerful people from which his
rank excludes him. It is in line with the paradoxes of his narrative that
it is rhetoric which enables him to present his tale in a persuasive and
provoking manner. The story itself becomes a consolation to that kind

of man excluded from, or embattled by, a superior, powerful estate, for Arveragus, the worthy knight who begins as the inferior of his wife, ends in a position of ascendancy. Dorigen's experience itself becomes an exemplum of the noble woman who harbours weaknesses that may be her downfall:

> But every wyf be war of hire biheeste!
> On Dorigen remembreth, atte leeste.
> *(1541–2)*

If this account of the Franklin is in danger of becoming a character study of a traditional sort, then it will be as well to remember that the Franklin is himself a rhetorical device, a voice, a point of view, through which Chaucer explores and articulates certain ideas within the larger design of the *Canterbury Tales*. Similarities in the profession, career and social standing of Chaucer and his fictional creation should make us consider from what, in this case, the potency of the device derives. Rhetoric for Chaucer the poet, no less than for the Franklin, was a means of expressing 'what the spirit feels'.

GENRE AND THE SENSE OF REALITY

Chaucer provides the Franklin with a strong sense of reality (Ferster 1986: 154). It is defined through contrasts and comparisons with the artificialities of aristocratic existence; these contrasts and comparisons are effected in the Franklin's representation of the courtly world, and through the attitudes and behaviour of Arveragus. The Franklin's 'real world' is a complex one, characterized by a co-existing fascination with and dismissal of the noble world to which he aspires. His is an outlook at once envious and proud – envious of that abstract, elusive quality of *gentillesse*, which is the preserve of the nobility, proud of the material values which give his own rank its status. Thus he is able to say 'Fy on possessioun' (686), rejecting 'twenty pound worth lond' (683), itself an ambivalent expression, in his admiration of the Squire's *gentillesse* (Storm 1984: 162–7), but later to relish the fate of another squire, Aurelius, who said '"Fy on a thousand pound!"' (1227), when he appears to be faced by economic and social ruin:

> *'Allas!' quod he. 'Allas, that I bihighte*
> *Of pured gold a thousand pound of wighte*
> *Unto this philosophre! How shal I do?*
> *I se namoore but that I am fordo.*
> *Myn heritage moot I nedes selle,*
> *And been a beggere; heere may I nat dwelle*
> *And shamen al my kynrede in this place ...*
> *(1559–65)*

As we have seen, the Franklin's 'real world' is also one in which suffering is a necessity; in which words should be made to count by being direct and effective; in which promises must be kept; in which the rhetoric of power-groups should be treated circumspectly; and in which actions may sometimes speak louder than words (a principle put into effect by the Franklin when he interrupts the Squire's Tale).

The courtly world, in opposition to which the Franklin's 'real world' exists, has by contrast a pervasive air of unreality, as Wood has observed (1970: 261–5). It is a world of exaggerated utterance, where words are a substitute for real power and action, where a promise may be made unthinkingly, where money is of no consequence, and where the participants adopt predetermined roles and conduct themselves accordingly. There is in fact an extraordinary sense of staginess about Armorik once Arveragus departs for England. This has to do not only with the courtly dialogue scripted for Dorigen and Aurelius and already discussed, but also with the melodramatic attitudes which they strike. Once Arveragus has gone, Dorigen 'moorneth, waketh, wayleth, fasteth, pleyneth' (819). Aurelius, set a seemingly impossible task, prays to Apollo in a disturbed state of mind,

> *Up to the hevene his handes he gan holde,*
> *And on his knowes bare he sette hym doun,*
> *And in his ravyng seyde his orisoun ...*
> *(1024–6)*

after which he falls down in a swoon and lies for a long time 'in a traunce' before being discovered by his brother (1080–1). The normality of Arveragus in the midst of this neurotic behaviour only helps to emphasize its strangeness. Returning home after a successful campaign, we are told that he loved Dorigen in an uncomplicated manner 'as his owene hertes lyf' (1093). Not for him the introspection which spawns anxiety and illusion – instead, action, as an expression of delight and affection:

> *No thyng list hym to been ymaginatyf,*
> *If any wight hadde spoke, whil he was oute,*
> *To hire of love; he hadde of it no doute.*
> *He noght entendeth to no swich mateere,*
> *But daunceth, justeth, maketh hire good cheere ...*
> *(1094–8)*

Aurelius, however, remains 'In langour and in torment furyus' (1101) for two years or more. And Dorigen, hearing that the rocks have 'disappeared', can hardly move:

> *For verray feere unnethe may she go.*
> *She wepeth, wailleth, al a day or two,*
> *And swowneth, that it routhe was to see.*
> *(1347–9)*

In reading the Franklin's Tale, one begins by entering a series of fictional worlds which become progressively make-believe. There is first, of course, a transition from the present day into the world of a medieval pilgrimage, although this, in its own terms, is represented with a considerable degree of vitality and realism. The Franklin's interruption of the Squire, the complexity of his attitude towards a higher social degree, the revelation of autobiographical detail (a wastrel son, a lack of education), all help to provide with an air of authenticity the journey from London to Canterbury and those who participate in it. From there, the reader steps into the world of Arveragus, a relatively recognizable world of common-sense values and well defined objectives, marked by marriage to Dorigen, maintenance of 'trouthe', foreign expeditions to win 'worshipe and honour' (811). In the absence of Arveragus, however, one enters a different sort of world – a world of misconceptions, mental aberrations, of exaggerated speech and posture, a world where words create the illusions of things, and which reaches its distillation in the hallucinatory 'dream-visions' created by theatrical magic (Luengo 1978: 1–12). Then, abruptly, the process of progressive make-believe comes to an end. For Arveragus continues to take 'trouthe' for what it is, and as a consequence the magical, illusory world is revealed as nothing more than an arrangement of stage-sets – and Aurelius, Dorigen and the clerk of Orleans are left to doff their costumes and assumed roles and to clean up after the show.

There is an extraordinary sense on Aurelius' part, in particular, of his suddenly coming to terms with the ethos which he, as a squire, is supposed to embody. Behind this, we detect that he has 'come to his senses', through the example of a man, Arveragus, who is his social inferior (Fyler 1987: 327). He has been outclassed by a 'worthy' knight. Instead of maintaining the fiction of being a despondent lover, pleading with his lady that she should show some pity, the tables are reversed and he now, involuntarily, feels pity towards Dorigen for the plight in which he has placed her. There is a flash of sympathy between the two such as has not existed before, and which finds its closest precedent in Arveragus' sympathetic response to his wife's confession. At the same time, Aurelius comes to a realization of how radically his 'churlish' behaviour must change if he is to practise in actuality, rather than in play, the *gentillesse* of his rank:

Aurelius gan wondren on this cas,
And in his herte hadde greet compassioun
Of hire and of hire lamentacioun,
And of Arveragus, the worthy knyght,
That bad hire holden al that she had hight,
So looth hym was his wyf sholde breke hir trouthe;
And in his herte he caughte of this greet routhe,
Considerynge the beste on every syde,
That fro his lust yet were hym levere abyde
Than doon so heigh a cherlyssh wrecchednesse
Agayns franchise and alle gentillesse ...

(1514–24)

So Aurelius releases Dorigen from her promise to become his mistress, to show that he, too, is worthy of his status: '"Thus kan a squier doon a gentil dede / As well as kan a knyght"' (1543–4).

Arveragus' example, and Aurelius' imitation of it, spread like a contagion. On hearing how matters have turned out, the clerk of Orleans releases Aurelius from his debt to demonstrate that he, too, has access to that moral quality and principle of behaviour which, increasingly, is revealed to be not the prerogative of a single rank:

'Everich of yow dide gentilly til oother.
Thou art a squier, and he is a knyght;
But God forbede, for his blisful myght,
But if a clerk koude doon a gentil dede
As wel as any of yow, it is no drede!'

(1608–12)

In the closing phases of the Franklin's Tale, the contrast between the values which Arveragus upholds, and the way in which Aurelius has failed to uphold the same values, is particularly marked. The contrast, we may say, is the Franklin's way of demonstrating in a persuasive manner his perception of the difference between an ideal the aristocracy is supposed to maintain, and its actual practice. In fact, the perception of this difference is present throughout the tale, and it appears in greater relief the more the story becomes make-believe. To put it another way: the make-believe world of the 'romance', in which Aurelius and Dorigen are the chief protagonists, is framed by an 'honesty to truth' world in which Arveragus is the prime mover, which is in turn framed by the fourteenth-century life of a pilgrimage, within which the Franklin expresses both admiration and distaste for the values of courtly life. And we read the 'romance' in relation to its frames.

We are using 'romance' loosely here to refer to the amorous adventure of Dorigen and Aurelius, and not as a generic term. But we do want to suggest that their experience is represented as typical of the romance genre, which is itself a reflection of aristocratic mores, and that to read the story of Dorigen and Aurelius is to step into and out of a romance world in relation to which the world managed by Arveragus is different, more down-to-earth, even though the story as received from Boccaccio is a romance which includes both the 'make-believe' of Aurelius and Dorigen and the 'realism' of Arveragus (Wallace 1983: 153–4; Pearsall 1985: 144–6; Davenport 1988: 178–83 and 194–7). For in many ways, the story of these three constitutes a romance which is not allowed to happen, a romance and anti-romance all in one. Beginning with near-perfect married love, the deserted wife makes a promise to be Aurelius' mistress, but only in play, and without any expectation that the task she has set can be completed. Arveragus does not come to his wife's defence, yet the affair is not consummated. The tale, considered as a romance, repeatedly belies expectation.

If the Franklin's Tale is a critique of aristocratic values and attitudes achieved through rhetoric, it is also a critique of such values and attitudes achieved through genre. In selecting a lay, a kind of literary composition which was perhaps passé (Burlin 1974: 188–9), but which nevertheless was well suited to his purposes (Hume 1972a), the Franklin chooses a genre suitable to an aristocratic milieu. In drawing attention to its supposed origins among 'olde gentil Britouns' (709), the narrator announces his intention to demonstrate how he, a Franklin, can command a genre not obviously associated with his class, while going on to show, through his story, how a man of lower status than Dorigen or Aurelius may behave in a *gentil*, free and generous manner to the point of being exemplary. We have already seen that, in other ways as well, the Franklin goes on to portray a romance world, reflecting aristocratic life, which is precious and introverted to the point of self-parody. In such ways, the Franklin's Tale is a riposte to the Squire's Tale rather as the Miller's Tale is a riposte to the Knight's Tale: through parallels and allusions it asks for another social perspective, another kind of reality, to be considered as equally, if not more, valid than the apparent omniscience of an aristocratic narrator.

The function of the larger genre, romance, of which the lay is a species, should not be allowed to conceal the existence of other, lesser genres within the romance, which also have significant functions. It has already been suggested that the regularity with which complaints appear in the Franklin's Tale is designed to underscore the self-absorbed quality of aristocratic life. Mention is also made of the compositions written by Aurelius in his attempt to woo and win Dorigen, part of the background of songs (919) which form the entertainment and distraction for the courtiers of Armorik. Aurelius' literary compositions, diverting and decorative as they may be, are also the means whereby, indirectly, he is able to express his feelings for Dorigen. The subject of his creations is himself, and the 'works of Aurelius' are written in a conventional code (Stevens 1961: 215–17) which, while releasing the emotion of the creator, does nothing to communicate his love to the one member of the courtly audience who really matters. The compositions are a protection, produced out of timidity and fear as much as out of desire:

> ... *nevere dorste he tellen hire his grevaunce.*
> *Withouten coppe he drank al his penaunce.*
> *He was despeyred; no thyng dorste he seye,*
> *Save in his songes somwhat wolde he wreye*
> *His wo, as in a general compleynyng;*
> *He seyde he lovede and was biloved no thyng.*
> *Of swich matere made he manye layes,*
> *Songes, compleintes, roundels, virelayes,*

How that he dorste nat his sorwe telle,
But langwissheth as a furye dooth in helle;
And dye he moste, he seyde, as dide Ekko
For Narcisus, that dorste nat telle hir wo.
(941-52)

It is perhaps worth noting that, while the lineaments of romance are closely associated with Dorigen and Aurelius, as are the lesser courtly genres of the complaint and lyric, Arveragus is not associated with any form of written composition except letters, letters which have as their practical aim and result the comforting and consoling of his wife during his long absence overseas (837–40).

The selection of an appropriate genre and the rejection of its clichés, so self-consciously undertaken by the Franklin, is, of course, a problem which must have frequently presented itself to the author of the *Canterbury Tales*. It may not be too fanciful to see the negative aspects of Chaucer's presentation of songs, complaints, and romance itself in the Franklin's Tale as a kind of retraction, such as that undertaken more directly elsewhere by that sometime squire-cum-son-of-a-wine-merchant, Geoffrey Chaucer, when he revoked his 'enditynges of worldly vanitees', including 'many a song and many a leccherous lay' (Ret. 1084 and 1086). For Chaucer, in relation to genre, was in as ambiguous a position as the Franklin in relation to rank, needing at once to preserve the kinds of composition familiar to himself and his audience and to break the mould of received genres with their accretion of customary meaning. In the Franklin's Tale, he at once presents and subverts genre, and in so doing transforms the meanings of which it is usually capable. Something of this process is reflected in the experience of responding to the tale. The narrative seems to reach a point of breakdown when Arveragus insists that his wife should keep her promise to Aurelius. The narrator is aware that audience reaction to this turn of events is likely to be mixed:

Paraventure an heep of yow, ywis,
Wol holden hym a lewed man in this

That he wol putte his wyf in jupartie.
Herkneth the tale er ye upon hire crie.
She may have bettre fortune than yow semeth;
And whan that ye han herd the tale, demeth.
(1493–8)

So the reader, unable to predict what will happen, is obliged to surrender a trust in genre to a trust in an unpredictable narrator. In particular, it is difficult to foresee that Arveragus' seemingly naive adherence to 'trouthe' will bring the artificial props of the romance world tumbling down. In a similar way, Chaucer may be represented as feeling his way forward, experimenting, admiring but disparaging the genres to which he aspires, mastering them, putting them to unusual tasks, and in the process achieving a new kind of fiction which more accurately expresses his own perception of reality.

ARISTOCRATIC *MENTALITÉ*

The sense of disturbance and distortion which permeates the central passages of the Franklin's Tale is exacerbated by the mental states of Dorigen and Aurelius. If the tale is a study of the *mentalité* of a Franklin, it is also a study of the *mentalité* of two members of the nobility who appear to have lost their grip on reality within their enclosed, exclusive world. With the departure of her husband, Dorigen is plunged into melancholic despair or depression, a state of extreme sorrow portrayed as characteristic of such women on such occasions, but which is nevertheless a serious, disabling emotional state (Jackson 1986: 54). Clearly, Dorigen does not yet possess that patience advocated by the Franklin as an antidote to suffering. Dorigen loves her husband 'as hire hertes lyf' (816):

For his absence wepeth she and siketh,
As doon thise noble wyves whan hem liketh.
She moorneth, waketh, wayleth, fasteth, pleyneth;

Desir of his presence hire so destreyneth
That al this wyde world she sette at noght.
(817–21)

Dorigen's friends partially succeed in driving away her 'derke fantasye' (844), but her psychological imbalance threatens to distort visual reality itself. Whatever she looks at is not what she desires to see – Arveragus – and so her visual world has meaning more according to the absence of her desired husband than according to the actual presence of perceived forms. From the 'bank an heigh' she sees 'many a ship and barge' sailing back and forth (849–51); yet the sight is not an entertaining distraction, which is presumably what the friends with whom she walks intend. Instead, she associates the vessels with the homecoming of Arveragus, and laments that none of those she sees will bring him back:

For to hirself ful ofte, 'Allas!' seith she,
'Is ther no ship, of so manye as I se,
Wol bryngen hom my lord? Thanne were myn herte
Al warisshed of his bittre peynes smerte.'
(853–6)

Similarly, the pleasure garden and dancing bring Dorigen no comfort. The great beauty of the place is ineffectual because of her excessive grief:

The odour of floures and the fresshe sighte
Wolde han maked any herte lighte
That evere was born, but if to greet siknesse
Or to greet sorwe helde it in distresse ...
(913–16)

So when others dance and sing, Dorigen sits alone, lamenting the absence of that sight which alone can bring her solace. She

> ... *made alwey hir compleint and hir moone,*
> *For she ne saugh hym on the daunce go*
> *That was hir housbonde and hir love also.*
> *(920–2)*

Dorigen's longing helps to explain why she is responsive, in some degree, to Aurelius' courtship. He is now introduced, an attractive figure who offers to fill the void left by Arveragus and become a surrogate lover.

The tendency of Dorigen to project her anxiety into the visual world, and to interpret it and respond to it in the light of her preoccupations, helps to explain one of the key passages of the Franklin's Tale, which concerns Dorigen's perception of the black rocks. It has already been noticed that there is an affinity between Dorigen's heart, the stoniness that is there because of Arveragus' absence, and the rocks themselves. In a sense they are the external, visible expression of her grief. So it is that Dorigen encounters the rocks with amazement and shock, as if meeting face to face an alter ego: her heart quakes for fear, she is unable to stand, and she sits on the ground to gaze 'pitously' (863) into the sea. Quite clearly, the issues raised by Dorigen in the course of her contemplation range more widely than the single one of her anxiety. In fact, the image of the rocks enables Chaucer to demonstrate the ramification of themes – particularly that of 'governaunce' – first mooted in the Franklin's exordium of Dorigen's marriage. At the simplest level of generality, the rocks threaten death, including that of the sea-travelling Arveragus: ' "An hundred thousand bodyes of mankynde / Han rokkes slayn"' (877–8). Such deaths seem arbitrary and meaningless if the universe was, after all, created by a benevolent God. God expressed his ' "chiertee"' (881) towards mankind in making man after his own image,

'... but how thanne may it bee
That ye swiche meenes make it to destroyen,
Whiche meenes do no good, but evere anoyen?'
(882–4)

This is a crisis of religious faith, but one which springs from a crisis of emotional faith – that is, the doubt that the loved Arveragus will ever return. At the same time, the spiritual dimension of Dorigen's Boethian speculations has serious and truly universal implications (Hume 1972b; Bachman 1977: 55–60). For the rocks are associated from the start with hell. Dorigen casts her eyes downwards 'fro the brynke' (858) to observe the ' "grisly feendly rokkes blake" ' (868), which suggest ' "a foul confusion / Of werk" ' (869–70) and which destroy mankind. It is not surprising that Dorigen at last consigns her speculations, unresolved as they are, to the ' "disputison" ' of clerks (890). For she appears to be encountering, through her experience, spiritual questions of a profound kind: What is the place of suffering and death in a world made by a good God? Why does an omnipotent God not destroy hell? Why is there chaos in an ordered universe? All of these questions entail a consideration of the 'certain governaunce' by which God rules his creation, and they all stem from an initial question which both the reader and Dorigen feel compelled to ask and to attempt to answer: What do the rocks mean? The question as asked by Dorigen may as well be asked of the adamantine anguish she experiences and for which the rocks form a visual correlative: What is the place and purpose of such extreme suffering in a world where she and Arveragus love each other? Or, to put the question another way, and from a reader's perspective: What order, what sense of 'governaunce', underlies the arrangement of human institutions when the loved Arveragus has to be absent for a long period in order to fulfil the expectations which society has of the husband of a woman of noble birth? As the tale reveals, this kind of 'governaunce', this kind of expectation, is the responsibility of the rank to which Dorigen belongs, and of others who aspire to it. The extremity of Dorigen's anxiety, her perception of the rocks, are, after all, figments, generated from her own susceptible and self-dramatizing outlook (Bachman

96

1977: 62–4). The profound questions which she ponders are, in every sense, academic. The meaning which experience has for her is seen to be a construct deriving from attitudes and postures characteristic of the nobility. It is perhaps revealing that when, eventually, the rocks do 'disappear', Dorigen does not verify this state of affairs. It is enough that Aurelius has said so, and that she believes his words (1342–5).

As Dorigen is susceptible to 'impressiouns', so the 'illusiouns' of magic find a suggestible subject in Aurelius. His prayer to Apollo suggests that he, at that stage, contemplates the possibility that the rocks can be made to disappear both by natural means and by the power of magic. He pleads for a ' "miracle" ' (1065), but one which might conceivably happen, that a ' "spryng flood laste bothe nyght and day" ' (1070) so that the rocks are covered by water. This, presumably, is what does happen, so that the efforts of the 'clerke of Orliens' are directed towards the task of discovering when the unusually high tide is going to occur. Natural events, more than magical power, secure the disappearance of the rocks (Wood 1970: 245–59). At the same time, Aurelius prays to Apollo that, as another means of achieving the desired result, the god should implore Lucina

> '... to synken every rok adoun
> Into hir owene dirke regioun
> Under the ground, ther Pluto dwelleth inne,
> Or nevere mo shal I my lady wynne.'
> (1073–6)

This is the effect that the clerk of Orleans strives to achieve, relying on ' "apparence ... / To mannes sighte" ' (1157–8), so that Dorigen

> ... and every wight sholde wene and seye
> That of Britaigne the rokkes were aweye,
> Or ellis they were sonken under grounde.
> (1267–9)

Thus the magician-clerk works not so much with actual, direct power over the natural world (an idea which, as we have seen, is given short shrift by the Franklin) but with the suggestibility of people, like Aurelius, who believe in magic. As long as Dorigen and others think and say that the rocks have gone, then to all intents and purposes, they have: 'It *semed* that alle the rokkes were aweye' (1296). The magic exists in the mind of the beholder. It is the magician's purpose to foster the illusions, desires and fears of his subject so that he or she is prepared to believe that they actually exist, that what they see is reality.

After more than two years of frustrated desire, a time during which his love rankles like an arrow in a hidden heart-wound (1111–15), Aurelius is more than ready to believe in the sleights of magic. He leaves his bed with alacrity 'In hope for to been lissed of his care' (1170) to journey to Orleans with his brother. There, he (though not his brother) is shown visions which appear to demonstrate the magician's power. On closer inspection, though, the 'sighte merveillous' (1206) conjured in the clerk's study, among his books, is curiously well designed to suit the unfulfilled desires of the young squire. The first is a hunting scene, in which some of the harts 'with arwes blede of bittre woundes' (1194). In view of Aurelius' own heart-wound, this may be taken as a symbolic version of his own condition. The following two scenes are more suggestive: two falconers on a river who have slain a heron with their hawks may refer to the 'hunting down' of Dorigen who later realizes that she has been caught in a 'trappe' (1341); and 'knyghtes justyng in a playn' (1198) perhaps indicates the contention between Arveragus and Aurelius for the love of Dorigen, jousting being an activity in which Arveragus habitually engages (as at 1098). The final scene is unambiguous: Aurelius sees Dorigen dancing, and he with her (1200–1). Earlier, Aurelius' brother had speculated on the sorts of ' "apparences" ' which ' "subtile tregetoures" ' might be able to conjure (1139–41). The scenes he imagines are different from those visions which Aurelius sees, but they are no less suggestive of a dreamworld corresponding to the preoccupations of Aurelius' mind. There is water and a barge (1144), such as might come and go once the rocks have disappeared (1158–60), a 'halle large' (1143), such as might be part of Dorigen's 'castel faste by the see' (847), a 'grym leoun' (1146), like the sign of Leo which, so Aurelius thinks, needs to be in a propitious relationship with the moon if a 'fyve fadme' flood is to occur in Armorik (1058–60), and so on. This magic fulfils in an illusory and shadowy manner the heart's desire of Aurelius. The two sets of magical scenes both invoke courtly worlds. They are epitomes of the romance worlds inhabited by Dorigen and Aurelius. Their evanescence suggests that the realm of aristocratic life is a never-never land inaccessible to a man like the Franklin; but also that it is itself an illusory place, out of touch with reality, and likely to disappear, like the 'sighte merveillous' of the clerk of Orleans, in the twinkling of an eye:

> *And whan this maister that this magyk wroughte*
> *Saugh it was tyme, he clapte his handes two,*
> *And farewel! Al oure revel was ago.*
> *(1202–4)*

LINES 761–798

Since Kittredge (1915: 204–10), it has become almost unavoidable to interpret the relationship between Dorigen and Arveragus as a 'knitting up' of problems first explored vociferously by the Wife of Bath. Here again is the theme of 'maistrye', which may also be traced through the Clerk's Tale and Merchant's Tale, with their emphasis on male dominance and the female response to it (patient suffering or infidelity), to the Franklin's Tale where, at last, the husband and wife appear to be equals, desirous of a marriage lived 'in quiete and in reste' (760). But it should now be clear that the marriage of Dorigen and Arveragus is not one made between equals. They are members of different social ranks, and this brings its own problems. So if the Franklin's Tale is to be seen as part of a 'marriage group' at all, then it does not express a resolution of recurrent dilemmas so much as an exploration of a further kind of marital problem. Here as elsewhere the marriage problem is part of a structure of problems much larger than itself so that Chaucer, through the relationships of Dorigen,

Arveragus and Aurelius, engages with issues with which his own society was much concerned (Jacobs 1985). The existence of keywords other than 'maistrye' – such as 'patience' and 'governaunce' (Mann 1982: 133–4; 1983: 168) – is an indication that the narrative situation of the Franklin's Tale has repercussions beyond its fictional world. It is the recurrence of debates using such terms, focusing as they often do on the microcosm of a marital relationship, that enables us to speak of 'a marriage group'. Yet that term is a misnomer, because the key terms are found as well beyond the confines of particular marriages and in such places as the final speech of Theseus in the Knight's Tale, where he speaks of the 'governaunce' of the universe and the virtues of 'patience' in the face of adversity and disorder.

The wider implications of the marriage of Dorigen and Arveragus are made clear in lines 761–98. They read as an interpolation, a rhetorical amplification whereby the significance of the marriage is elaborated. The action of the tale is put in suspended animation as the Franklin indicates the implications of the unusual arrangement to which the married partners have come. He indicates, in rapid succession, a concatenation of topics which the nature of the marriage raises, ones deeply disconcerting to critics devoted to the principle of hierarchical order (Robertson 1974: 281–4). These are, in order, friendship, love, freedom, patience in adversity, and 'governaunce'. That the audience (of pilgrims, of listeners, of readers) is being asked to consider the relationship of Dorigen and Arveragus in a wider context is clear from the form of address which the narrator here adopts. With an eye on his audience, on the fellowship of pilgrimage (which has had its share of contention), and on the community in general, he offers the observation:

> For o thyng, sires, saufly dar I seye,
> That freendes everych oother moot obeye,
> If they wol longe holden compaignye.
> (761–3)

There follows a series of further adages which gain in substance and complexity the more one attempts to apply them to the particular case of Dorigen and Arveragus. 'Love wol nat been constreyned by maistrye' (764) might seem to be a straightforward reference to Arveragus' success in preserving the love between himself and Dorigen by allowing her the maximum amount of freedom in marriage. On reflection, though, it is clear that the love between these two already exists within certain constraints brought about by their difference in social status. It is as if the reader is being provoked to say 'Yes, but ...' to the adage. For Arveragus has preserved his premarital relationship not simply by putting into practice a truism about the nature of love; instead, he has acted in a canny and realistic manner in order that their love should survive. He has recognized that, social inferior that he is, it would hardly be appropriate, advisable, or even possible, for him to exert the traditional mastery of husband over wife. If love is to have a chance of survival within marriage, he must allow Dorigen the room, the independence, which her aristocratic status has led her to expect.

The next two lines state that

> *Whan maistrie comth, the God of Love anon*
> *Beteth his wynges, and farewel, he is gon!*
> *(765–6)*

They emphasize that mastery, were it a real option for Arveragus, would have disastrous results. What is also interesting about these lines is the inclusion of 'rhetorical colour' of the sort earlier eschewed by the Franklin. The image of the god of Love beating his wings for a hasty departure comes oddly from the Franklin's mouth. As we have seen, he tends to reserve ornate, artificial language for those of noble birth. References to Love's dart are not uncommon, for example, in his account of Aurelius' passion. The image of the god of Love's flight is not entirely consonant with Arveragus' mode of loving, and so there is a harder edge to the image than at first appears. It suggests that the refined, courtly conception of love is inappropriate to the case of Arveragus and Dorigen. Its articulation in this context helps to indicate the enduring distance between Arveragus and the 'polite' world which, by his marriage, he has entered, but which still remains to some extent inaccessible and alien.

If the following statement – 'Love is a thyng as any spirit free' (767) – is true, how can love survive within *any* constraints, even those of a marriage which allows the partners a maximum of latitude? In the case of Arveragus and Dorigen, love survives in spite of the minimal restraint introduced and later enforced by the husband, who will keep 'the name of soveraynetee, / ... for shame of his degree' (751–2). And there is a second consideration which recoils on the adage. It is that love brings its own constraints – for Dorigen, after all, does not want to take Aurelius as a lover because of the love she bears for Arveragus. It is truth to *this* kind of constraint which the tale explores. It is, therefore, a study of what may be called 'natural', self-imposed constraint as opposed to the constraints exercised through conventional marriage or through society.

The transition has now been made from the subject of love to the related subject of freedom. Again, there is a statement which is too bald, uncompromising and featureless to be accepted at face value. It is that women, 'of kynde, desiren libertee, / And nat to been constreyned as a thral', and so do men (768–70). The 'Yes, but ...' response follows hard on the heels of this assertion, to the effect that if men and women jockey for their freedom the result will be social chaos. The objection is anticipated, for there is now an abrupt further transition to the subject of patience, and the reader is led to consider the paradoxical notion that the survival of individual freedom depends on the toleration of individual constraint, just as the survival of friendship depends on mutual respect and obedience.

The idea of patience seems to be poles apart from the idea of a love of liberty which men and women share. For the practice of patience means enduring oppression and 'maistrye'. Yet those who suffer adversity for love not only preserve love but gain a moral ascendancy, a mastery over self:

> *Looke who that is moost pacient in love,*
> *He is at his avantage al above.*
>
> *(771–2)*

Patience is represented as ultimately more effective than enforcement, or control. It is 'an heigh vertu ... / For it venquysseth ... / Thynges that rigour sholde nevere atteyne' (773–5). Thus patience itself is full of internal contradictions: practising it, on the one hand, could lead to a form of quietism easily manipulated by a cynical husband, overlord, or government; on the other hand, its ability to be more effective than enforced control makes it potentially disruptive of 'governaunce', whether personal, marital or social.

The Franklin argues that, like it or not, patience is a virtue which must be cultivated because suffering is unavoidable, a fact of human existence. In the first place, it is impossible to take exception at every word that infringes personal liberty (776–8). Again, just as we may be on the receiving end of oppression, so we may be the means of causing suffering in others (779–80). Further, the cause of suffering –

> *Ire, siknesse, or constellacioun,*
> *Wyn, wo, or chaungynge of complexioun*
> *(781–2)*

– may be out of the control of the agent, let alone the recipient. The practice of patience, obligatory as it may be, is intimately bound up with control. Whoever would be skilled in government, whether of self or others, should respond temperately to suffering:

> *After the tyme moste be temperaunce*
> *To every wight that kan on governaunce.*
> *(785–6)*

The last word has manifold applications: to the arrangement of marital relations, to the obligations of friendship, to the government of society and ultimately, as Dorigen's meditation on the threatening rocks makes clear, to the ordering of the universe itself.

The reader returns to consider the marriage of Dorigen and

Arveragus with a renewed understanding of its implications. Among the other philosophical conundrums the paradoxes of Arveragus' situation and of his practical wisdom, inculcated by necessity, are expressed here. He is a 'wise, worthy' knight who, in order to live harmoniously with Dorigen, 'in ese', has accepted the need for toler-ance, for suffering (787–90). How has Arveragus suffered? How is he to suffer? He has undertaken 'many a labour, many a greet emprise' (732) in order to win Dorigen, and he has experienced 'wo … peyne, and … distresse' (737) in the process of courtship. Dorigen's promise to Aurelius is to cause Arveragus more anguish. True to his ideal of 'verray love' (1477), he tells Dorigen 'in freendly wise' (1467) that she is to maintain her integrity by keeping the promise (1479), though to do so costs Arveragus a sudden outburst of weeping, causes a recognition of sorrow in store, and makes him resolve to put on a brave face in order to guard his wife against suspicion of infidelity:

> '*As I may best, I wol my wo endure –*
> *Ne make no contenance of hevynesse,*
> *That folk of yow may demen harm or gesse.'*
> *(1484–6)*

In return for her husband's preparedness to suffer, Dorigen had pledged that she would be free from blame:

> *And therfore hath this wise, worthy knyght,*
> *To lyve in ese, suffrance hire bihight,*
> *And she to hym ful wisly gan to swere*
> *That nevere sholde ther be defaute in here.*
> *(787–90)*

It is an unequal arrangement, and not only because Dorigen does commit the fault of making a rival promise to Aurelius. For Dorigen does not, in return, acknowledge that she is prepared to suffer.

Instead, 'ful wisly', she takes another option. Yet, as the Franklin has reminded us, she, as a human being, must needs experience suffering and learn patience – and not only the predictable, contrived suffering of a chatelaine deserted by an adventure-seeking husband, but a more genuine suffering which comes from the recognition that she has actually put in jeopardy her love for Arveragus, and from the realization that, morally speaking, Arveragus is her superior, a man whom she must, finally, obey.

This passage at the beginning of the Franklin's Tale is an accumulation, as well as an abstraction, of those contradictions which give the plot and its themes their intrigue. It culminates in a language of paradox well suited to its subject matter, in lines which point to both the complexity and the fragility of the marriage arrangement:

> Heere may men seen an humble, wys accord;
> Thus hath she take hir servant and hir lord –
> Servant in love and lord in mariage.
> Thanne was he bothe in lordshipe and servage.
> Servage? Nay, but in lordshipe above,
> Sith he hath bothe his lady and his love;
> His lady, certes, and his wyf also,
> The which that lawe of love acordeth to.
>
> (791–8)

It is a 'humble, wys accord' more for Arveragus than for Dorigen. The nature of Arveragus' wisdom has already been discussed; the agreement suggests humility on his part because the marriage strategy (which is Arveragus' proposal) is one brought into existence by a husband in a relatively inferior social position. It is a wise arrangement for Dorigen because it allows her to keep the best of both worlds – the continued 'service' of a lover-husband, and a husband who is lord in name only.

Arveragus is thus in the ambiguous position of being both lord and servant, and these lines ask us to evaluate the nature and respective advantages of the two roles. He is 'in service' but he has the name of lordship. Service preserves the love; marriage gives him, nominally, higher status than his wife. So he has both lady and love – a lady who is a wife on terms which preserve their love. The 'lawe of love', love 'a thyng as any spirit free' (767), is preserved through Arveragus' refusal to exert actual dominance. The arrangement seems too good to be true and the 'prosperitee' (799) is brief. The honeymoon lasts only 'A yeer and moore' (806) before Arveragus leaves for England to seek 'worshipe and honour' (811) in order to improve his social standing. From that point onwards, it is Dorigen's turn to learn more about the nature of love's law, about the constraints on freedom, about suffering and patience, about 'governaunce', about humility, indeed about Christian ideals (Bachman 1977: 59; Davenport 1988: 188).

WHY DID ARVERAGUS CRY?

Our consideration of the Squire's Tale and the Franklin's Tale has been predominantly occupied with the language and form of those tales and the relationship which language and form have to social condition. The danger in this approach is that an emphasis upon social satire of a literary kind ignores the thematic content of the stories themselves which arguably expresses the nature of the crisis which the satire is fundamentally designed to address. In whatever form, both the Squire's Tale and the Franklin's Tale address certain crises in aristocratic society and suggest solutions to those crises which Chaucer's audience is invited to consider. To take the two tales as part of a dual consideration of certain critical problems is to recognize that the perception of the crises and the identification of their solutions are essentially part of the problems themselves. We may have more sympathy for one set of views rather than another, and we may feel we are being led to one set of conclusions rather than another, but we must recognize that the views presented are deliberately chosen to represent interests closely aligned on either side of the dividing line of the argument.

It is important to note what would seem to be a deliberate parallelism between the story of the falcon in the Squire's Tale and the story of Arveragus in the Franklin's Tale. Both stories employ the device of the separation of the recently married. In the Squire's Tale the departure of the tercelet comes when the falcon is blissfully innocent of the tercelet's duplicity (as she later sees it):

> 'This laste lenger than a yeer or two,
> That I supposed of hym noght but good.
> But finally, thus atte laste it stood,
> That Fortune wolde that he moste twynne
> Out of that place, which that I was inne.
>
>   ....
>
> 'And resoun wolde eek that he moste go
> For his honour, as ofte it happeth so ...'
>   (574–8 and 591–2)

In the Franklin's Tale the separation arises when

> A yeer and moore lasted this blisful lyf,
> Til that the knyght of which I speke of thus,
> That of Kayrrud was cleped Arveragus,
> Shoop hym to goon and dwelle a yeer or tweyne
> In Engelond, that cleped was eek Briteyne,
> To seke in armes worshipe and honour –
> For al his lust he sette in swich labour –
> And dwelled there two yeer; the book seith thus.
>   (806–13)

The similarities encourage close comparison between the stories. From the beginning, however, there would seem to be a marked difference between the reasons for the departures of the tercelet and Arveragus. For the tercelet, the need to depart is described as though it were a conventional obligation, whereas for Arveragus it is a passionate necessity. For the tercelet honour needs to be maintained by appropriate ritual; for Arveragus worship and honour must be won to provide him with a status sufficient to uphold his own dignity, and publicly be recognized as equivalent to his wife's inherited aristocratic

rank. The differences between the two perceptions of the need to leave
in order to attain honour derive from the difference in social standing
between the tercelet and Arveragus and also between the Squire and
the Franklin. Squire and Franklin are intent upon telling stories which
address similar problems of social crisis from social positions which
are crucially located on the very boundary which determines the narrative developement of the stories they tell and the psychological experience of their protagonists. In view of Chaucer's own social position
and his special role as poet it is only a small step to argue further that
in the Squire's Tale and the Franklin's Tale Chaucer is exploring
matters of profound contemporary concern at both a general and a
personal level and exploring them additionally in ways of great personal significance to himself.

In both cases the consequence of the separation is anguish and
betrayal. Significantly, the anguish of the falcon is represented as
different from that of Dorigen. The falcon declares

> 'That I made vertu of necessitee,
> And took it wel, syn that it moste be.'
> (593–4)

As for Dorigen, 'She moorneth, waketh, wayleth, fasteth, pleyneth'
(819), and although in describing her the Franklin parodies conventional descriptions – 'As doon thise noble wyves whan hem liketh'
(818) – it is as though the unconventional nature of the relationship
between Arveragus and Dorigen does generate an unrestrained
anguish by comparison with that described by the falcon.

When betrayal comes, moreover, the stories diverge significantly.
The female falcon is betrayed by the male tercelet with the female kite,
the betrayal being by the aristocratic husband of his aristocratic wife
with a bird of lower rank. The worthy knight, Arveragus, is betrayed
by Dorigen, his aristocratic wife, with the squire Aurelius, and here it
is the lower-ranking Arveragus who is betrayed by members of the
same aristocratic rank. Both stories are concerned with aristocratic
betrayal but for the Squire, characteristically, the betrayal involves the

seduction of the tercelet by the newfangled kite, whereas for the Franklin, approving as he does of the relationship between the aristocratic lady and the worthy but less aristocratic knight, what amounts to a betrayal is brought about by the action of a squire behaving as conventionally such men do in aristocratic society but in such a way as to disturb what the Franklin believes to be the proper social order. Two views of social and political order are being set against each other. For the Squire, right order implies the hierarchical separation of the aristocracy from the lower orders, and within his tale it is the seduction of the lower orders which seems to precipitate (as far as the development of his story before its interruption permits us to discover) the crisis which is signalled earlier at the court of Cambyuskan. For the Franklin, right order is necessarily established by a quality of relationship determined by more than blood or traditional rank order, a quality characteristic of true aristocracy but not necessarily heritable, namely *gentillesse*. Within the Franklin's Tale it is the socially inferior Arveragus who is invested with power to effect the restoration of this true aristocratic quality. To extend this debate into fourteenth-century English society: the Squire argues, at a time of rapid social and economic change and social mobility in which the traditional authority of the aristocracy is commonly perceived as being under threat, for traditional values and the traditional social order. The Franklin argues for a system of values and a social order which draw on the spirit of traditional values (as he sees it) but are better suited to accommodate the social and political problems which confront contemporary society. In this debate the concept of *gentillesse* is clearly crucial. It retains the aristocratic ethos while permitting its redefinition. In changed times it is no longer possible, in the Franklin's view, to depend upon the rules which formerly governed personal, social and political relations. What has become of central importance is to identify the essential spirit of those rules. Unless this is done then the social order is in danger of collapse. Subtly exploring this debate from positions only narrowly separated at the heart of the conflict, Chaucer provides his audience with an exquisite description of the mechanisms of social change.

The perception of an aristocratic society in crisis informs the narrative in both tales. It is not just that the Squire's Tale is jejune, superficial and incompetent that leads to its rejection and the alienation of its audience or reader; it is also condescending. In other words, the Squire's values, which are aristocratic and traditional, are made to represent part of the problem under discussion. There is an over -emphasis upon aristocratic distance which insults its audience with its snobbishness. And we may read this snobbishness as an attitude (perhaps defensive in nature) which is inappropriate among the company of the pilgrims and thus as a social and political attitude which is inappropriate to prevailing conditions in English society in the late fourteenth century, certainly in its capacity to initiate a process of restorative social change. The Franklin's values, however, lead him, as has been argued earlier, to satirize both the genre and the rhetoric of aristocratic convention and behaviour, and that very mode of comic discourse is symptomatic of a view which looks to new forms of convention and behaviour or, at least, to their revitalization. It is a mode of discourse, moreover, implicitly more acceptable to his fellow pilgrims and to audience and reader.

This perception of crisis, however, is not articulated by narrative voice alone. Three images or metaphors are particularly interesting in their identification of crisis and the inadequacy of the response of aristocratic society to the difficulties which confront it. All three convey a sense of damage deliberately concealed or ignored. The first, from the Squire's Tale, which was discussed earlier, concerns the hypocrisy of the tercelet (as perceived by the falcon) and describes a tomb, fair above but concealing the dead body below; the second, from the Franklin's Tale, portrays Aurelius 'In langour and torment furyus' (1101), suffering from his self-inflicted wound:

> *Under his brest he baar it moore secree*
> *Than evere dide Pamphilus for Galathee.*
> *His brest was hool, withoute for to sene,*
> *But in his herte ay was the arwe kene.*
> *And wel ye knowe that of a sursanure*
> *In surgerye is perilous the cure,*
> *But men myghte touche the arwe or come therby.*
> *(1109–15)*

And the third involves the magical solution to Dorigen's dread and despair when '... for a wyke or tweye, / It semed that alle the rokkes were aweye' (1295–6). Here the concern with outward and inner reality extends the awareness of the problems under consideration. The Squire's apparent suggestion that in some way aristocratic society can mend itself is unacceptable; all it can do is suppress and temporarily defer the crisis.

The Franklin's solution, however, is far from revolutionary. Indeed, it seeks to provide the smoothest possible social transition. Arveragus may be the instrument by which social adaptation is made possible but he does so from within the ethical codes of aristocratic society. What indicates the critical nature of the process of change, even so, is the anguish which Arveragus suffers as the agent of transition. Nowhere is this better demonstrated than at the point of Arveragus' return when confronted by Dorigen's confession. The deliberately dramatic delay of this return has heightened the reader's expectation of its climactic importance:

> *Arveragus, with heele and greet honour,*
> *As he that was of chivalrie the flour,*
> *Is comen hoom, and othere worthy men.*
> *O blisful artow now, thou Dorigen,*
> *That hast thy lusty housbonde in thyne armes,*
> *The fresshe knyght, the worthy man of armes*
> *That loveth thee as his owene hertes lyf.*
> *(1087–93)*

And yet before Arveragus returns, to the reader and to Dorigen the whole episode of Aurelius' distress, and the magical achievements of the clerk in concealing the rocks, are described at length. When, at last, Arveragus and Dorigen meet before the reader, Arveragus finds his wife not joyful at his return but in tears. The loving simplicity of his initial response to Dorigen's confession, and his emphasis upon the importance of truth, provide a remarkable turning point in the whole narrative. None the less, it is equally significant that having uttered these words 'he brast anon to wepe' (1480).

Arveragus cries because, having won honour and achieved the
social status which he sought, he now faces shame. What is more, the
only way in which he can avoid public shame within the aristocratic
society to which he sought full admission is by accepting private
shame. Thus, he commands Dorigen, through his tears,

> '... I yow forbede, up peyne of deeth,
> That nevere, whil thee lasteth lyf ne breeth,
> To no wight telle thou of this aventure –
> As I may best, I wol my wo endure –
> Ne make no contenance of hevynesse,
> That folk of yow may demen harm or gesse.'
> (1481–6)

Linked to the descriptions of an outward and inward reality, the
themes of public and private constraints run throughout the
descriptions of personal relations in the tale. Driven to seek honour by
'shame of his degree' (752), having entered into a relationship in
which his wife 'pryvely ... fil of his accord / To take hym for hir
housbonde and hir lord' (741–2), he now finds his world turned
upside-down. What is more, it is a further aspect of the ethical system
which he seeks to embrace which has caused this inversion. Unable to
cope with the disappointment and contradiction, he breaks down and
weeps.

Taken at the level of the discussion of crisis in aristocratic society,
Arveragus' emotional outburst is symptomatic of the tensions of
social change. The contradictions within the ethical system of aristocratic society are also depicted in the stress and anguish of Dorigen,
especially when Aurelius declares that the rocks have gone and seeks
to hold her to her promise. Her list of suffering heroines undoubtedly
enables the Franklin to parody a conventional genre of complaint but,
at the same time, it explores ideas of honour and shame in terms of
male violence and female oppression. In social and political terms the
price paid by Arveragus and Dorigen for the unconventional nature of

their relationship is the painful duality which the aristocratic system inevitably imposes upon them.

But, by a most ingenious irony, Arveragus' perception of his own actions is identified to have been imperfect. His acceptance of personal shame may symbolize the tensions of social change, but his very acceptance (and, thereby, his very admittance into aristocratic society) itself triggers a series of changes of far-reaching social and political consequence. Only partially aware of Arveragus' motives, Aurelius sees only his 'grete gentillesse'; and this essential spirit of true aristocracy, redefined through the accident of the social acceptance of the worthy knight of insufficient degree, resolves the narrative and, by implication, restores right social order. The Franklin's Tale, in contrast to the Squire's Tale, argues for the resolution of the crisis within aristocratic society by means of the acceptance of a new social order. For the Franklin, no doubt, this implies an order in which the exclusivity of the Squire is rejected. It is an order, none the less, in which an aristocratic ideology still prevails, albeit redefined. For Chaucer, perhaps, the outcome of this dual investigation through Franklin and Squire is the identification of a radical if conservative solution in which the traditional structures of society are revitalized.

3

The Pardoner

The Pardoner's Prologue and Tale, in their discussion of gluttony, 'hasardrye', false-swearing and avarice, directly confront central tenets of Christianity. In themselves the teachings of the Pardoner are orthodox. What transforms these teachings is the context within which the audience hears them. From the beginning it is clear that the Pardoner's statements may be seen as a devastating self-criticism. Demonstrating the rhetorical devices by which he dupes his other audiences he invites the criticism and resistance of the pilgrims, just as the prologue invites the reader to reject such blatant hypocrisy from a servant of the papacy. The sense of desecration and sacrilege brought about by wilful spiritual blindness becomes progressively offensive. At the same time the deliberately cultivated sensitivity to rhetorical techniques leads the audience to question both prologue and tale and the position of Chaucer in their telling.

The comedy of prologue and tale is employed to serious satirical purpose. If the Pardoner's words are to be seen as an attack upon the condition of the late medieval English church in the long term, they must also be seen as biting criticism of conditions in England in the 1370s. Directed against the English clergy and the management of international affairs, at a time when these were peculiarly interlinked, the satire includes among its targets both Archbishop Simon Sudbury and John of Gaunt. Religious metaphors are used to convey corruption, degradation and dishonour, with the contemporary controversy over the eucharist informing all levels of the argument. Frequently the criticism echoes that of Wycliffite polemic. The Pardoner becomes the 'fool' who has denied the existence of God and his tale provides a picture of a betrayed kingdom in which church and court have been consumed by corruption and avarice.

DRUNKENNESS

The passages in the Pardoner's Tale which treat of drunkenness are concerned with the shame and dishonour brought to great men because of the influence of wine. The shame may be of sexual or military origin but it arises from the mental confusion promoted by drink, a kind of madness entailing the destruction of reason, discretion and sense of honour, rendering the victim like an animal. The discussion is rich in biblical and other allusions and many of these do more than reinforce a traditional argument or suggest wider applications of the central theme. They become sub-texts with a life of their own, providing a metaphorical depth and complexity for the simple morality of the sermon.

When the Pardoner begins

> *The hooly writ take I to my witnesse*
> *That luxurie [lechery] is in wyn and dronkenesse*
> *(483–4)*

he refers his listeners to Ephesians 5 with its condemnation of fornication, uncleanness and covetousness; its warning that 'no fornicator or unclean or covetous person (which is a serving of idols) hath inheritance in the kingdom of Christ and of God' (Douay Bible 1609); its injunction 'see therefore ... how you walk circumspectly; not as unwise, / But as wise redeeming the time, because the days are evil', as well as its command 'be not drunk with wine, wherein is luxury; but be ye filled with the Holy Spirit'; and its later instructions to wives to submit to husbands 'Because the husband is the head of the wife, as Christ is the head of the church', instructions which contain phrases used in the Merchant's Tale. Similarly, the example

Lo, how that dronken Looth, unkyndely,
Lay by his doghtres two, unwityngly;
So dronke he was, he nyste what he wroghte
(485–7)

possesses a context which has a rich cluster of associated meanings for its immediate audience. The episode with Lot and his daughters comes after the burning of Sodom and Gomorrah and is concerned with preserving the seed of the father at a time when the father is old and there is no one to follow him. Here, as before, the references are to a corrupt society in need of reform, faced by the problem of succession. The discussion of drunkenness has swiftly taken on social and political dimensions as well as religious ones.

Describing the 'dronke man' the Pardoner makes him snort through his nose

As though thou seydest ay 'Sampsoun, Sampsoun!'
And yet, God woot, Sampsoun drank nevere no wyn.
(554–5)

The drunken heavy breathing of the disfigured and disgusting creature ironically sounds like the powerful man who had nothing to do with wine. Yet the same reference at the same time recalls the betrayal of Samson by a woman and the destruction of the temple, so that the breathing of the drunken man also contains that strand of meaning. As to precisely what it is that causes the drunkenness and confusion, the Pardoner has a specific warning:

Now kepe yow fro the white and fro the rede,
And namely fro the white wyn of Lepe
That is to selle in Fysshstrete or in Chepe.
This wyn of Spaigne crepeth subtilly
In othere wynes, growynge faste by,

116

Of which ther ryseth swich fumositee
That whan a man hath dronken draughtes thre,
And weneth that he be at hoom in Chepe,
He is in Spaigne, right at the toune of Lepe –
Nat at the Rochele, ne at Burdeux toun –
And thanne wol he seye 'Sampsoun, Sampsoun!'
(562–72)

Commenting on this passage historians have noted Chaucer's awareness of Anglo-Castilian trade (Russell 1955: 9) and seen in his warning
the expertise of a member of a family of vintners who knew well the
strength of the sweet and heady wines of Lepe (Childs 1978: 127–8).
But as the discussion of drunkenness becomes more specific, moving
from a general sense of the evil of the times through confusion and
delusion to contemporary London, the extended metaphor takes on a
still more complex range of possible meanings.

Rochelle, Bordeaux and Lepe are more than sources of wine for
Englishmen in the 1370s. The revival of war with France after 1369
meant that English interests in Calais, Normandy, Brittany, Poitou
and Gascony were the principal preoccupation of the court, at least
until 1374 (Holmes 1975: 21–32). At the same time, the alliance
between Edward III and Peter I, one of the two rival claimants to
the throne of Castile, and the part played by the Black Prince in
reinstating Peter as legitimate ruler, established close links between
England and Spain – links which Chaucer had experienced in 1366 at
first hand (ed. Crow and Olson 1966: 65) – and especially with the
Black Prince's court at Bordeaux. In 1369, however, Henry of
Trastamara killed and usurped his rival Peter I and, in the following
year, Gaunt replaced the Black Prince in Gascony. Gaunt's marriage
in Gascony to the daughter and eldest surviving child of Peter I,
Constanza, gave a new direction to relations between England and
Castile. Henceforth Gaunt styled himself 'King of Castile and Leon'.
The war with France became entangled with the Duke of Lancaster's
ambitions in Castile.

Whatever the truth of the matter, contemporaries interpreted
English foreign policy in the 1370s as inextricably involved with

Gaunt's own interests, and increasingly those interests came to be seen as not only encompassing the Castilian throne but also the English crown. As the question of the succession to Edward III became a central political concern, so rumours of Gaunt's intentions multiplied. His desire to oust the claims of Richard, the son of the Black Prince, was widely believed, and it was thought that he had formed foreign alliances with the purpose of furthering this end. What is more, as the outcome of English foreign policy in these years was invariably disastrous for England's traditional interests, suspicion of Gaunt deepened, and fear of humiliation and even invasion grew strong.

In June 1372 the destruction of the Earl of Pembroke's fleet off La Rochelle ushered in a series of military reverses in which the alliance between France and Castile proved superior. Pembroke was imprisoned in Castile and, while an abortive English naval expedition planned between August and October failed to set out, the French recaptured Poitou, Saintonge and Angoumois. Despite the limited successes of expeditions to Brittany by Neville and Montague, in October 1372 and March 1373, by the summer of 1373 the French had restored control in Brittany and English influence in France had been severely reduced. Culminating these disastrous episodes came Gaunt's expedition, begun in July 1373 and ending at Bordeaux in December of the same year. Long planned, this *chevauchée* proceeded from Calais around Paris via Reims, Troyes, the upper Loire valley, the Cher above Montluçon, and down to Tulle, Brive and the valley of the Dordogne, before reaching Bordeaux. If it had been intended as a manoeuvre to relieve Brittany it was a complete failure, the force being diverted from its original intention and losing more than a third of its men (probably more than 2,000) and 24,000 of its horses out of 30,000.

Contemporaries, however, were deeply suspicious of Gaunt's intentions and interpreted his ill-conceived expedition through the winter months as part of plans to invade Castile. English foreign policy, and Gaunt's personal responsibility for it, might seem to be both dangerous and intoxicated ambition leading to personal and national humiliation, and the action of one prepared to gamble with honour and reputation. The consequences of such drunkenness and 'hasardrye' were to be worked out in the Treaty of Bruges when representatives of England, France and the papacy produced a settlement which reflected the changed balance of power and interest which had emerged in the previous five years (Perroy 1952; Holmes 1975: 33–62). There is a possibility, but no more than that, of Chaucer having attended the peace commission (ed. Crow and Olson 1966: 44).

The history of Anglo–papal relations in the years before Bruges might also be seen as the history of a threat to the independence of the English church, an independence also threatened by the actions of a government led by Gaunt. Taken with developments in foreign policy it was possible to identify a deepening crisis and Gaunt's malign responsibility. The Pardoner's accusations of avarice and gluttony take on a very specific significance. The demands of the papacy for subsidies became a central issue in the second half of 1373 as Gaunt's *chevauchée* worked its way towards Bordeaux. The papal representative, Garnier, pressed hard the claims for taxation. At a Great Council in June 1373, presided over by the Black Prince and Archbishop Whittlesey, the demands were discussed and counter-demands subsequently put which were tantamount to a rejection of the claims of the papacy and a substantial reduction of its rights in England. The parliament which met between October and December 1373 maintained a firm position, complaining about papal reservations and provisions which impeded free elections and which resulted in an outflow of bullion, and complaining about the influence of Italian merchants and alien clergy.

If the demands of the papacy were thought to be excessive on the one hand, the demands of the English crown on the other were seen as also providing a threat. The king's request for clerical subsidies, when seen in conjunction with the removal of episcopal influence in government in 1371, appeared as two aspects of a policy of ecclesiastical oppression in which the church was being made subservient to the interests of an unsuccessful war policy prosecuted for personal aggrandizement. Increasingly there was a refusal to pay clerical subsidies. At the Convocation of Canterbury in December 1373, however, when a deputation from the Council represented the king's case for financial aid to support the war, the Bishop of London, Simon Sudbury, argued in favour of granting a subsidy. Only after some opposition was a grant made and then not as fully as some of the bishops would have wished. What is more the subsidy was accompanied by a list of grievances and a declaration by Courtenay, Bishop of Hereford, that payment by his clergy would be conditional upon redress of injuries.

The accusations of the Pardoner in respect of covetousness may seem, from the mouth of a papal representative, to recoil upon himself and indeed upon a church whose worldly concerns were widely criticized. His charges of gluttony may seem similarly to stink of hypocrisy. If the position of the English church is threatened it might seem to have only itself to blame. But within the church, as the Pardoner tacitly acknowledges, are those critical of it. In choosing the conflict over the eucharist to illustrate the views of the enemies of the church, Chaucer exposes the self-deception of the Pardoner and the weakness of those critics who might be counted sympathizers of John Wyclif, anti-papal apologist for Gaunt – both, in different ways, are involved in rendering substance into accident. Chaucer's criticism is of the church as a whole. The English church is under threat from the papacy, from the policies of Edward III and Gaunt, from 'accidentalists' within its ranks and from its own corruption. In the developments of the Treaty of Bruges the position of the English church may be seen to have reached a critical phase.

Within the Pardoner's Tale the reference to Stilboun provides a link between the crisis in the church, the disasters of foreign policy under Gaunt, and the Treaty of Bruges. Among those chosen to attend the negotiations at Bruges on behalf of England was John Wyclif, as a client of Gaunt presumably intended to argue the case against papal demands (McFarlane 1952: 62–6; Daly 1962: 39–41). The history of his involvement seems strikingly similar to that of Stilboun at Corinth, for in less than two months Wyclif had returned from Bruges earlier than expected. Chaucer's gentle but serious mocking of the 'wys embassadour' (603) and 'wise philosophre' (620) seems applicable to Wyclif, the stern critic who priggishly washed his hands of the crisis and who might, therefore, be seen as implicated by default in the outcome of the discussions.

The Pardoner's digressions at the opening of his tale on the themes of drunkenness, gluttony and 'hasardrye', arising from the behaviour of the

...compaignye
Of yonge folk that haunteden folye,
As riot, hasard, stywes, and tavernes
(463–5)

and the 'riotoures thre' (661), allusively suggest those matters in church and government which were to be critically considered at Bruges in 1375 between the three major parties of England, France and the papacy. The description of the three rioters in the Flemish tavern proves to possess a bitterly satirical dimension, as has been argued before in another context (Norris 1933). In his tacit condemnation of the conduct of these diplomatic affairs Chaucer was not alone. Not only did such criticism surface in the political and constitutional crisis of the Good Parliament of 1376 but it was voiced by contemporary chroniclers, perhaps most notably in the *Anonimalle Chronicle* (ed. Galbraith 1927: 79). Speaking of the Bruges treaty and the involvement of Gaunt and Sudbury the chronicler wrote:

> *...et demurrerent illeoqes tanqe la Pentecost*
> *a excessive costage saunz profit ... A quel*
> *tretee le dite duk fist graunt despens et*
> *graunt riot al count de Aungeoy, fitz al*
> *roy de Fraums, qare chescune iour a poy furount*
> *ensemble par revelers et dauncer; et despendist*
> *passaunt xx mille li. saunz ascune esploit*
> *profitable de les biens Dengleterre.*

Similar views were expressed by Walsingham in his *Historia Anglicana* (ed. Riley 1863: I. 318) and Higden in his *Polychronicon* (ed. Babington and Lumby 1882: VIII. 381).

Chroniclers were no less clear about the disastrous outcome of the negotiations for English interests. For the informed observer there might seem to be a profound interconnection between the matters under discussion. There was a widespread fear of a conspiracy designed to humiliate and disinherit; there was the fear of the subjugation of the English church to papal *and* royal power; there was the

121

fear of invasion and defeat by France and Castile, coupled with the shameful loss of English territory in France; and there was fear of the emergence of Gaunt as King of England and Castile. Rumour fed such anxieties: Flemish envoys at the court of the King of Navarre, for example, were told in 1375 of a secret treaty between the King of France and Gaunt by which Charles V would help secure Gaunt's succession to the throne by persuading the pope to declare Richard, son of the Black Prince, illegitimate, and by which Charles would stand aside while Gaunt attacked Henry of Trastamara in Castile.

The terms of the Treaty of Bruges, moreover, could only have confirmed most suspicions. For contemporaries there was a clear connection between what appeared to be a humiliating submission to France and an expensive submission to the papacy. The depth and seriousness of the situation was such that it not only provoked a political crisis with widespread repercussions throughout England at all levels of society, but remained long after as a determining and influential force in English political life. Anxious for peace after a military failure exacerbated by mismanagement and internal conflict, the English crown was prepared to concede territory, leaving England with little more than Calais and a strip of coast from Bordeaux to Bayonne. Furthermore, the Anglo–papal Concordat agreed to allow the raising of a papal subsidy of 60,000 florins from the English clergy with few, if any, concessions by the papacy. If the policies of the court had been unpopular it was because they were the unsuccessful pursuit of traditional strategies. The radical changes of policy embodied in the Treaty of Bruges were widely offensive because they were a humiliating abandonment of tradition, one which seemed to threaten church and kingdom. And the danger seemed that much more acute when on 10 August 1375, only a week after the truce should have become effective, the Castilians inflicted off La Rochelle what the *Chronique des quatre premiers Valois* called 'the greatest loss that England ever suffered on sea' (Holmes 1975: 56–7).

But for the court there may have seemed to be some advantages. Above all the agreement enabled it to tighten its control over ecclesiastical appointments, especially in the choice of the new bishops Gilbert, Wakefield, Erghum and Sudbury. Sudbury – a product, like the Pardoner, of the papal curia – was one of the few who benefited from the negotiations at Bruges. His ensuing promotion to Canterbury gave the royal court 'an archibishop exceptionally sensitive to royal wishes' (Holmes 1975: 48), however unpopular he might otherwise become, who was to prove an important apologist for the court in the turbulent months of 1377 in his sermon to parliament and his instructions to the church. But when Wyclif was summoned to St Paul's to answer before Courtenay, now Bishop of London, for his seditious preaching, the confrontation which developed between Courtenay, Lancaster and Percy seems to have started a riot which fed on the hostility between the court and the London oligarchy. Noticeably, Gaunt was a principal target for the Londoners' hostilities and he was never again to be sure of the city's support.

If the Pardoner's Tale incorporates the satirical treatment of this profound political and ecclesiastical crisis, the dynamics of the original story are allowed to carry the satire to a bitter conclusion of poisoning, self-destruction and sacrilege. The confrontation between the old man and the three rioters, moreover, may raise the vital matter of succession to Edward III and point to the appalling prospects for the kingdom. Finally, in the Host's rejection of the representative of the church there may be allusions, if not to the rejections of the Londoners, then to the sense of resistance and rebellion which pervades these last months of Edward III's reign and the opening years of Richard II's. The reconciling action of the Knight may reflect the widely held opinion that it was time that a supine aristocratic estate fulfilled its social role. The influence of Seneca, noted below, gives a special dimension to the tale. The poem possesses a twofold warning by a latter-day Seneca of the consequences of the destruction of the authority of the church and of the dangers of the personal ambition of a prince.

BLOOD AND WINE

If the intoxication of Gaunt's political influence 'crepeth subtilly', so does the significance of wine within the text. As well as being the cause of the rioters' death, excessive drinking has a moral and spiritual importance. The gradual accumulation of weighty meanings around the image of wine makes Gaunt's activities, and those of Sudbury, appear heinous and reprehensible.

The Pardoner is, of course, the prime exemplum of the avarice against which he preaches. But he is also the embodiment of another fault which he castigates – excessive drinking. He insists on pausing at an alestake and drinking before beginning his contribution to the game of story-telling (321–2 and 327–8). His ideal existence is to 'drynke licour of the vyne / And have a joly wenche in every toun' (452–3), although on the pilgrimage he is obliged to loosen his tongue with a 'draughte of corny ale' (456).

The tale of the three rioters illustrates the consequences of immoderate drinking. They 'drynken over hir myght' (468), and are seated in a tavern to drink 'Longe erst er prime rong' (662) when they hear the passing bell for their friend. He has been slain 'Fordronke, as he sat on his bench upright' (674). The rioters vow to seek revenge 'al dronken in this rage' (705). Having unexpectedly found untold wealth, one of them calls for bread and wine (797). The youngest member of the trio fetches three bottles from a nearby town, two of which he adulterates with poison (872–3). He is murdered on his return, his fellows drink the poison and come to hideous ends, the wine their downfall (885–94).

Told like this, the story of the three rioters might seem to be little more than a medieval temperance tract, a moral tale on the evils of drink, though even at this level it is effective and pointed enough. For the narrative is directed not at drink itself, but at excess or 'superfluytee abhomynable' (471), at a man who drinks so much 'That of his throte he maketh his pryvee' (527). Drunkenness causes its victim to be quarrelsome and wretched (550); it is disfiguring and unattractive – 'Sour is thy breeth, foul artow to embrace'; (552); it atrophies wit and discretion, being their 'verray sepulture' (558); and whoever is dominated by drink 'kan no conseil kepe' (561).

These exhortations, addressed as they are to 'lordynges' (573), are made more precise and authoritative by reference to the Old Testament, where 'alle the sovereyn actes . . . / Of victories . . . / Were doon in abstinence and in preyere' (574–7). One example following the

exhortations is taken from Proverbs 31 and its subject, as glossed by
Chaucer, is 'Of wyn-yevyng to hem that han justise' (587):

> *Give not to Kings, O Lamuel, give not*
> *wine to Kings: because there is no*
> *secret where drunkenness reigneth:*
> *And lest they drink and forget judgements,*
> *and pervert the cause of the children of*
> *the poor.*
> *(Proverbs 31: 4–5)*

The Pardoner's reference to Lamuel is preceded by one to Attila,
although the biblical material is given more weight: 'over al this,
avyseth yow right wel / What was comaunded unto Lamuel' (583–4).
Attila's story, with its brief, pointed moral – 'A capitayn sholde lyve
in sobrenesse' (582) – is self-explanatory:

> *Looke, Attila, the grete conquerour,*
> *Deyde in his sleep, with shame and dishonour,*
> *Bledynge ay at his nose in dronkenesse.*
> *(579–81)*

There is a warning here to great lords to exercise moderation in the
use of heady policies.

The immorality of those who are drunk with the wine of power is
made more serious by the linking of drunkenness with deadly sin. It is
an aspect of gluttony to which lechery is 'annexed' (482) for 'luxurie is
in wyn and dronkenesse' (484) – the words are taken from Ephesians
5: 18. Here, and in the examples which follow, the Bible is again
introduced as a testimony to the truth: 'The hooly writ take I to my
witnesse' (483). There follows a reference to the story of Lot (Genesis
19: 30–8), who in old age was made drunk by his daughters so that,

unknown to him, they were able to lie with him and conceive children. The emphasis in the Pardoner's version falls on how the stupefying effects of wine lead to acts done unnaturally, 'unkyndely' (485): 'So dronke he was, he nyste what he wroghte' (487). Unnatural sexual relations are also a feature of the next story, concerning Herod and John the Baptist. According to the biblical account (Mark 6: 14–30), John had condemned Herod's marriage to Herodias, his brother's wife; consequently, Herodias sought John's death. Chaucer's version, that Herod acquiesced in his wife's demand for John's head, 'Whan he of wyn was repleet' (489) is apocryphal. It accentuates the injustice of the act through the innocence of the 'ful giltelees' victim (491). Chaucer's final authority is Seneca, to whose moral letters Chaucer had recourse as a fount of rational wisdom (Ayres 1919). He attributes to Seneca the idea that there is no difference between madness and drunkenness, except that madness lasts much longer (492–7), although Seneca had actually said in Epistle 83 that the habit of drunkenness is like recurrent fits of madness in its ability to affect even periods of sobriety (ed. and trans. Gummere 1920: 274–5).

The deepening significance of wine and drunkenness is taken a stage further when gluttony, of which drunkenness is symptomatic, is represented as the original sin responsible for man's fall from grace in the garden of Eden:

> O glutonye, ful of cursednesse!
> O cause first of oure confusioun!
> O original of oure dampnacioun...
> ....
> Corrupt was al this world for glotonye.
> (498–500 and 504)

Adam and Eve were driven from paradise when Adam ceased fasting and ate from the forbidden tree (505–11) – a point made by Pope Innocent III in his De Miseria Condicionis Humane, II. 18. 5–7 (ed. and trans. Lewis 1978: 166–7) and by Jerome in his Against Jovinian II. 15 (trans. Fremantle 1893: 398–9), as a gloss to one manuscript of the Canterbury Tales indicates (Manly and Rickert 1940: III. 516).

Theologically speaking it is a short step from the Fall to the Crucifixion, and the Pardoner weaves into his apostrophe to gluttony and its consequences a reminder of how the second Adam atoned for the first's disobedience. He was damned

> *Til Crist hadde boght us with his blood agayn!*
> *Lo, how deere, shortly for to sayn,*
> *Aboght was thilke cursed vileynye!*
>
> *(501–3)*

The linked series wine–gluttony–Fall–Christ's blood is now complete, a set of associations with parallels in penitential literature (Tupper 1914: 560–2; Yeager 1984). The final significance of wine is as a eucharistic emblem of man's redemption.

The Pardoner's Prologue and Tale are in fact studded with allusions to Christ's sacrificial blood. Before the Pardoner begins, the Host swears ' "by nayles and by blood" ' (288), a curse echoed by those rehearsed by the Pardoner which, appropriately enough, include reference to relics: ' "By Goddes precious herte ..." ', ' "By his nayles ..." ', ' "By the blood of Crist that is in Hayles ..." ', ' "By Goddes armes" ' (651–4). One of the rioters swears ' "By God! and by the hooly sacrement" ' (757). In a more heartfelt vein the old man addresses the rioters, ' "God save yow, that boghte agayn mankynde" ' (766). And the Pardoner, commenting on the rioter's murder, laments:

> *'Allas, mankynde, how may it bitide*
> *That to thy creatour, which that the wroghte*
> *And with his precious herte-blood thee boghte,*
> *Thou art so fals and so unkynde, allas?'*
>
> *(900–3)*

Given the presence of these persistent reminders of the Crucifixion and the doctrine of redemption, it is difficult not to read the Pardoner's cake and ale (321–2) and the bread and wine of the rioters (797) as travesties of the eucharistic bread and wine, symbols of the body and blood of Christ (Nichols 1967; Millichap 1974). But neither the Pardoner, nor the rioters, are able to grasp the spiritual significance of what they perceive and do. The rioters, for example, believe that death can be overcome, which is Christ's prerogative (Stockton 1961), and that florins, not Christ's sacrificial blood, are what buy mankind. Consequently, they are doomed to die unredeemed. The shadow of the Crucifixion falls across the final scene of their story (Delasanta 1973) but, chillingly, the protagonists are bereft of any inner understanding of their tableau with its tree, dice, betrayals for money and painful deaths. The moral for those intoxicated with 'wine' could hardly be clearer. What is more, the rioters may also be seen as the victims of Saturn: some of the key images of the story also occur in the iconography of his rule (Plates 1 and 2).

FLESH AND BONE

The sense of desecration and sacrilege brought about by wilful spiritual blindness, and channelled through the references to sacramental blood, also finds an outlet in allusions to Christ's body. In blaspheming, the rioters

> Oure blissed Lordes body they totere –
> Hem thoughte that Jewes rente hym noght ynough ...
> (474–5)

And on vowing to kill Death they swear 'many a grisly ooth ... / And Cristes blessed body they torente' (708–9) – an idea repeated by Chaucer's Parson (ParsT 590) and found in contemporary sermons and treatises (Owst 1961: 414–25; Miller and Bosse 1971: 178–9).

The actual tearing of flesh, whether threatened by one gambler to another,

'*By Goddes armes, if thou falsly pleye,*
This daggere shal thurghout thyn herte go!'
(654–5)

or enacted by Death – 'And with his spere he smoot his herte atwo'
(677) – or by the rioters against their friend (825–36 and 880–1), are
sufficient reminders of Christ's violent death. Indeed the final betrayal
is not of one rioter by another but a betrayal of Christ in which
narrator and rioters share. As the theological locus shifts from Fall
to Crucifixion so there is suggested the orthodox idea that the 'first
gluttony' can be redeemed through eating the body and drinking the
blood of Christ in the eucharistic act. Only then will death through sin
be overcome. But the rioters and Pardoner continue to seek death
through their dedication to vice.

Far from offering a sense of the spiritual benefits of Christ's body
and blood, the Pardoner, in describing the evils of gluttony, focuses
instead on the visceral aspect of the human body (Stevens and Falvey
1982: 148–54) – on flesh as flesh, and food as food:

'*O wombe! O bely! O stynkyng cod,*
Fulfilled of dong and of corrupcioun!
At either ende of thee foul is the soun.'
(534–6)

Cooks, for their part, make concoctions to go 'thurgh the golet softe
and swoote' (543). The Pardoner, who is supposedly a healer of souls
as the Physician is of bodies, in practice directs his attentions, for what
they are worth, to the ' "pokkes and ... scabbe, and every soore" ' (358)
which afflict sheep. Similarly, the lives of the rioters are reduced to an
animalistic existence when the poisoner among them seeks a substance
that will kill rats, or a polecat, telling the apothecary that he wants to
destroy the 'vermyn' that are troubling him (851–8). Ironically, his
victims – expecting food and desperately in need of sacramental wine

– 'storven' (888) and die deaths which exhibit all the classic symptoms of poisoning as set out by Avicenna (889–94).

Bones, as the final component to which the body can be reduced, are also used to convey the spiritual conditions of the rioters and the Pardoner (Lawton 1985: 25). 'Goddes digne bones!' (695) might form a curse, but the only bones which carry significance for the rioters are in the shape of dice, at which they play 'bothe day and nyght' (467). 'The bicched bones two' (656) are the means whereby they gamble, oblivious (832–4) to the dice associated with Christ's death (Miller and Bosse 1971: 178) and to the menacing appearance of Death, as a skeleton. To the Pardoner, bones mean relics, 'cristal stones, / Ycrammed ful of cloutes and of bones' (347–8). Any bones will do, as long as they can masquerade as the real thing – 'Relikes been they, as wenen they echoon' (349) – like the sheep's shoulder bone set in latten (350–1), or pigs' bones (GP 700).

As the irreducible elements of human and animal existence, the bones of the Pardoner's Prologue and Tale suggest something of the Pardoner's and rioters' obdurate sinfulness. Their outlook is materialist not only in the sense of being avaricious but also in the limitation of their perceptions to the physical and tangible. It is appropriate that the Pardoner's appeal to the Host to kiss the relics should be met with a retort that, while it denigrates, sums up the fleshly and materialist religious attitude of this pilgrim. The Host begins with a reference to the true cross, unlike the 'croys of latoun ful of stones' (GP 699) which the Pardoner carries:

> '...by the croys which that Seint Eleyne fond,
> I wolde I hadde thy coillons in myn hond
> In stide of relikes or of seintuarie.
> Lat kutte hem of, I wol thee helpe hem carie;
> They shul be shryned in an hogges toord!'
> *(951–5)*

The Pardoner is himself reduced to a thing, to the status of a false and worthless relic.

THE PARDONER AS FOOL

The construction of the Pardoner's character can profitably be studied in relation to the idea of the fool, with whom he shares many traditional features: drink-induced eloquence tending to loquacity, then sudden silence; a display of 'masks'; a confrontation with 'reality' in the form of the Host; burlesque of sacred authority; incitement to desecration and obscenity; a close identity with death; an ability to speak truthfully through apparent folly; a capacity to act as scapegoat; a desire to break down received ideas of moral and social order; ambivalent sexuality (Rowland 1979); self-division; an existence as a social outcast and parasite fond of food and drink; dependence upon an audience; eye-catching clothes (Welsford 1935; Willeford 1969).

More specifically, the Pardoner is a fool because he is a trickster, a liminal figure who inhabits the boundaries between opposite states of being (Movshovitz 1977). In the General Prologue we are told that 'with feyned flaterye and japes, / He made the person and the peple his apes' (GP 705–6). The Host expects from him 'myrthe or japes' (319), and can hardly be disappointed by the account of a 'gaude' and 'an hundred false japes moore' (389 and 394) which follows. Indeed his pose at the alestake to 'drynke and eten of a cake' (322), while he thinks of a tale, may have suggested to a medieval audience one of the customary images of a fool, of a monk devouring bread (Plate 3; Gifford 1974: 337).

The image gives pause for thought because it indicates a much more serious framework of meaning for 'the fool' than that of the successful prankster. Painted fools are often found in psalters as part of the historiation of the initial D to Psalm 52, *Dixit insipiens*, 'The fool said in his heart: there is no God' (Newton 1980: 82–5). Seen in this context, Chaucer's representation of the Pardoner as fool becomes a portrait of a man whose folly neither conceals wisdom (Wenzel 1982), nor derives from holy innocence, but which lies in denying the existence of God. This negative representation of the fool is consonant with Chaucer's remarks in the *House of Fame*, where the fools exclaim 'We ben shrewes... / And han delyt in wikkednesse' (*HF* 1830–1). More generally, fools who are the Pardoner's kin occur in the mystery plays, often at moments of intense piety, mocking, deriding, and inverting orthodox values (Billington 1984: 1–31), and in the anti-clerical satire of the seasonal Feast of Fools (Mann 1973: 146), in which clerics might mock prelates, travesty the mass, personify hypocrisy, and preach bogus sermons (Welsford 1935: 202–4; Neaman 1975: 58–9; Billington 1979: 36–44). The cake-eating Pardoner is, then, like his counterpart in the Psalms, one of 'the workers of iniquity ... who eat up my people as they eat bread' (Psalm 52: 5). This is an affinity first noticed, to our knowledge, by Lynne Griffin, a graduate student of the Universities of Kent and Manchester, in a series of unpublished papers.

There are two *Dixit insipiens* psalms, Psalms 52 and 13. Their opening and closing verses are virtually the same, but both contain some unique material. The way each elaborates the nature of the God-denying fool has a bearing on the meaning of Chaucer's Pardoner. A translation of the psalter into Middle English, which achieved 'immense popularity' (Alford 1984: 42), that done by Richard Rolle before 1349, was available to Chaucer (ed. Bramla, 1884 Everett 1922: 217–23). Rolle himself provided a commentary to his translation of the Psalms, loosely based on Peter Lombard (Deanesly 1920: 144–6). At some time in the last quarter of the fourteenth century Lollard interpolations were added to what Rolle had written (Everett 1923; Hudson 1984: 255; 1988: 259–64). It is this interpolated version of Rolle's commentary (e.g. British Library MS Royal 18 D.I., ff. 19v–20v and f. 94) which provides some intriguing parallels to the Pardoner's Prologue and Tale. The relevant verses of the *Dixit insipiens* psalms begin with the later part of verse 3 of Psalm 13 (not found in Psalm 52):

> *A byriel openyng is þe þrote of hem*
> *wiþ her tungis triccherously þei wrouȝte:*
> *venym of snakis vndir þe lippis of hem.*
> *Whos mouþ is ful of cursyng and bittirnesse:*
> *swifte ben her feett to spille blood.*
> *Soruwe and vnhap in þe weyes of hem: and*

þe weye of pees þei knewe not, þe dreede of
god is not bifore þe eyen of hem.

Verses 4 and 5 of Psalm 13 are close to Psalm 52: 5–6:

> *13:4 Ne shal þei not knowe all þat worchiþ*
> *wikkednesse: þe whiche deuouriþ my folk*
> *as mete of breed.*
> *13:5 God þei in callide not: þer þei qwoke*
> *for drede whar dreede was not.*

Psalm 13: 6 is unique:

> *For oure lord is in ryȝtwis getyng:*
> *þe counceyl of helplees you shamed,*
> *for oure lord is þe hope of hym.*

So is the second part of Psalm 52: 6:

> *For god haþ scaterid her boonys þat*
> *plesedyn to men: þei ben schamyd*
> *for god haþ dispisid hem.*

The phrase 'byriel openyng' of Psalm 13: 3 is taken by the Lollard commentator in two senses. First, it can mean the mouth of an evil man who leads others astray 'þoru euel eyr and swelewyþ hem', because he is devoted to 'vicious and delicaat lyuyng'. Such persons are like walking graves for they are 'biried in obstynacion þat is þei ben endurid to dwelle in her synne al her lyf to her deeþ'. Second, the words 'bitokneþ glotenye þat wastiþ boþe bodyli goodis and goostly and euere gapynge to take for vndiscreet etynge and drynkynge', which can lead to sickness and death. 'Venym of snakis' is glossed as 'vncorrigyble malyce vndur þe tunge of hem in whos hertis for vaynglorye of þe world goddis loue ne his dreede may not synke'. On 'cursyng and bittirnesse' the commentator writes: 'Her mouþ is euere redy to mysseye and reproue and to manace wiþ boost for her owne heyȝnesse and couetyse not in charite mekely for cristis sake to amende synne'. Their desire to spill blood means 'to sleen her oune soulis for doyng of synne and of oþir mennes þoru her yuel ensaumple'. Sorrow and misfortune ('Soruwe and vnhap') will follow 'for her pryde and her malyce'.

Those who 'deuouriþ my folk as mete of breed' (13: 4 and 52: 5) are seen as those who 'comeþ falsly to þe offy of holy churche for to take richesse and honours of men not for heele of mannis soule'. They 'rauyshe fro symple man vndisserued here good but þei disserue it not. Her askyng and her takyng is vniuste robberye of oþre mennes goodis to her owne dampnacion.' Psalm 13: 5 (52: 6) concerns 'couetouse men comynge in to þe churche more for delyt to gete richessis of þe world þan for þe loue of god suche as her werkis shewen'. Such men have not called God with love into their hearts and so become hypocrites: 'For hou meke þat þey seeme to þe puple þei ben þoru her false lyuyng and takyng gredily of goodis raueshyng wolues'. Knowing their falseness they 'shulde dreede of the wraþþe of god'.

'Ryȝtwis getyng' (13: 6) concerns tithes and offerings which are 'goddis trewe part' and 'trewe men takyn hem riȝtwisly ... but in vntrewely getyng and ȝeuyng is not god but þe deuel'. The commentator warns that 'preestis þat þoru pryde and couetyse disspisiþ heere to folewe crist in mekenesse and wilful pouert shal of god be shamed'. In the commentary to 52: 6 those shamed by God who have their bones scattered are those guilty of 'glosyng'. They are wicked men beneath their guise of being healers of souls: 'god haþ dispisid hem for her traitorie for he þat feyneþ hym a leche to kunne heele woundis and pryueli sleiþ hym for his substaunce whom he schulde heele is an open traitoure'.

The image of ecclesiastical corruption developed by the commentator is too close to the Pardoner's self-portrait to be easily ignored. In general terms and in detail the Pardoner fits the Lollard stereotype of a corrupt churchman. There is, for example, his vindictive loquacity, infectious in its maliciousness, as when he uses preaching to attach his enemies, to 'quyte ... folk that doon us displesances' (420). Devoted to vicious and delicate living, to being 'a ful vicious man' (459) enjoying 'moneie, wolle, chese, and whete' (448), 'licour of the vyne / And ... a joly wenche in every toun' (452–3), he is a prime example of a proud man 'buried in obstynacion', of a man who is condemned to re-enact his sins until his life's end:

> *My theme is alwey oon, and evere was –*
> Radix malorum est Cupiditas.
> *(333–4)*

His life is a closed system, for he spends it preaching for the money against which he preaches: 'Thus kan I preche agayn that same vice / Which that I use, and that is avarice' (427–8). Consequently he is doomed to unredeemed death.

The way to death and damnation, the open grave, is indeed what the Pardoner and his tale reveal. His own gluttony, and that against which he preaches, has already been discussed. The Pardoner, like the commentator, notes its wastefulness (537). It too leads to hell (imaged in the description of frenzied cooks at lines 538–46) and spiritual death: 'he that haunteth swiche delices / Is deed, whil that he lyveth in tho vices' (547–8). Like the biblical commentator, the Pardoner represents the mouth, 'the shorte throte, the tendre mouth' (517) as the opening which leads to the grave, while drunkenness 'is verray sepulture / Of mannes wit and his discrecioun' (558–9). As for the Pardoner's own mouth, as well as being gluttonous, it is venomous and serpentine, like that of the treacherous speakers of the Psalm. Admitting that preaching may be motivated by 'ypocrisye, / ... veyne glorie ... hate' (410–11), he goes on to describe how he attacks an opponent from the pulpit:

Thanne wol I stynge hym with my tonge smerte …
....
Thus spitte I out my venym under hewe
Of hoolynesse, to semen hooly and trewe.
(413 and 421–2)

An officer of the church as described by the Lollard commentator –
one whose objectives are wealth and power – the Pardoner also typi-
fies the false cleric's exploitation of the poor and ignorant. It is these
'lewed peple' who are duped by his pulpit rhetoric (392), who are
enthralled by his stories (437), and from whom he extorts gifts,

Al were it yeven of the povereste page,
Or of the povereste wydwe in a village,
Al sholde hir children sterve for famyne.
(449–51)

Apostolic poverty (447), to 'lyve in poverte wilfully' (441), and manual labour (444–5) are not for him. Instead, the Pardoner looks
forward to offerings, obtained under false pretences, of 'nobles or
sterlynges, / Or elles silver broches, spoones, rynges' (907–8). As the
General Prologue makes clear, he is capable of obtaining more in one
day than a 'povre person' (GP 702) is able to gather in two months
from the tithes and offerings which are lawfully due. Like the Lollard
stereotype, the Pardoner (a man of scattered bones) is a gloser shamed
when his shamming is openly rejected by the Host. This supposed
curer of souls with his paraphernalia of relics, following hard on the
heels of the Physician with *his* paraphernalia (304–7) is revealed as a
false curer who actually cares nothing for the state of others' souls, a
betrayer of trust whose real interest is in the 'substance' he can acquire
from his victims.

Of course, both commentary and the Pardoner's Prologue and Tale
are heirs to a tradition of anticlerical satire, and this in part explains
their similarities (Hudson 1984: 244). The tradition is well represented,

in Chaucer's case, by the apocalyptic figure of Faux-Semblant in the *Romance of the Rose,* lines 11006–12380 (trans. Dahlberg 1971: 194–9) by Jean de Meun, on which he drew, as he drew on other sections of the *Romance* (Lawton 1985: 29–31; Emmerson and Herzman 1987). A hypocritical preacher who is contemptuous of the poor and of apostolic models, a pilgrim who is well schooled in avarice and in malicious defamation, Faux-Semblant is adaptable to Chaucer's purposes. But Jean de Meun's satire is directed against friars and the bulk of it is too general to be easily transferable to the Pardoner (Kean 1972: II. 96–100). We must, of course, look to as many other works as possible for a full explanation of the genesis of Chaucer's Pardoner, especially in the present state of research, where the absence of prototypes is more evident than their presence (Mann 1973: 145). But it is perhaps not claiming too much to say that the Lollard image of corruption is closer to the Pardoner in conception and realization than any other model so far advanced.

It is nevertheless difficult to assess the precise relationship between the Pardoner's Prologue and Tale and the interpolated Lollard commentary on Rolle's English Psalter. It is possible that Chaucer knew of it in one of its versions. He certainly seems to have been familiar with Lollard sentiments about corrupt, predatory churchmen, views which were widespread in their writings (ed. Hudson 1983: I.195; Hudson 1988: 390–4), and which are indeed well represented elsewhere in the interpolated commentary (Everett 1923: 287–91); that on Psalm 25: 10 (f. 43v), for example, includes some interesting remarks on avarice as a source of ecclesiastical corruption. Such views Chaucer uses as a platform from which to condemn the Pardoner, and what he represents, out of his mouth. But the nexus of issues in the *Dixit insipiens* commentary, coinciding as it does with the same nexus of issues in the Pardoner's Prologue and Tale, reveals a basic affinity between it and Chaucer's composition. In indicating that the Pardoner is a fool of the god-denying, self-destructive variety, Chaucer is perhaps inviting his audience to consider the Pardoner in the light of the Lollard commentary on the *Dixit insipiens* psalms, a commentary which his own composition echoes verbally, with the Pardoner adopting a posture at the beginning of his prologue as if he were the fool in the historiated initial to Psalm 52.

THE PARDONER AS SATIRIST

Other features of the Pardoner's Prologue and Tale make him the kind of target favoured by the Wycliffites: his sale of indulgences, carrying of false relics, encouragement of image-veneration, his participation in the pilgrimage and in tale-telling, the degree to which he represents the power of the papacy (Lawton 1987: 26–40; Besserman and Storm 1983). On all of these topics the Wycliffites were outspokenly critical, seeing them as evidence of church corruption (Jones 1972; Hudson 1984: 251; Aston 1984: 136–92; Hudson 1988: 301–9 and 327–34). The Pardoner might therefore seem to be the embodiment of those practices identified by the Wycliffites as being rife in the institutional church.

But it would be a mistake to align Chaucer too closely with a Wycliffite position, however perennially tempting that might be (Tatlock 1916; Jeffrey 1984). His attitude is more complex (Olson 1986: 129 and 184; Peck 1986), for he provides the Pardoner with material that also makes him a satirist of Wycliffite doctrine. This is suggested by the excessive vehemence with which he attacks the uttering of oaths (Hudson 1988: 371–4), but is nowhere more clear than in lines 538 to 548 in which the Pardoner travesties the Lollard position on the eucharist (Stevens and Falvey 1982: 154–6). He does this by speaking in the persona of a preacher embroiled in the debate on transubstantiation.

The traditional position of the church, developed over many centuries, and formulated in a decretal of Innocent III in 1215, was that after the words of consecration the eucharistic bread and wine become the body and blood of Christ. Although the bread's colour, texture, taste and dimensions (its accidents) remain, the bread changes its reality, transforming its 'substance' into Christ's body as known on earth and as present in heaven. In the *De Eucharista* (*c*.1379) and subsequent writings Wyclif denied the presence of Christ's body, arguing that the substance of the bread and wine remains unchanged, a view that was to cause his denunciation as a heretic (Leff 1967: II. 497–8). For Wyclif, the bread and wine are to be though of as potent sacramental images directing man's thought towards the truth of Christ. If materially the bread and wine remain unchanged, spiritually they are indeed transformed into the body and blood of Christ (Leff 1967: I. 549–57; ed. Hudson 1978: 142; Kenny 1985: 80–90; Keen 1986; Hudson 1988: 281–90). From Wyclif's position it is mistaken to believe either that the substance of bread changes, 'that this sacrament is Goddus body and no brede, for it is bothe togedur', or that the bread is no more than bread: 'the most heresie is to trowe that this sacrament is an accident withouten a substance' – statements found in *Wyclif's Confessions on the Eucharist*, dating from *c*.1381 and composed by a disciple (ed. Hudson 1978: 18). The *Confessions* go on to indicate the extent of the difference between 'heresie' and the Wycliffite position:

> *Owe! howe grete diuersite is bitwene vs*
> *þat trowes þat þis sacrament is verray*
> *brede in his kynde, and betuene heretykus*
> *þat tellus þat þis [is] an accident*
> *wiþouten a subiecte.*

Such differences are also brought out in the examination of the Lollard William Thorpe (active *c*.1387–1407) before Thomas Arundell, Archbishop of Canterbury (ed. Pollard 1903: 130–3).

The Pardoner, for his part, refers to:

> *Thise cookes, how they stampe, and streyne, and grynde,*
> *And turnen substaunce into accident*
> *To fulfille al thy likerous talent!*
>
> *(538–40)*

These lines are based on a passage from a work which Chaucer claimed to have translated, *De Miseria Condicionis Humane* (II. 17) by Innocent III (ed. and trans. Lewis 1978: 164–5), a pope whom Wyclif's follower, John Purvey, condemned as Antichrist for his views on the eucharist (Leff 1967: II. 579). Indeed, anyone familiar with the contemporary controversy over the eucharist would have recognized in the criticism of those who turn substance into accident a reference to the Wycliffite attack on a doctrine they themselves regarded as heretical (Nichols 1967: 501–2). Here the consecrating priest is represented in a belittling manner as no more than a cook dedicated to the preparation of fleshly food and drink (Leff 1967: II. 553; Keen 1986: 15). In view of the customary association of cooks, with their meathooks and boiling cauldrons, with devils, the attack is made even more pointed. Nor is Christ the only person subjected to the processes of a theological cuisine; so is his mother:

> *Out of the harde bones knokke they*
> *The mary, for they caste noght awey*
> *That may go thurgh the golet softe and swoote.*
> *(541–3)*

The stimulus to the soul's taste-buds, the 'spicerie of leef' (544), is but an appeal to gluttony, making the devout but erring consumer want ever more exotic sensations as the 'accident' glides down the throat. As a temptation to vice it can have fatal consequences:

> *Of spicerie of leef, and bark, and roote,*
> *Shal been his sauce ymaked by delit,*
> *To make hym yet a newer appetit.*
> *But, certes, he that haunteth swiche delices*
> *Is deed, whil that he lyveth in tho vices.*
> *(544–8)*

That Chaucer's presentation of a Wycliffite position on the eucharist is not to be taken at face value is clear from the fact that it is the Pardoner who speaks – a man who, as we have seen, could hardly be further from the Wycliffite ideal. What also undermines the force of his remarks on transubstantiation is the rhetoric with which they are introduced, itself a parody of Lollard vernacular utterance and its tendency towards what McFarlane, in another context, called 'dreamy cant ... a farrago of pulpit commonplaces' (McFarlane 1972: 210 and 204). Thus the Pardoner captures the Wycliffite habit of referring directly to the gospel for authority, of investing that authority with emotional appeal, and of sensationalizing moral issues by painting them in lurid colours:

> *The apostel wepyng seith ful pitously*
> *'Ther walken manye of whiche yow toold have I –*
> *I seye it now wepyng, with pitous voys –*
> *They been enemys of Cristes croys,*
> *Of whiche the ende is deeth; wombe is hir god!'*
> *O wombe! O bely! O stynkyng cod,*
> *Fulfilled of dong and of corrupcioun!*
> *At either ende of thee foul is the soun.*
> *How greet labour and cost is thee to fynde!*
>   *(529–37)*

Such preaching is sensational, but not exceptional (Lawton 1985: 21–2).

There are in the Pardoner's Prologue and Tale many other examples of this technique. They have antecedents in the *De Miseria* II.18, 2–5 (ed. and trans. Lewis 1978: 166–7), in later penitential literature (Tupper 1914: 560–2; Yeager 1984), and would also bear comparison with the diction found in vernacular Lollard works as a means of establishing more securely the mainsprings of Chaucer's satire. What might also emerge from a wider study of Lollard texts is their tendency, like that of the Pardoner's Prologue and Tale, to return to a relatively small number of interlinked preoccupations, or network of obsessions, one leading to another with sudden movement. The nature of those preoccupations might also shed light on the Pardoner's treatment of such topics as drunkenness, gluttony, blasphemy and dice-playing (Hudson 1984: 260–1).

There may be in what Chaucer writes an indication of his sense of distance not only from certain features of Wycliffite doctrine but also from the activities of Wyclif himself. If, as has been argued, the ambassador 'Stilboun' may be taken as a reference to Wyclif and his embassy to Bruges, then the representation of this event is done in such a way as to imply criticism. Quite apart from the implications of 'Stilboun' (= stillborn?) itself, the wisdom of this envoy-cum-philosopher is made to look questionable. He is, first, a victim of life's ironies: on arriving at his destination the man opposed to 'hasardrye' finds out by chance that the greatest people of the land are addicted to gambling:

> And whan he cam, hym happede, par chaunce,
> That alle the gretteste that were of that lond,
> Pleyynge atte hasard he hem fond.
>
> (606–8)

Faced with an affront to his moral beliefs, and fearful for his reputation, he hurriedly and stealthily returns home, like the academic who would rather reaffirm his principles and ideals than sully himself with the compromises of practical politics. Stilboun's repetition of the word 'hasardours' suggests a man holding the world at arm's length, a man too morally disdainful and self-righteous to be of much practical use. He takes refuge in an ivory tower of rhetoric:

> ... as soone as it myghte be,
> He stal hym hoom agayn to his contree,
> And seyde, 'Ther wol I nat lese my name,
> Ne I wol nat take on me so greet defame,
> Yow for to allie unto none hasardours.
> Sendeth othere wise embassadours;
> For, by my trouthe, me were levere dye
> Than I yow sholde to hasardours allye.
> For ye, that been so glorious in honours,
> Shul nat allyen yow with hasardours
> As by my wyl, ne as by my tretee.'
>
> (609–19)

In the wake of this speech the last line of the passage becomes bitingly ironic: 'This wise philosophre, thus seyde hee' (620). Behind Chaucer's lines may lie the recognition that Wyclif who, like him, knew Gaunt's patronage, is also, like him, in the position of being expected to act as a wise counsellor. One of the purposes of the Pardoner's Prologue and Tale may be to enact that very function. Chaucer, as the discussion of the Merchant's Tale will show, is no stranger to the role of counsellor to princes.

The sources of the 'Stilboun' passage have not been fully traced. There is a 'Stilbo' in Seneca's *Moral Epistles*, book IX, introduced as an example of the self-sufficient philosopher who remains unaffected by personal and political disaster. But Seneca does not mention the episode described by Chaucer: that is found in John of Salisbury's *Policraticus* (Tupper 1941: 438) where the protagonist is Chilon. Chilon is represented as thoroughly admirable in rejecting an alliance with a country whose elders are addicted to gambling. The contrast with Chaucer's version is revealing, but there may be another source to consider, say in the commentary on Wisdom by Holcot, who makes frequent recourse to Seneca, and which Chaucer knew.

Chaucer's representation of the Pardoner is therefore founded on much more complex principles than might at first be suspected. An embodiment of the God-denying fool and hypocrite identifiable in Lollard writings, he also acts as a mouthpiece through which Wycliffite views are satirized. Through him the Pardoner's Prologue and Tale contain a powerful critique both of ecclesiastical corruption and of one kind of would-be reformer. At one point the critique becomes an *ad hominem* attack on one who, like the church he castigates, attempts to mix politics and religion. Chaucer's perception of the church is of an institution divided against itself.

STRUCTURE AND SOURCES

Repeated changes of voice, tone, register and implied audience make of the Pardoner's Prologue and Tale a teasing composition which is structurally complex. To some extent structural divisions may be linked to the source material which lies beneath different sections.

What follows is an attempt, first, to identify the nature and peculiarities of the poem's organization and, second, to examine the tale proper in the light of that organization.

After the Physician has told his tale and the Host has passed comment, the Pardoner's contribution gets under way with the Host's invitation to this man who looks 'lyk a prelat' (310) – a word which invites connections with actual prelates, such as Sudbury, but which in Lollard parlance could be denigratory (Hudson 1981: 22–3) – and the Pardoner's response as he lounges at a tavern door (309–28). There follows an address to the pilgrims (329–51), then the Pardoner's exposition of his preaching techniques and the announcement of his theme, avarice (352–462). As we have argued, much of the material finds a context in the Wycliffite commentary on *Dixit insipiens*. At line 463 the tale begins, set in Flanders. The vivid opening is no sooner given than it is frozen by a digression on drunkenness, gluttony, 'hasardrye' and false swearing running from lines 485 to 660. Here a context might also be found in Wycliffite writings. Within this section are two further digressions (562–628) concerning political material: the influence of Gaunt and the role of Stilboun/Wyclif. At line 661 the tale resumes and continues uninterrupted until its end at line 903. The type of audience address favoured in the earlier preaching exposition then recurs (904–14) before the Pardoner switches to a direct address to the Canterbury pilgrims (915–45), one which culminates in a quarrel with the Host and the intervention of another pilgrim, the Knight (946–68).

It would be possible to represent diagrammatically the structure of the Pardoner's Prologue and Tale as a nest of boxes. At the centre would be the passages on topical political events, contained within a larger box indicating the digression on drunkenness and associated vices. Surrounding that would be the beginning and ending of the tale. The next largest box would stand for the Pardoner in the process of demonstrating his homiletic art, itself framed by direct addresses to the pilgrims and then by exchanges with the Host. The drawback of using such a model to describe the arrangement of the poem's parts is that it suggests too much balance and symmetry and too great a degree of separation among the components.

In practice the divisions between structural units are frequently

fractured and broken. In reading the poetry one is often in an ambiguous border country between one kind of utterance and another. For
example, the following lines might seem to belong within the body of
the tale, illustrative as they are of the rioters' habitual blaspheming:

> *'By Godde armes, if thou falsly pleye,*
> *This daggere shal thurghout thyn herte go!'*
> *(654–5)*

In fact they occur as an example of one kind of oath among others in a
catalogue of blasphemings given by the Pardoner as instances of 'gret
swering'. He appears to be demonstrating his skills as a preacher,
although the passage is the final part of the moral excursus prompted
by the beginning of the tale. A more famous example of structural
no-man's-land occurs once the tale is finished and the Pardoner
addresses the pilgrims as if they were a gullible rural congregation of
the sort he habitually dupes (919–45).

The structural units of the Pardoner's Prologue and Tale ought
therefore to be thought of not as discrete, but as interactive. The 'nest
of boxes' model will stand provided that the demarcating lines are
broken, to indicate the possibility of allusive cross-referencing. The
model is also useful in drawing attention to the central position
occupied by the political material. In terms of its effect on an understanding of the other parts of the Pardoner's Prologue and Tale it is,
of all the structural sections, not so much interactive as explosive. A
measure of its impact may be gained by removing it temporarily from
Chaucer's poem. The prologue and tale would then run without a
break from line 329 to 561, followed immediately by lines 589 to 602,
before picking up again at 629, where the Pardoner speaks on the last
member of the moral quartet — false swearing — having by then
rehearsed the other three: gluttony, drunkenness and 'hasardrye'. If
this were the received state of the Pardoner's Prologue and Tale then
it would read as an account of the condition of the church which
draws on Wycliffite views of clerical hypocrisy and of the eucharist.
Such a composition might indeed have been one version of the work.

Events involving Sudbury and Gaunt may then have made the composition potentially more pointed and topical, causing Chaucer to insert new material (the digressions on the influence of Spanish wine at lines 562 to 588 and on Stilboun at lines 603 to 628), and to set the tale in Flanders.

Such a hypothesis cannot be tested and is therefore of limited use. But it nevertheless expresses a conception about Chaucer's method of composition which is worth considering – namely that, far from writing a work such as the Pardoner's Prologue and Tale all of a piece, he crafted it incrementally, through a process of revision which would have entailed the insertion of substantive new passages capable of altering the entire meaning of the poem. This way of thinking about Chaucer's writing would help to account for the sense created by a number of Canterbury tales (the Wife of Bath's Prologue and Tale form another instance) that they are compilations, some of them with their rubrics still intact – rubrics which may reveal a particular mode of address, such as that pertaining to a preacher or clerk, but which may also indicate the transition between one block of material and another ('Now wol I speke of othes false and grete', line 629).

To move within a single work from one unit of meaning to another is often to move from one kind of source material to another. What then becomes of interest, beyond identifying particular sources and analogues and rhetorical tropes, is the principle of selection which Chaucer has employed. Why that narrative and not another? Why that convention and not another? Why that transition and not another? To answer such questions it is necessary to form some estimate of the 'pressures' which are forming the particular work. These, we would argue, are not to be found exclusively in 'the genius of Chaucer' but in his considered and creative response to certain specific circumstances. The clues to those circumstances, which are of a political and social nature, are to be found within the poetry and the issues it raises.

To place Chaucer's writing securely in relation to specific events and topical subjects, and to argue that one of his attitudes towards composition was that of a compiler, is to raise the question of dating. The Pardoner's Prologue and Tale are customarily dated on internal evidence to the mid-1390s (Pearsall 1985: 7) and yet it alludes to events in 1376 and would seem to be addressed to problems current then. If the later date is to stand, is it likely that Chaucer would have included material about a twenty-year-old controversy? Two other dates need to be taken into account. Wyclif's *De Eucharista* appeared in 1379 and from then may be dated the dissemination of his views on substance and accident. Second, in his revision to the *Legend of Good Women*, dated on fairly firm evidence to 1386–7, Chaucer refers to his (now lost) prose translation of Innocent III, the *Wreched Engendrynge of Mankynde*, used on several occasions in the course of writing the Pardoner's Prologue and Tale.

Clearly certain parts of the poem do belong to a period centring on the last years of Edward III. Yet the implications of the other datable evidence destroy the supposition, earlier rehearsed, concerning Chaucer's method of composition, which saw the political matter as a final addition, a 'depth charge' dropped into the poem when the surrounding material was already intact. That material could not have been in existence if it depended in part on a treatise by Wyclif that had not been published and a work by Innocent III with which Chaucer had not had any dealings.

A more plausible hypothesis concerning the composition of the Pardoner's Prologue and Tale would see the political centre as indeed the nucleus of the poem, its germ from which developed later accretions. Thus the passages on Gaunt and Wyclif could well have been composed when they would have been most topical. Around them at later dates, as Chaucer built up prologue and tale syncretically, were set 'units of meaning' deriving from Wyclif's views on the eucharist and the *De Miseria*, as these became available. Eventually, the poem was incorporated into the Canterbury sequence. According to this theory, 1376 and the mid-1390s would both be dates of composition, because the poem was in a process of revision and development during that period (although the argument from the dated components suggests that the Pardoner's Prologue and Tale were substantially complete years before the work was included in the *Canterbury Tales*). The idea that Chaucer's compositions were in a state of perpetual authorial revision is one to which textual scholars are increasingly drawn (Fisher 1988: 784).

In that case, the question still remains as to why Chaucer, so long after the event, should have wanted to incorporate such a work, rooted as it was in a twenty-year-old crisis. There are various explanations. First, although the root and origin of the work does indeed lie in the Bruges conference and its impact, that is not the be-all and end-all of the poem's existence. It is not a political allegory to be seen in those terms alone, but an ever-widening attempt to expose political and ecclesiastical corruption, issues of which the Bruges conference was a culmination and example but not an end. For, second, Chaucer's satire, devastating though it is when applied to figures like Gaunt and Sudbury, does not cease to be highly effective when applied to church–state relations in the final quarter of the fourteenth century. Finally, events at Bruges were so sensational, had such ramifications, that they were not forgotten but were seen as a turning-point in the triangular accord of pope, English church, and state. During the reign of Richard II, when Gaunt's power was extensive, the figures and issues associated with Bruges had not lost their contemporaneity and relevance.

Whether the Gaunt–Wyclif passages are thought of as later insertions, or as providing the original impetus for the Pardoner's Prologue and Tale, their position at the centre of the poem is crucial. They have a retroactive effect on prologue and tale to that point, and create certain expectations concerning what is to follow. It will be reasonably clear from the preceding discussion how allusions to Wyclif and Gaunt serve as a focus for the preceding matter. For example, drunkenness becomes a metaphor for the intoxications of power, 'hasardrye' for the gamblings of policy-making, avarice a by-word for the demands of papal taxations. With something of a shock, we recognize that the Pardoner, 'lyk a prelat', may figure Sudbury himself. And so on. At the same time (and this is part of the interactive capacity of the poem) the central political sections are placed within a context that exposes the likes of Sudbury, Gaunt and Wyclif to a devastating moral attack.

The satirical mechanisms at work here are evident enough. What is less clear is the way in which the 'Bruges sections' function in an anticipatory way and colour the meaning of the tale of the three

·SATVRNVS·

S aturno huomini tardi er rei produce
R ubadori er buxardi er affasini
V illani er usai er fensa alchuna luce
P aston er zoppi er fiindi meschini :·

Plate 1 Dicing, gaming and sudden death: the children of Saturn, *De sphaera* by
Johannes de Sacrobosco, Modena, Biblioteca Estense, MS. α. x. 2. 14 (Lat. 209),
f. 4v.

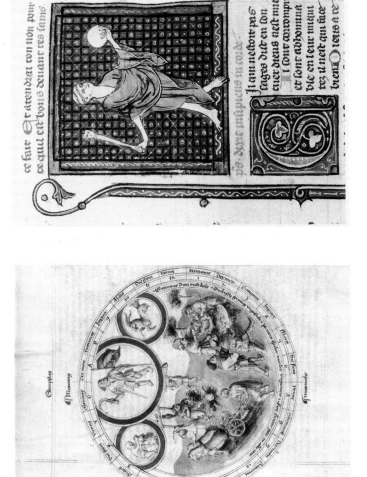

Plate 2 Dicing and its dangers, hanging, arduous work: the children of Saturn. Kassel, Gesamthochschul-Bibliothek, 2° MS. astron. 1, f. 62v.

Plate 3 The monk as fool. Psalm 52: *Dixit insipiens*. Oxford, Bodleian Library, MS. Douce 211, f. 258v. Paris, early 14th century.

Plate 4 Ploughing and digging, mutilation and butchery, stocks and shackles: the children of Saturn. Master of the *Hausbuch*. Schloss Wolfegg, collection of Graf Waldburg-Wolfegg, f. 11. Mainz region, *c.*1480.

Plate 5 Imprisonment, stocks, mutilation and carrying water: the children of Saturn. Attributed to Maso Finiguarra. Italy, after 1450.

Plate 6   Counting money: the children of Saturn. Tübingen, Universitatsbibliotek, MS. Md. 2, f. 267. German, early 15th century.

Plate 7   Hanging, woodcutting, threshing, ploughing, stocks, mutilation: the children of Saturn. German, *c.*1470.

Plate 8   The architect as a follower of Saturn. Wolfenbüttel, Herzog August Bibliotek, MS. 29. 14 Aug. 4°, f. 90v.

Plate 9   The castration of Saturn by Jupiter. Dresden, Kupferstich Kabinett.
Before 1435.

rioters. The Flanders setting (also found in one analogue) is an obvious enough signal. But beyond that a detailed examination of Chaucer's manipulations of the story, manipulations which would reveal how it is keyed in to the Gaunt–Wyclif sections, is impossible because a written version of the folk-tale Chaucer used is not extant. The published analogues are from printed collections made in the sixteenth century, or from manuscripts dating from 1400 or after. Cumulatively the analogues provide a reasonably accurate impression of what Chaucer knew, but close comparison between source, or even analogue, and adaptation is out of the question. There is a further difficulty of procedure. Contemporary responses to the Bruges conference, though they are likely to have been extreme, are not known. So a historical context is lacking as well as a literary one. The tale is therefore a tantalizing one to read because it seems so often to suggest a precise contemporary allusion, and to imply multiple variations on the received narrative.

In the circumstances, one viable approach is a reading of the tale on the reasonable assumption that the references to the Bruges conference are intended to be kept in mind and applied to what follows. The three rioters meeting in a Flanders tavern, devotees of 'hasardrye', drunkenness and false swearing, therefore become representative of the Bruges triumvirate of Gaunt, Sudbury and Garnier. It should be stressed that (no more than in the case of the Pardoner–Sudbury connection) this is not intended to be a reductive account of Chaucer's poetry, forging one-to-one connections between politics and literature in the manner of an allegorical tract. Chaucer is more subtle and more devious. He works by suggesting strong possibilities of connection, leaving it to his audience to think through the consequences. In the present case he is not fictionalizing the political careers of the Bruges politicians and their demise so much as representing their spiritual death as a consequence of the vices practised and exemplified at their conference. It is therefore, within the Pardoner's Prologue and Tale, a section with its own distinct register and volition, factors which increase the difficulty of interpretation.

The tale, then, depicts the 'rioters' as the embodiment of those vices so effectively described by the Pardoner. They are, above all, ignorant blasphemers, because they believe that death can be overcome through human agency (lines 699 and 710). Although the tale may be seen as an exemplum illustrative of the Pardoner's themes, its ability to escape the morally qualifying voice of the narrator, and to make its points unaffected by the speaker's own corruptions, are remarkable. An increased narrative economy, achieved by an absence of self-consciousness in the use of language, and of digression after line 661, contributes to this effect, to the sense that Chaucer is speaking more in his own voice. By the time the end is reached, the tale has become less a pyrotechnic display of the Pardoner's oratorical powers, more a thought-provoking and morally realistic analysis of the inexorable logic of inveterate vice. The collocation of gluttony, luxury, 'hasardrye', blasphemy and pride, causing the rioters' downfall, is the very antithesis of the salvation made possible by another, virtuous death – that of Christ:

> O cursed synne of alle cursednesse!
> O traytours homycide, O wikkednesse!
> O glotonye, luxurie, and hasardrye!
> Though blasphemour of Crist with vileynye
> And othes grete, of usage and of pride!
> Allas, mankynde, how may it bitide
> That to thy creatour, which that the wroghte,
> And with his precious herte-blood thee boghte,
> Thou art so fals and so unkynde, allas?
>   (895–903)

Such lines are written in deadly earnest, one critic seeing in them 'spiritual magnificence and passionate intensity' (Lawton 1985: 27), even though the rhetoric continues to recall the flamboyance of Lollard utterance. Regarded as part of a 'counsel to princes' they are the climax of a sustained warning of a particularly arresting and devastating kind to all those betraying church and state.

The tale distinguishes among the roles and characteristics of the protagonists, but not to the point where each becomes identifiable with an actual counterpart. Thus one is the youngest (804), one a dullard (816), one the proudest (716). Although lacking specificity in this respect, Chaucer's narrative does mirror a world which those familiar with the activities of Gaunt and Sudbury would have had no difficulty in recognizing. It is a world where promises and treaties of mutual help are easily made, bound by solemn oaths (702–4), only to be broken when a new set of less convenient circumstances arises. The value of sworn bonds and friendship is nugatory (808). Self-interest rules the day, self-interest that concerns the acquisition of money for personal motives and the enjoyment of power which riches bring (779–81). In the achievement of their ends the rioters practise stealth and subterfuge (791–2), both symptoms of their habitual malevolence and scheming greed (813–15). In short, the Pardoner's Prologue and Tale present a world in which moral and spiritual values are inverted, even to the point where the Crucifixion and its significance are ignored and travestied. The rioters are irredeemably devoted to vice (831–4) and incapable of repentance (850).

What is of extreme importance in anchoring the tale, ethically speaking, of providing a contrast with the rioters' topsy-turvy world, and of removing the tale out of range of the ambivalent and corrosive effects of the Pardoner's narration, is the presence of the 'oold man' (713). He is standing at a stile which the rioters are about to cross, a stile which, as it emerges, is a threshold between moral torpor and wilful perdition. The rioters resolutely ignore the significance of him and what he says, and blunder on to their own death.

What exactly the old man does signify is one of the great debating points of Chaucer scholarship and criticism. Indeed, the entire episode of the old man at the stile (711–67) is an epitome of the teasing, allusive nature of the work and of the problems posed by the lack of reliable sources and contexts. For Kittredge he was Death (1915: 215). According to another early study he is to be placed in the tradition of the wandering Jew (Bushnell 1931). Hamilton (1939) saw him as Old Age, heralding Death. The details of old age, longing for death, knocking on the ground with a staff and asking the earth to receive him with pity, appear to derive from the first elegy of Maximian (Tupper 1941: 437). For Robertson (1962: 173) he stands for the unredeemed man of the Old Testament. Beidler (1981) praises him as a Noah figure. There is also, perhaps, a reminiscence of apocalyptic material of which Chaucer may have been reminded by the *De Miseria*, III. 8 (ed. and trans. Lewis 1978: 214–15):

> *And in those days men shall seek*
> *death and shall not find it. And*
> *they shall desire to die; and death*
> *shall fly from them.*
> *(Apoc. 9: 6)*

David (1965) was wise to avoid too exact a symbolic interpretation. Whatever the precise stratification and interconnections of Chaucer's sources it is at least possible to make certain observations on the function of the old man and of his dialogue with the rioters. Quite clearly he is intended as a foil, as everything they are not (Dean 1968: 47), being not only old and seemingly immortal (Hatcher 1975), but also having the best moral and spiritual credentials. His appearance, his words, his advice, condemn the rioters. He is, first, a meek man where they are proud, greeting them with a humility most unlike their own impudence and presumption. He is poor where they desire wealth; he is old, 'pale and welked' (738), where they are young. Their respective attitudes towards death are also at opposite poles. Death does not threaten the old man – it eludes him. He desires to be overcome by death, whereas the rioters seek to vanquish it. Ironically, it is they who are vanquished. They wilfully seek death whereas the old man searches patiently – 'I moot go thider as I have to go' (749). Death shuns the old man but welcomes the rioters. The old man desires rest as against the restlessness of his present life; the rioters know nothing but restlessness (720–38).

Their attitudes to language are also contrasted. Not only are the rioters disrespectful, speaking 'vileynye' where they should speak 'curteisye' (739–40), but the old man, who is himself partially constructed from an Old Testament passage (Ecclus. 7: 1–9), introduces biblical material into his discourse to give it extra weight, effectively diminishing further the moral status of the rioters. He quotes from Leviticus 19: 32 – '"Agayns an oold man, hoor upon his heed, / Ye sholde arise"' (743–4) – a verse from a chapter which includes advice on doing the very opposite of what the rioters practise: honouring the ordinances of God; not stealing, lying or deceiving; not swearing falsely by God's name or profaning it; not standing 'against the blood of thy neighbour'; not hating 'thy brother in thy heart'; loving friends. The note of authority which the old man strikes is further augmented by two exempla, cited as analogues, in which the part of the old man is taken by Christ himself (Tupper 1941: 422).

As the dialogue continues, the authority of the old man continues to increase. He has about him elements of the seer or prophet, with a knowledge beyond himself of what lies at the end of '"this croked wey"' (761). Finally his blessings – '"God be with yow, where ye go or ryde!"' (748), '"God save yow, that boghte agayn mankynde"' (766) – are intended as exactly that, with none of the blasphemous distortions or intentions to curse which such words would have in the mouths of the rioters. That is not to say that the second blessing does not incorporate a deeper suggestiveness and irony. Its reference to the Crucifixion follows hard on the old man's directions to the tree under which death lies; and the use of the word 'boghte' to describe the redemption alludes to a realm of spiritual values which the money-obsessed rioters know only through travesty.

The manner and language of the old man are ennobling. They are directed towards accepting the rioters for better than they are and facilitating the achievement of what they really need. At the same time the presence and attitude of the old man open up for them the possibility of abandoning their pursuit of death, of changing their behaviour. As they cross the stile and run down the crooked way to the tree it is not without first being confronted by an individual whose moral and spiritual propriety is unimpeachable and who, if listened to, might redirect them. But they are oblivious to the deeper reaches and implications of the old man's words. Far from responding to his acceptance of them they become more virulent, hostile and defensive, as if threatened at one level of their precarious existence but determined to assert brute force at another. The nature of their language reveals this. It is increasingly vehement: the old man (in a word indicating presumed social differences between them and him) has become a ' "cherl" ' (749). The blasphemy returns, ironically: ' "by the hooly sacrement" ' (757). The old man is accused of being an ' "espye" ' (755), in cahoots with ' "thilke traytour Deeth" ' (753), out to kill ' "us yonge folk" ' (759), a ' "false theef" ' (759) who must reveal what he knows or bear the consequences (755–6). Thus for all the old man's authoritative and allusive utterances, marking as they do the introduction of a deeper spiritual dimension, the rioters persist in perceiving only their literal significance. As they leave to discover the gold florins, it is clear that they do so in wilful ignorance of a world now beyond their ken, a world whose informing principles are more powerful and more pervasive than those of greed and self-interest.

THE EFFECTS OF RHETORIC

Other sections of this chapter have argued that the Pardoner's Pro-logue and Tale are to be taken seriously as a satirical commentary on events centring on Sudbury and Gaunt, events which highlighted the interdependent corruption of lay and ecclesiastical power. A major objection to such a reading is that it ignores the tone of the writing, its tendency to strive for lurid rhetorical effects (especially in the pro-logue and earlier part of the tale). Such features of the poetry might seem to dissipate the moral force the content might otherwise have.

Of course it is the Pardoner's intention to reveal rhetorical sensa-tionalism as precisely that. His exposé of working methods, like the carefully calculated gestures – ' "Thanne peyne I me to strecche forth the nekke .../ Myne handes and my tonge goon so yerne" ' (395 and 398) – or his signalling of one bravura piece in the wake of another –

> And now that I have spoken of glotonye,
> Now wol I yow deffenden hasardrye.
> (589–90)

– allows the audience to step back and appreciate the performance for its stylistic flair and for its success in achieving the desired ends. A sense of distance is also maintained by the Pardoner's making it clear that the type of audience on which his oratory has most impact is one of ignorant, illiterate people: '"For lewed peple loven tales olde"' (437); '"... when the lewed peple is doun yset"' (392). No self-respecting pilgrim would be likely to include himself or herself among the uneducated. When, at the end of the tale, the Pardoner *does* confuse his audience, the result is personally humiliating.

In the process of anatomizing his practices the Pardoner allows the distanced audience to anatomize him. The illusion of moral authority which his words can provoke casts no spell once the mechanisms of deceit are revealed. But the stripping away of the forms and disguises which words weave does not mean that the content of the Pardoner's utterances is annulled. Christian morality and Christian theology remain unassailed in spite of all that the Pardoner, the false curer of souls, can do:

> ... *Jhesu Crist, that is our soules leche*
> *So graunte yow his pardoun to receyve,*
> *For that is best; I wol yow nat decyve.*
> *(916–18)*

In effect, the Pardoner's corruptions, laughable though they may be, recoil not on the ideas of sin and pardon but on himself. His account of avarice is self-reductive and self-destructive because his own practices, from which he is unable to escape, are his best illustration of the nature of greed. He has become the most vivid and telling exemplum of sin and its consequences (Burrow 1982: 111).

For this reason, if for no other, the Pardoner's Prologue and Tale have a considerable moral impact. Beneath the amusement which his antics provoke is a horror that such a monster might exist. At the same time there is relief that the morality which he appears to discount has justly claimed the Pardoner as its victim. Given this underlying seriousness, it is necessary to reappraise the tone and rhetorical colour of the Pardoner's utterances, for at the core of them lie ideas central to Christian thinking. Thus the content of his statements on gluttony, 'hasardrye' and false swearing, as well as on avarice, ought not to be confused with their form. Their basis is in received Christian dogma, just as the glosses given to biblical authority are orthodox, if partial, accounts of received interpretations. Indeed, the rhetorical virtuosity with which sin is described, and the care taken to frame the set pieces with spoken rubrics – 'Now wol I speke of othes false and grete' (629) – function as mnemonics: prologue and tale leave a vivid memory of certain sins, graphic details associated with them, and their outcome, as demonstrated in the story of the rioters and in the life of the Pardoner himself. In fact the rhetoric used is as much that of a commentary, with its divisions and headings for ease of reference and recall, as that of the sermon.

Thus the Pardoner's rhetoric, no more than his dubious moral status, does not finally erode the power of his accusations. The language which Chaucer uses, and the narrator which he employs, are to be seen as reflexive masks (Howard 1976: 376; Aers 1980: 89–106) which allow him to make certain criticisms. The role of truth-telling jester was no doubt conducive to a court poet who, while he may have depended on aristocratic patronage for his professional occupation (Hulbert 1912: 79–84; Williams 1965: 20–55), could not close his eyes to the iniquities of powerful men. That the Pardoner's utterances are capable of, and are intended to have, a serious impact, irrespective of the nature of the speaker, is clear from the pilgrims' response to the conclusion of his tale: stunned silence. And in the prologue, Chaucer is careful to raise the issue of intention and effect. The Pardoner is able to wean others from avarice although he himself is guilty of the sin (429–31), and ' "though myself be a ful vicious man, / A moral tale yet I yow telle kan" ' (459–60). Gluttony, false swearing, avarice, hypocrisy and 'hasardrye' are likely to have been just those faults which certain contemporaries saw embodied in Archbishop Sudbury and his associates.

4

The Merchant

The bitter, black comedy of the Merchant's Tale is extraordinarily but deliberately rich in ambiguity and in its invitation to varieties of interpretation. At once romance and fabliau, it undermines the conventional use of genres. Inviting debate and permitting the simultaneous existence of many levels of related meaning in its original use of iconography and allegory, it none the less directs its audience to notions of delusion, degradation, deceit, travesty and shame. The treatment of marriage and sexual relations, the development of the metaphors of the court, the seasons, and the garden, emphasize the absence of love and the dominance of sexual appetite, the cultivation of sycophancy, the unnatural relations of January and May, and the corruption of paradise. These topics are pointed by meaningful rhetorical insinuations which suggest a consciously elaborate coding of information about contemporary affairs.

In this chapter we suggest that Chaucer, as with many of his contemporaries, was concerned in the Merchant's Tale to explore directly the political crisis of 1376/7 and the contribution made to it by developments in the preceding seven years. Taking as its centre the political and constitutional crisis which came to a climax in the Good Parliament of 1376, the tale sees the relationship between Edward III and his mistress, Alice Perrers, as the source of a profound malaise in the king's declining years. At every level the microcosm of the tale draws upon and illuminates the political crisis, concentrating especially on the role of the church and the court, but also taking the viewpoint of the mercantile community who were particularly involved in the developments of those years. If the bleak conclusion of the tale suggests a crisis unresolved, Chaucer none the less argues once again for a radical reform in which kingship can only recover its dignity through the acknowledgement of the will of the subject.

SEXUALITY: BODY AND LANGUAGE

The treatment of sexuality in the Merchant's Tale is affected by its association with religion, the mental world of January, and the disenchanted outlook of the narrator. Within the narrative, sexuality is represented as a powerful force, directing the behaviour of the three main protagonists. This is not an unusual feature of Chaucer's compositions, yet in the Merchant's Tale the greater the power of sex the more degraded it and its victims appear. The sense of degradation and shame is modulated through references to and descriptions of the human body, and through innuendo, puns and genital images (Richardson 1970: 141–6).

The iconography of January as an old man feasting in his hall makes it appropriate that the ruler of Pavia should be represented on several occasions – and notably at the wedding feast, so like a miniature for the month of January – eating and drinking (E. Brown 1979: 254–559; 1983: 84–6). The assuaging of January's appetite is linked with his appetite for sex. This is quite clearly the case when he takes aphrodisiacs to increase his 'corage' on the wedding-night (1807–12). But January also sees his prospective bride in terms of food: a young woman is to be savoured as ' "yong flessh" ' and ' "tendre veel" ', unlike older women who are ' "Oold fissh" ', ' "old boef" ', ' "bene-straw and greet forage" ' (1415–22). The representation of sex as animal appetite is extended to January's squire and wife. Once Damian is assured of May's feelings towards him he becomes excessively courteous and deferential:

> *And eek to Januarie he gooth as lowe*
> *As evere dide a dogge for the bowe.*
> *(2013–14)*

For her part, May is so desirous of the '"smale peres grene"' (2333) which the pear tree, concealing Damian, can supply, that she appears to feign pregnancy in order to satisfy her cravings:

> '...a woman in my plit
> May han to fruyt so greet an appetit
> That she may dyen but she of it have.'
> (2335–7)

Post-digestive functions of the human body are alluded to in the course of May's affair with Damian when she conceals his love-letter, written 'In manere of a compleynt or a lay' (1881), by tearing it to shreds and throwing the pieces 'softely' into the privy (1952–4). This is a fitting start to an affair which must perforce be conducted with 'privee signes' (2105).

The effect of linking sexual feelings with hunger and excretion is to divest them of any romantic trappings. Similarly, the human body itself tends to be represented in an uncompromising and unadorned manner – naked, or in the process of being stripped, with clothes at best a hindrance to urgent sexual activity. The Merchant describes God creating Eve for Adam's company when he saw him in Eden 'al allone, bely-naked' (1326). January asks May to

> ...strepen hire al naked;
> He wolde of hire, he seyde, han som plesaunce;
> And seyde hir clothes dide hym encombraunce ...
> (1958–60)

Damian, for his part, makes short work of May's dress: he 'Gan pullen up the smok, and in he throng' (2353). But the most vivid impression of bodies and their response (or lack of response) to sexual stimuli is created by Chaucer's account of the unlovely coupling of January and May on their wedding-night. Pretentiously, January anticipates his possession of May's body as if it is to be a rape on a heroic scale. He thinks he will 'manace' her and 'streyne' her in his arms harder than Paris did Helen, and expresses his anxiety that May will not be able to endure his sexual fervour (1752–61). She is brought to bed in an appropriately passive state, 'as stille as stoon' (1818). In practice, January treats the sexual act more prosaically, as a job to be done. He promises May that it will be a long time ' "Er tyme come that I wil doun descende" ' (1830) and goes on to draw an analogy with a careful workman setting about his labour – an analogy which, we suspect, is being used to conceal the absence of genuine sexual potency:

> 'Ther nys no werkman, whatsoevere he be,
> That may bothe werke wel and hastily;
> This wol be doon at leyser parfitly.
> It is no fors how longe that we pleye ...'
> *(1832–5)*

So January labours on until daybreak (1842) when, his obligation to spend the night in love-making fulfilled, he lies down exhausted (1855–6).

The grotesque and unnatural elements in the conjunction of January and May are achieved through contrasting the appearance of their bodies. May's is young and beautiful, with its 'myddel smal, hire armes longe and sklendre' (1602), she is 'fresshe May' (1822) with a 'tendre face' (1827). Against it, January rubs the 'thikke brustles of his berd unsofte' (1824) with its rough, scratchy texture 'Lyk to the skyn of houndfyssh, sharp as brere' (1825). The allusion to fish here echoes ironically January's early distaste for older women, 'Oold fissh' (1418), as unpalatable food – *he* is the old fish whose slack skin trembles at his neck as he sings in a cracked voice (1850) and who, on a later occasion, is roused from sleep to 'han som plesaunce' with May not by sexual desire but by a cough (1955–9). The switch to May's point of view at the end of the wedding-night scene, with her perception of January 'up sittynge in his sherte, / In his nyght-cappe, and with his nekke lene' (1852), only makes January seem the more repulsive in his attempt to act the young man.

As some of the preceding remarks will indicate, there is a high occurrence of *double entendre* in the Merchant's Tale and its presence adds further to the sense that there is something covert, furtive and shameful about the sexual activities which the tale describes. There is a fairly systematic attempt to introduce puns and images both verbal and visual referring to male and female genitalia. Appropriately enough for a man who has sex on the brain, January complains to his advisers that ' "o thyng priketh in my conscience" ' (1635), thereby giving lewd meaning to a phrase which was also the title of a devotional manual containing an unflattering portrait of old age (Coffman 1934: 261–4). At the wedding feast, Venus dances before the bride and company with a phallic firebrand (1727), and although January claims that he is enflamed with desire, ' "my corage, it is so sharp and keene!" ' (1759) it is actually Damian who is affected by the goddess, 'So soore hath Venus hurt hym with hire brond' (1777). Priapus, the god discovered with an erect penis and then mocked (E. Brown 1970: 31–8), is associated with January's garden (2034), although it is Damian's sexuality, not her husband's, which is rampant there. The Merchant remarks that love will find a way for a 'sleighte ... thogh it be long and hoot' (2126); this, with Damian's 'smale peres grene', slake May's appetite. The suddenness of their coupling indicates that it has not happened a moment too soon, while the evocative word 'throng' suggests both 'thrust' and a satisfying, crowding fullness. January's 'slakke skin' is no match for such virility, and he is left, pathetically, grasping the tree.

There are two composite images which are used to convey both male and female sexuality. Like so much of the innuendo in the Merchant's Tale, they are off-colour jokes. The first is the image of the key in the lock, so blatantly a sexual symbol, with a pedigree which includes the *Romance of the Rose* and the Song of Songs (Bugge 1973; Wimsatt 1973: 86), and here presented with much nudging and winking:

> *Som wonder by this clyket shal bityde,*
> *Which ye shul heeren, if ye wole abyde.*
> *(2123–4)*

January (so he thinks) possesses the only key to the 'smale wkyet' (2045) which he uses to open it in order to 'paye his wyf hir dette' (2048), that is to enter his garden or 'paradys', a word which is synonymous with May herself (1822). But Damian, through May's agency, makes a counterfeit key with which he also enters a sexual heaven (2120–1). The counterfeiting takes place through the medium of wax: May

> *In warm wax hath emprented the clyket*
> *That Januarie bar of the smale wyket,*
> *By which into his gardyn ofte he wente ...*
> *(2117–19)*

The logic of the sexual imagery is such that the wax reads as a metaphor for female genitalia. As such, January's desire for a younger woman because she may be more malleable becomes all the more distasteful:

> *But certeynly, a yong thyng may men gye,*
> *Right as men may warm wex with handes plye.*
> *(1429–30)*

In practice, the manipulation works in different directions, as Chaucer uses metaphors of impression to signal visual and psychological events (Burnley 1979: 104–15). It is May who takes an 'impression' of Damian, Damian who deceives January be making an impression in real wax, and January who confesses that he is May's to command, for 'Ye been so depe enprented in my thoght' (2178).

The second composite image is that of the scorpion. In context, the apostrophe to this creature equates it with

> *...Fortune unstable!*
> *Lyk to the scorpion so deceyvable,*
> *That flaterest with thyn heed whan thou wolt stynge ...*
> *(2057–9)*

because January, at the height of his happiness and prosperity, has been struck with blindness. But there are further layers of significance. For the deceiving and flattering is not only Fortune's work – as was recognized in one chronicle dealing with Alice Perrers (Amyot 1829: 233) – but that of Damian and May who, under a pretence of friendship, respect and love for January enact their sexual desires. Thinking of the scorpion iconographically, as Chaucer invites us to do here, two further meanings emerge which associate the image even more securely with vicious sexual behaviour (Pace 1965). First, the scorpion is that sign of the zodiac which was held to have a particularly strong influence over the human genitals, as pictures of 'zodiac man' remind us. Thus there is the suggestion that the change in January's fortunes is in part due to stellar influence, a factor which ought not to be left out of account in a tale in which the two main characters are named after months of the year, themselves associated with dominant signs. Second, the scorpion is, as the Parson puts it, following Solomon, an image of woman's deadliness. The devil has five fingers with which to take people into the sin of lechery:

> The seconde fynger is the vileyns touchynge in
> wikkede manere. And therfore seith Salomon that
> 'whoso toucheth and handleth a womman, he
> fareth lyk hym that handleth the scorpioun that
> styngeth and sodeynly sleeth thurgh his
> enveynmynge': as whoso toucheth warm pych,
> it shent his fyngres.
>
> (ParsT 853)

On rereading the Merchant's lines, the application of the scorpion image becomes only too obvious: it fuses the erect phallus and the deadly vagina, with plays on the bawdy words 'heed', 'tayl', and 'queynte':

> ...the scorpion so deceyvable,
> That flaterest with thyn heed whan thou wolt stynge;

Thy tayl is deeth, thurgh thyn envenymynge.
O brotil joye! O sweete venym queynte!

(2058–61)

The scorpion passage is extraordinarily vituperative, its tone suggesting that the lines have an application beyond the confines of the narrative to a world where those in the know will understand what is meant by the 'poisoning' of January's life by sexual obsession. The impression that the narrator is, here and elsewhere, hinting at enormities and scandals almost too horrible to contemplate, is fostered by the pervasive doubleness of the sexual language as discussed in this section, and by his professed coyness which, while pretending in asides to his 'polite' audience to be discreet, then shocks by the baldness of a sudden, blurted statement (E. Brown 1978: 145–6). Receiving Damian's love letter, May

...feyned hire as that she moste gon
Ther as ye woot that every wight moot neede;
And whan she of this bille hath taken heede,
She rente it al to cloutes atte laste,
And in the pryvee softely it caste.

(1950–4)

The love scene in the pear tree is similarly bleak. Damian waits in the branches: January, 'stoupyng age' (1738), bends to receive May, for it is now her turn to be ascendant:

He stoupeth doun, and on his bak she stood,
And caughte hire by a twiste, and up she gooth –
Ladyes, I prey yow that ye be nat wrooth;
I kan nat glose, I am a rude man –
And sodeynly anon this Damyan
Gan pullen up the smok, and in he throng.

(2348–53)

ALLEGORY

Like irony, punning and innuendo, allegory is a way of saying one thing to mean another. It is therefore an attractive mode to a poet who may be contemplating dealing with delicate and controversial contemporary issues. Allegory is present in the Merchant's Tale to a much greater degree than in the other tales under discussion (Burrow 1957: 207–8), and it is possible to discern three distinct allegorical mechanisms which lift the narrative out of a purely naturalistic existence. Each in its way requires the reader to probe surface meaning in order to find, and assess, a deeper significance or 'symbolic spread' (Frye 1976: 59). Chaucer requires of his audience a fairly strenuous analytical temper, a dedication to 'truth' as defined by the text, which is quite unlike the easy, self-serving speculations of January himself. By interpreting the allegory the reader undergoes a mental exercise which makes the thought processes of the old knight seem deficient.

On two occasions, January calls together his 'freendes' (1397 and 1611) to ask their advice. On the first occasion the matter at issue is marriage itself, and particularly the advantages of January's marrying a young woman. It is easy to imagine, at Chaucer's prompting, a medieval court scene. January sends for his friends/advisers on a certain day to tell them of his intentions (1397–8). A debate ensues, with different men offering different opinions of marriage: 'Somme blamed it, somme preysed it, certeyn' (1471). Eventually, two spokesmen, who are 'bretheren' of January, emerge from each side of the debate and they state their opposing cases:

As al day falleth altercacioun
Bitwixen freendes in disputisoun,
Ther fil a stryf bitwixe his bretheren two ...
(1473–5)

The picture of a court council in session, and one strained with controversy and animosity, is made clearer in other incidental details. The second disputant 'ay stille sat and herde' (1519) while the first makes his case. He then offers a criticism of his lord's policy. January is unable to countenance the opinions of a man who disagrees with him:

> *'Wel,' quod this Januarie, 'and hastow ysayd?*
> *....*
> *'...Wyser men than thow,*
> *As thou hast herd, assenteden right now*
> *To my purpos.*
>
> *(1566 and 1569–71)*

And so, after a brief rejoinder from the first adviser, the session comes to an abrupt end and without any judicious weighing of opinion on January's part. Instead, he simply gets his way and the counselling emerges as nothing but a formality:

> *And with that word they rysen sodeynly,*
> *And been assented fully that he sholde*
> *Be wedded whanne hym liste, and where he wolde.*
>
> *(1574–6)*

On the second occasion, after choosing May, January is even less inclined to listen to advice:

> *Hym thoughte his choys myghte nat ben amended.*
> *For whan that he hymself concluded hadde,*
> *Hym thoughte ech oother mannes wit so badde*
> *That inpossible it were to repplye*
> *Agayn his choys; this was his fantasye.*
>
> *(1606–10)*

This is a court at which the arbitrary decisions of an old but still powerful ruler hold sway, impervious to constructive criticism and leading to personal discredit and disaster (Bloomfield 1978). January tries to pre-empt further hostility to his plan by insisting that his 'freendes', now reconvened, grant him a 'boon' to

> ...*none argumentes make*
> *Agayn the purpos which that he hath take,*
> *Which purpos was plesant to God, seyde he,*
> *And verray ground of his prosperitee.*
> *(1619–22)*

The tactic is not entirely successful, for the ensuing debate on earthly and heavenly bliss, instigated by January himself as an abstract question somewhat removed from the actualities of his marriage to May, allows the second adviser to bring matters down to earth by reminding his lord that a wife may be purgatory, not heaven. After this, recognizing that there is no alternative, the brother advisers join forces in putting January's desires into effect 'by sly and wys tretee' (1689–95).

To describe the two council scenes in these terms, as reflections of fourteenth-century court life (Green 1980: 162), is to ignore the names of the two opposed advisers, Justinus and Placebo. They appear first as spokesmen for the two sides of the debate on marriage. But they are more than delegates or representatives of two factions. They represent the *arguments* which they voice: the debate is articulated, polarized and dramatized through them. The debate itself is more complex than at first appears for, as we have suggested, the immediate subject of marriage is set within a larger but no less urgent discussion of the nature of the ruler's counsel. Placebo urges flattery and sycopancy in response to January's dilemma, and full agreement with his lord's wishes. January, he says, is right to ask for '"Conseil"' (a word that is often on Placebo's lips), yet his own wisdom is the best guide (1478–90). Placebo goes on to reveal that his long survival as a '"court-man"' (1492) to high ranking lords is due to his careful avoidance of '"debaat"' (1496) and contradiction of their wishes. He has simply mouthed his lord's opinion: '"I seye the same, or elles thyng semblable"' (1500). Any counsellor who presumes, by offering advice, to "'passe his lordes wit'" (1504) is a fool. Placebo then returns to the point and praises in fulsome terms January's decision to marry a young wife. His counsel amounts to

> 'Dooth now in this matiere right as yow leste,
> For finally I holde it for the beste.'
> (1517–18)

Placebo emerges, therefore, as a counsellor who has abrogated his responsibilities in order to preserve his own skin. His 'confession' is a further indication that his contribution is meant to be construed not as that of an individual or character but as a type of false adviser.

At the other extreme, Justinus' view of women appears justified by the outcome of January's marriage. His comments on marriage hit the world-weary tone of the Merchant in his prologue: 'God it woot, I have wept many a teere / Ful pryvely, syn I have had a wyf' (1544–5). He advocates a careful appraisal of the pros and cons of marriage, dealing not in platitudes but in a hard-headed assessment of what might go wrong. He is the type of realist who anticipates the worst: young men have a difficult enough time in controlling their wives, so how will January fare? "'Trusteth me, / Ye shul not plesen hire fully yeres thre'" (1561–2). Justinus perceives his lord's folly, hates it (1655), and does his best to offer a critique and a remedy. In Placebo's terms, he is a fool to do so, but in the context of the tale his is the voice of wisdom. As with Placebo, the status of Justinus as an individual or character is broken with a device indicating that what matters here is not character but the debate on marriage and counsel: he refers beyond the bounds of the primary fiction to the Wife of Bath as an authority on marriage, as if January and he were part of the pilgrim audience (1685–7).

Placebo and Justinus embody the two sides of the debate and articulate the drama of ideas. But there is another, complementary way of reading the allegory, and one which is fostered by the notion that January and his two advisers are close kin. Placebo and Justinus could be seen as externalized representatives of two conflicting mental processes taking place in the ruler's mind: the desire to get his own way regardless of the consequences of doing so; and the need, as ruler, to take advice and weigh it carefully in order to formulate a wise policy. By viewing Placebo and Justinus as elements in a psychomachia, an anatomy of a ruler's mind, then the diagnosis must be that it is a mind dangerously deficient in the judiciousness normally associated with a wise ruler: the promptings to be 'realistic' have become entirely subject to the desire for self-gratification.

The Merchant's Tale contains an allegory of time as well as one of mind. The temptation and possibility of discussing the characters and human relationship of January and May is much stronger than in the case of Placebo and Justinus, whose function within the narrative is more obvious and limited. Nor is it a temptation which need be resisted as long as it is tempered with the recognition that, whatever else they may be, January and May are personifications of months of the year. This is to say a great deal more than that they are each appropriately named because the old ruler is associated with the waning year and his young wife with its renewal, an idea which Chaucer may have taken from a ballade by Deschamps (Matthews 1956). The medieval iconography of January and May reveals that Chaucer has carefully selected many of the details concerning the appearance and behaviour of January and May from traditional representations of these months (Adams 1974; E. Brown 1983). It is on these foundations that Chaucer has built the illusion of character.

Chaucer has also been careful, within the tale, to assign to January and May appropriate times of the day, week and year when their influence predominates. In the earlier part of the story, until the time of January's blindness, he is the active partner, May the passive. The wedding-night is preceded by a description of gathering darkness, which might be seen as a more 'natural element' for the wintry January:

Parfourned hath the sonne his ark diurne;
No lenger may the body of hym sojurne

On th'orisonte, as in that latitude.
Night with his mantel, that is derk and rude,
Gan oversprede the hemysperie aboute . . .
                              (1795–9)

He is now in the ascendant, and promises May that it will be a lengthy interval '"Er tyme come that I wil doun descende"' (1830). With the arrival of dawn, he sleeps (1856–7). In spite of the conjunction of January and May, they maintain a certain distance, a different pace, appropriate to two months which are four months apart in the calendar. So, after the wedding-night, May 'Heeld hire chambre [an astrological term] unto the fourthe day' (1860). May's tarrying is represented as customary for a noble bride, but it does carry an astrological significance, for by the time May leaves her chamber the moon has changed its position in the zodiac:

> *The moone, that at noon was thilke day*
> *That Januarie hath wedded fresshe May*
> *In two of Tawr, was into Cancre glyden;*
> *So longe hath Mayus in hir chambre abyden,*
> *As custume is unto thise nobles alle.*
>   *(1885–9)*

Coinciding with Damian's infatuation with May is the narrator's intimation that celestial influence has shifted in favour of the lovers: the stellar clock has moved on:

> *Were it by destynee or aventure,*
> *Were it by influence or by nature,*
> *Or constellacion, that in swich estaat*
> *The hevene stood that tyme fortunaat*
> *Was for to putte a bille of Venus werkes –*
> *For alle thyng hath tyme, as seyn thise clerkes –*
> *To any womman for to gete hire love,*
> *I kan nat seye . . .*
>   *(1967–74)*

May, 'fresshe May, that is so bright and sheene' (2328) now becomes progressively active and dominating as the time of year favourable to her approaches. As already suggested, matters may be aided by the influence of Scorpio, who rules the genitals. On the fateful day when May and January enter the garden it actually is, or is close to, the month whose name May bears: 'er that dayes eighte / Were passed [of] the month of [Juyn]' (2132–3) emends 'er the month' (before the month of June), as found in the two earliest manuscripts. As January remarks, the time of year in which his own influence is likely to predominate has waned: '"The wynter is goon with alle his reynes weete"' (2140). He now takes on a more submissive role, expressing his fear of offending May (2163–4), whereas earlier January boasted of his intention to commit a sexual offence against her (1828–30). The knight of Pavye proceeds to give away '"heritage, toun and tour"' (2172). With Damian poised in the garden, and swearing fidelity to the blind old man, May has January utterly in her power. Broad daylight is her favoured time; the sun, not the moon, is the luminary of her season – and it is now in Gemini, one of the dominant signs of springtime:

> Bright was the day, and blew the firmament;
> Phebus hath of gold his stremes doun ysent
> To gladen every flour with his warmnesse.
> He was that tyme in Geminis, as I gesse,
> But litel fro his declynacion
> Of Cancer, Jovis exaltacion.
>
> (2219–24)

The time is propitious for May, who now gains the ascendancy over January in more senses than one (2348–9).

If it is accepted that the Merchant's Tale is in part an allegory about the interaction of the months January and May, the next question to arise concerns Chaucer's choice of months: for surely the marriage of January with May is far-fetched and unnatural. That is an important part of the point which the tale is making: January and May are naturally ill-matched (Halverson 1960: 606–12), their marriage is ill-fated from the start, and their struggle for supremacy over each other is an indication of its unhappiness. January exerts a close, claustrophobic control of May, and especially so when blindness brings jealousy in its train. He bestows melancholic blackness on a month elsewhere associated with light and colour:

> *For neither after his deeth nor in his lyf*
> *Ne wolde he that she were love ne wyf,*
> *But evere lyve as wydwe in clothes blake,*
> *Soul as the turtle that lost hath hire make.*
> *(2077–80)*

The jealousy begins to lessen, but remains 'outrageous' enough (2087) for January to keep his 'hond on hire alway', much to May's distress (2091–2), but January's blindness also enables her to escape his control.

The third allegorical mechanism is devoted to place. January's garden undergoes a repeated transformation of meaning so that it is impossible to arrive at a stable point of interpretation. Chaucer here exploits the capacity of allegory to be polysemous, but without making obvious one dominant meaning to which the others are related. The equation of 'May' and 'paradys' (1822) has already been noted, as has the consequence, reinforced by suggestive remarks, that January's garden serves as a topography of May's body, originally as 'stille as stoon' (1818). Its 'smale wyket', opened by January's silver 'clyket' (2045–6), May's 'herte as hard as any stoon' (1990) like the garden which is 'walled al with stoon' (2029) and which is penetrated by Damian (1990), give it this meaning. In representing May, the garden also represents that spring month, for she is 'lyk the brighte morwe of May, / Fulfild of alle beautee and plesaunce' (1748–9). The garden landscape, with its warm, bright sunshine, blue sky, glad flowers (2219–21), 'turves, fressh and grene' (2235) and 'fresshe leves grene' (2327) is an epitome of spring, a place where 'This fresshe May, that is so bright and sheene' (2328) is completely at home, and where the very deity, Proserpina, to whose struggle, rape, abduction and temporary release by Pluto the creation of spring is credited (Donovan 1957), likes to walk (2038–41 and 2225–326). Again, January creates his garden as a place devoted to his own kind of erotic pleasure, and it is specifically compared to its counterpart in the *Romance of the Rose* (2032), although in that work old age is categorically excluded from the experience of sexual love. There, entry to the garden and winning the rose are the prerogative of the young lover. The role is, in the event, enacted by Damian, while the well, tree, 'melodye' and dancing (2040–1) are also reminiscent of Guillaume de Lorris's 'plesaunce'.

January's address to May before entering the garden indicates that there are further levels of meaning somewhat different from those which associate the place with nature and sexuality. As is well known (Wimsatt 1973; Wurtele 1977), his words form a pastiche of phrases from the Song of Songs, an erotic Hebrew love-song interpreted allegorically by the medieval church as concerning the relationship between Christ (the bridegroom) and his bride (the church, Mary or the human soul). The Song of Songs is full of garden and food imagery and so the language used by January is appropriate, if disconcerting, in his mouth:

> 'Com forth now, with thyne eyen columbyn!
> How fairer been thy brestes than is wyn!
> The gardyn is enclosed al aboute ...'
> *(2141–3)*

When Chaucer concludes this passage with 'Swiche olde lewed wordes used he' (2149) it is clear that January's words are lewd both because they are erotic and because his use of them as only erotic reveals a blind ignorance about their theological meaning.

Finally, Chaucer invites his audience to interpret January's garden as a version of Eden (Bleeth 1974). January's preoccupation with earthly and heavenly bliss is evident from the second council with Justinus and Placebo when he expresses his concern that he may have to forgo heavenly bliss because "'I shal have myn hevene in erthe heere'" (1647). How can those "'that lyve in swich plesaunce'"

(1650) come to '"the blisse ther Crist eterne on lyve ys?"' (1652). Earlier, January had declared that '"wedlock is so esy and so clene, / That in this world it is a paradys"' (1264–5) and the Merchant had traced the origins of marriage to the Genesis garden, concluding, if ironically, that woman is man's 'paradys terrestre, and his disport' (1332). So, on the wedding-night, May is for January 'his paradys, his make' (1822). The two of them and Damian (demon), who is compared to 'the naddre' (1786), enact a parodic version of the fall of man, complete with tree and forbidden fruit, although the participants have no inkling of their roles.

The garden as May's body, spring, a *Romance* 'plesaunce', as the garden of the Song of Songs, and as Eden – January's garden accommodates all of these meanings and more (White 1965: 398; Rosenburg 1971), and it accommodates none. They are offered as possible alternatives, and ones which critics have been eager to accept singly to the exclusion of the others, but nevertheless they are alternatives with equivalent status. The overall impression is of a garden rich in cumulative significance, although the point of that sense of significance is not immediately clear. The reader is constantly required to read the image of the garden from a different perspective, but the advance beyond this point of view to a final evaluation of the image and stratification of its meanings is thwarted either by the disturbing context in which any one meaning is encountered, or by the speedy replacement of one meaning by another, as they shift constantly from body of May to spring to Eden and back again. The one stable point to be grasped, and one which is a common denominator of the garden allegories, is January's ignorance about the significance of the place he has created. It is, for him, simply a private preserve where he can take sexual pleasure of May:

> In somer seson, thider wolde he go,
> And May his wyf, and no wight but they two;
> And thynges whiche that were nat doon abedde,
> He in the gardyn parfourned hem and spedde.
>
> (2049–52)

January's inability to look beyond the immediate, the superficial, is evident in other spheres of his life. For instance, he is aware of the orthodox view that heaven can be bought only with tribulation and penance, yet he cannot see its application to his own case (1648–52). The large disparity between his one-dimensional view of the garden, and the wide variety of interpretations which the poem makes available, points to the seriousness of January's limitations. Chaucer reproduces in the experience of reading his allegories, and particularly that of the garden, the kind of dilemma with which January refuses to take issue: the need to discriminate between the greater and lesser good, to look beyond the literal to the deeper significance and consequence of what he sees, what he thinks, and what he does. As Burnley has argued, the moral significance of January's attitudes would have been all too clear to a medieval audience familiar with the marriage liturgy (Burnley 1976).

ICONOGRAPHY

The multiple meanings activated through allegory are often, but not always, anchored in a visual image. That is true of January's garden and of January and May themselves, but not of Justinus and Placebo, who remain shadowy and formless, abstract voices. Modern readers of Chaucer need to take account of the vocabulary of visual symbols used by Chaucer and shared by him and his audience as a commonly understood language of signs. An awareness of the appropriate medieval iconographies is particularly useful in the case of the Merchant's Tale because the poem is in many ways a study in envisaging. As the allegorical content, and the problems of interpretation which it sets, mirror January's mental processes, so the stimulation of the reader's visual imagination creates in the audience's reception of the tale an experience and problem analogous to those which have such a profound effect on January's mental life. His fixed image of an ideal sexual partner, which in his eyes corresponds with May herself, blinds him to his own folly. The lesson provided by January exhorts the

reader to pay careful attention to visual imaging, its relative importance, and its meaning.

The earlier discussion of the scorpion may have indicated the
importance of referring to traditions of image representation because
of the way in which Chaucer's poetry here takes traditions for granted
and, by alluding to them, builds up strata of significance. The acerbic
tone of the Merchant's rhetorical address to the scorpion leaves no
room for doubt that, from all aspects, it is to be regarded as a malevolent creature with designs on January. The same note of certainty is
absent from other iconographic images, which are presented in a
much more open-ended and suggestive manner, allowing for
possibilities of interpretation rather than directing the reader towards
a particular judgement.

By way of contrast and comparison with the scorpion, the trees of
the Merchant's Tale deserve attention. There is, for example, the ever-
green laurel, a tree which has its place in January's garden, signifying,
when it is first mentioned, enduring life and associated as such with
January (1465–6 and 2037). January also associates himself with a
blossom- and fruit-bearing tree, suggesting regeneration (1461–2), a
tree such as the pear tree at the centre of the final action. As we have
seen, this tree, which 'charged was with fruyt' (2211), is a parodic
version of the tree of knowledge. There is a third tree, mentioned by
January in passing, and by which he sets little store because he is so
assured of reaching a state of bliss through his marriage to May:

> 'I have,' quod he, 'herd seyd, ful yoore ago,
> Ther may no man han parfite blisses two –
> This is to seye, in erthe and eek in hevene.
> For though he kepe hym fro the synnes sevene,
> And eek from every branche of thilke tree,
> Yet is ther so parfit felicitee
> And so greet ese and lust in mariage...'
> (1637–43)

A critic might be tempted to take the image of the tree of vice, so
common as a verbal and visual metaphor of the ramifications of sin, as

offering a moral standard from which to make a final judgement of January. Indeed it would not be difficult to argue how, from the standpoint of Christian orthodoxy, January commits the sins of lechery and pride if not of gluttony as well. In a sense, January brings down this judgement on himself by flaunting and disregarding accepted Christian standards of behaviour. But it would beg too many questions to argue that the moralist's standpoint, all-encompassing though its tree-like system might seem, is final, or indeed all that secure. For it leaves out of account that other January, the month of the year, which, because it is part of a natural cycle, is not subject to the systematizations of theology. Thus the shifting nature of the meaning of 'the tree' in the Merchant's Tale is similar to that of the garden: the reader is left with the problem of evaluation and interpretation, with possible meanings, and not a final resolution.

The case of May is similar. Her behaviour could be considered reprehensibly adulterous, or entirely understandable in the circumstances, but such opinions depend finally on the cast of the reader's mind. Chaucer encourages prolixity of interpretation and stimulates debate about meaning. Viewed from an iconographic standpoint, what May does is entirely natural. Calendar representations of the month, as they were known in the fourteenth century, show a burgeoning spring landscape, sometimes in the form of a garden, in which a squire rides, perhaps accompanied by his lady love. Alternatively the twins of the dominant zodiac sign, Gemini, are incorporated within the composition as lovers. What happens at the end of the Merchant's Tale is entirely in keeping with what might be expected of May in May.

The iconography of January contains details which Chaucer exploited to create what a modern reader is inclined to call the character of the duke of Pavye. Feasting is a necessary part of the traditional image, as Chaucer notes in the Franklin's Tale (FrankT 1252–4). So is the idea that Janus looks to both past and future, being simultaneously young and old. He is the god of entrances, thresholds and doorways, of comings and goings, and his natural habitat, unlike May's, is an interior, where he sits like a lord in a hall. Outside, the trees are barren and bare. Chaucer invites his audience to project complementary images and meanings on to his figure of January. He is old age, 'stoupyng age' whose stoop enables May to clamber into the pear tree. Old age should be excluded from the experience of love, and when January persists in his amorousness he becomes a figure of fun:

> *Whan tendre youthe hath wedded stoupyng age,*
> *Ther is swich myrthe that it may nat be writen.*
> *(1738–9)*

Finally, January must have looked like Saturn himself, who rules January's signs of Capricorn and Aquarius (Frontispiece), as an old but powerful king blighting with blackness the lives of those under his sway (2077–80). His mythic counterpart and king of the dark region of faery invokes Saturn's weapons, 'wylde fyr and corrupt pestilence' (2252). For that matter, January must have looked uncomfortably like Edward III, whose portrait in old age includes the 'double berd' so often included in representations of Janus (FrankT 1252), and whose interest in romance appears to have centred on representations of feasting (Green 1980: 135). To venture into this kind of interpretation is to realize that the allusiveness of both iconography and allegory, their capacity to offer simultaneous coded meanings, provides Chaucer with a means of articulating complex interrelations of ideas, and of indirectly expressing criticism of those whose power extended even to his own circumstances.

THE FAERY AND CLASSICAL WORLDS

An effort of imagination is also needed to respond constructively to the presence in the Merchant's Tale of the gods Venus, Pluto and Proserpina. It is too easy to see them as *dei ex machina* introduced to ginger up a creaking plot. The discussion of the iconography of January will have shown that, at one level of reading, he is himself a pagan deity domiciled in a Christian calendar. January's 'split personality' is important, for it is the meeting-point not just of opposed personal urges but also of wider cultural forces. January, one of the 'fooles that been seculeer' (1251) has lived for sixty years a life in which he has freely indulged his 'bodily delyt / On wommen, ther as was his appetyt' (1249–50). In deciding to marry May, he is aware of entering into a Christian sacrament. Yet his former behaviour, in effect, continues unabated. So January's marriage becomes a ground of conflict between pagan and Christian standards of sexual conduct (Dalbey 1974: 409), a conflict perhaps deriving from the classical attitudes embedded in the tradition of writings on which Chaucer drew for his portrait of a senile lover (Coffman 1934; Hartung 1967: 6–21).

There are indications of the uneasy relationship of the two cultures in the role allotted to Christian ceremony: the church wedding seems like a whitewash as the priest goes through the motions; the ceremony is a matter of form rather than content. He

> ...seyde his orisons, as is usage,
> And croucheth hem, and bad God sholde hem blesse,
> And made al siker ynogh with hoolynesse.
>
> (1706–8)

As church ritual is relegated to a subservient position, so the feast which follows is a predominantly pagan celebration. The music is compared with that of Orpheus and Amphioun and Theodomas of the doomed city of Thebes, all figures associated with marital loss or civic destruction, as is the one biblical musician, Joab (1716–21). The real spirit of the occasion is captured by 'Bacus' who 'the wyn hem shynketh al aboute' (1722); Venus, laughing at the prospect of January who would 'bothe assayen his corage / In libertee, and eek in mariage' (1725–6); and 'Ymeneus, that god of weddyng is', who 'Saugh nevere his lyf so myrie a wedded man' (1730–1). The pagan deities erupt into the tale at this point, animated by the spirit in which January has approached his marriage. Their energy is the energy of a mirth so extreme as to be inexpressible – 'Ther is swich myrthe that it may nat be writen' (1739) – because the incredible has happened: 'tendre youthe hath wedded stoupyng age' (1738). The prevalence of pagan forces, the absurd yoking of youth and age, and the mirth it provokes, are not to be thought of as restricted to Pavye. There may be instances closer to the experience of the Merchant's audience, equally inexpressible, which they can test for themselves:

> *Assayeth it youreself, thanne may ye witen*
> *If that I lye or noon in this matiere.*
> *(1740–1)*

May herself is affected by the pagan forces which January's marriage releases: 'Hire to biholde it semed fayerye' (1743). January is under the spell of a magical force channelled through May; he is 'ravysshed in a traunce / At every tyme he looked on hir face' (1750–1). The pagan deities present at the feast are denizens of the other world, faery. Characteristically, when they intervene in human affairs, their activity is signalled by a dance, such as that performed by Venus who 'Daunceth biforn the bryde and al the route' (1728). The forces of faery are particularly potent within January's garden, for it is a favoured place of the king of faery, Pluto, 'and his queene, / Proserpina, and al hire fayerye' (2039), who dance there. Perhaps their magical influence is the cause of the sexual achievements which the garden promotes, for January finds that 'thynges whiche that were nat doon abedde, / He in the gardyn parfourned hem and spedde' (2051–2).

The parallels between Pluto and January and Proserpina and May are close and they are stressed. Like January the would-be ravisher, Pluto seized his wife, the granddaughter of Saturn (2265) by force: she was 'ravysshed out of [Ethna]' (2230) and, so the story goes, he took her to his dark and baleful underworld kingdom: 'in his grisely carte he hire fette' (2233). Proserpina, for her part, is associated with a spring landscape: she is seized 'Whil that she gadered floures in the mede' (2231). Chaucer refers his readers to the *De Raptu Proserpinae* of Claudianus for further details of the story. At this spring time of the year (2219–24), Proserpina returns to earth and so avoids Pluto's control. He now appears as subservient to her, for he is described as

'Pluto... / And many a lady in his compaignye, / Folwynge his wyf' (2227–9). Evidently she is not the first (or last) woman to be taken by Pluto. The discussion which follows between the 'kyng of Fairye' (2234) and the 'queene of Fayerye' (2316) sounds for all the world like a debate between the Wife of Bath and one of her husbands. Proserpina wins the argument, forcing Pluto to concede defeat: 'I yeve it up!' (2312). Nevertheless, both continue to support their respective parties, January and May. The closing episode and dialogue of the tale are conducted by humans who are under the control of the gods of faery. May's final piece of trickery, to 'visage it hardily' (2273) and persuade January that his eyes have deceived him, seems truly magical, evidence of the astonishing power she now wields over January.

The published analogues of the ending of the Merchant's Tale provide no precedents for the intervention of Pluto and Proserpina. The introduction of a powerful faery kingdom is Chaucer's innovation and is surely a response to the particular meanings which he wished to elicit from the narrative. Quite apart from this modification of his source, the sequence of events at the end of the Merchant's Tale comes as a surprise. As the analogues indicate, the ending derives from a fabliau plot, and the hallmarks of the genre present here – fast pace of events, quarrelling, ludicrous sexual antics – seem in a different spirit from those of the body of the tale, where the prevailing ethos is that of a courtly romance. Thus the transition from one genre to another, from romance to fabliau, is a major source of the surprise effect: a sense of romance decorum is upset in the sudden, graphic revelation of basic facts about human motivation, facts represented so bleakly as to qualify the fabliau effect itself (E. Brown 1978: 149–51).

This is not the only occasion in the *Canterbury Tales* on which Chaucer juxtaposes romance and fabliau in order to offer a more comprehensive view of human experience through 'inorganic unity' (Jordan 1963). The Miller's riposte to the Knight's Tale, or the Wife of Bath's Tale, a romance which follows a prologue ending with a fabliau episode, might be cited as examples. Unlike these, however, there is in the Merchant's Tale no break between the romance and fabliau sections, but instead a startling transition, within a single narrative, from one genre to another. In retrospect, once the business in the pear tree is over, it becomes clear that fabliau elements are latent in the body of the tale, only waiting their opportunity to burst into life. The crude treatment of sexuality as little more than a function of bodily appetite contributes to this impression, as does the pantomine of gesture and posture in which May and Damian engage, which is more characteristic of fabliau than of romance (Benson 1980: 59–60): to acknowledge that she reciprocates the sentiments Damian has expressed in his love-letter, May 'taketh hym by the hand and harde hym twiste' (2005); they continue to communicate 'by writyng to and fro / And privee signes' (2104–5); May signals Damian into the garden before she and January enter (2150–1), and 'in he stirte' in a covert manner to sit motionless under a bush (2153–5); and May coughs 'And with hir fynger signes made she' (2209) to cue Damian's climb into the pear tree. For that matter, the *senex amans* theme itself is one more readily associated with a fabliau (such as the Miller's Tale) than a romance.

Such characteristics of the earlier part of the Merchant's Tale combine to encourage the feeling that it is a romance without romance, or that it is a romance world into which fabliau characters, ones not worthy of elevated roles, have wandered. There is a point to this undermining of one genre by another. Although the audience for both fabliau and romance was aristocratic, there is a clear distinction between the types of protagonist usually to be found in each genre. Those found in romances are almost exclusively members of the nobility, while fabliaux generally concern individuals from the low or middle ranks. January, May and Damian, though of noble birth, behave in a manner normally associated with their social inferiors. The fabliau genre is therefore more appropriate to the motivation and behaviour of those three. The choice of genre – which in a sense they choose for themselves – reinforces the impression that, through his experiences with May, January is undergoing a process of degradation, and of belittling of his nobility. Indeed, Chaucer stresses May's relatively inferior status (1625), one which she shares with Alice Perrers who, her conquest complete, also persuaded her socially elevated lover to part with 'heritage, toun and tower' (Amyot 1829: 233; Holmes 1975: 68–9 and 88–90; Given-Wilson 1986: 147).

The ambiguous status of romance as it occurs in the Merchant's Tale raises questions about the genesis of Chaucer's narrative. It has no known romance source or analogue. The plot has its roots in the fabliaux which provide their closest parallels in the ending of the tale. Here is a further reason for maintaining that the entire story is a fabliau at heart. Indeed, the Merchant's Tale begins in an odd way for a romance, with an extended debate about marriage. Debate is also an important part of the tale's generic constituents: the impulse for telling it is the Merchant's response to the Clerk's tale of patient Griselda, with whom his own wife contrasts; there follows a lengthy and provocative mock-praise of marriage; January initiates and participates in two court sessions in which the same subject is disputed by Placebo and Justinus; the latter refers to the Wife of Bath and the wider debate on marriage which she initiated; and finally, Pluto and Proserpina discuss the relations between men and women. These debates – or parts of a continuing debate – are framed and interlinked by a romance narrative. The romance may therefore be thought of as emerging under pressure from the debates, in order to provide their abstract, static natures with direction, movement, and a location in a recognizable world. If the form developed in response to content, it may also have been moulded to an unusual extent by material drawn from Chaucer's own experiences and observations: the absence of a romance model left him ample space for invention.

The romance element in the Merchant's Tale provides more than a skin-deep *modus vivendi* for January and May, more than a convenient linking device for the debates. Chaucer actively encourages his audience to begin by categorizing the narrative as a romance when he includes and elaborates conventional features of the genre. The court setting is a case in point, and so is the illicit love affair of Damian and May. But in both instances what is noticeable is the purposeful manipulation of convention to make it speak with a pointed and perhaps topical relevance. The similarities between the court of January and that of Edward need no further urging. In the case of the love affair its conventional, clandestine nature is used as an epitome of the betrayal and subterfuge bred by January's misguided policies.

The court relationship of Damian and January is the formally close one of squire to knight, which only makes the behaviour of the 'hoomly fo' (1792) more heinous, fostered as it is unwittingly by a January 'dronken in plesaunce / In mariage' (1788–9). Damian has carved before January for some time (1773), and is valued by his lord as a 'gentil squier' (1907):

> *'He is as wys, discreet, and as secree*
> *As any man I woot of his degree,*
> *And therto manly, and eek servysable,*
> *And for to been a thrifty man right able.'*
> *(1909–12)*

Ironically, the very qualities which January cherishes in Damian are of great use in his betrayal of the old, blind, man. Damian pursues May 'In secree wise' (1937), appropriate enough behaviour for a noble lover, but here so much part of the covert nature of court life which has become exacerbated under the rule of January. Even a clichéd utterance of Damian to May –

> *'Mercy! and that ye nat discovere me,*
> *For I am deed if that this thyng be kyd'*
> *(1942–3)*

– has a cutting edge, for January remains a powerful man whose jealousy would not stop at the death of the offender.

May's thoughts and actions are also hidden from January. She 'studieth' (1955) while lying down by the old man's side. The 'excellent franchise' (1987) with which she is now credited is not in fact creditable because it is directed towards admitting her desire for Damian (1982–4), an admission produced by women's ability to 'hem narwe avyse' (1988). The famous line, couched in terms which evoke the courtly ethos, 'Lo, pitee renneth soone in gentil herte!' (1986), points only to May's considered, calculating, self-serving schemes. Again, the language used to describe the customary attitude of a desired romance heroine, who

> *Som tyrant is, as ther be many oon,*
> *That hath an herte as hard as any stoon,*
> *Which wolde han lat hym sterven in the place*
> *Wel rather than han graunted hym hire grace,*
> *And hem rejoysen in hire crueel pryde,*
> *And rekke nat to been an homycide ...*
> *(1989–94)*

has a hard and sinister side to it within this particular court setting. Under January's rule, such terminology has a powerful effect because tyranny, insensitivity, the cheapening of life, typify the attitude of January to May and of May to January.

The court intrigue, designed to satisfy the lust of the participants, gathers momentum through secret messages (1995–2008). The duplicity of Damian and May becomes more outrageous. May keeps up appearances while Damian acts the obsequious, dissembling courtier: he curries favour with all and wins a good reputation – partly in order to be admired by May, and partly as a strategy for diverting suspicion, '(For craft is al, whoso that do it kan)' (2015). The language of love, ironically expressed, is not allowed to lapse. May loves Damian 'benyngnely', to the point of dying unless she 'han hym as hir leste' (2093–5). She has become a travesty of a romance lady of the court, a woman with a sharp sexual appetite who must slake her craving for her husband's squire. She is able to act more naturally in the relatively unrestrained, informal and uninhibited world of fabliau.

There is another type of composition which the Merchant's Tale is in the process of becoming: a mirror for the wise ruler, a genre of perennial interest to poets at this period, as the case of Gower's *Vox Clamantis*, VI. 8. 18 (trans. Stockton 1962: 233–44), who was also exercised by the malign influence of Alice Perrers, illustrates (Stillwell

1948; Ferguson 1965: 70–85; Coleman 1981: 66, 81 and 105; Coleman 1983: 60; Peck 1986: 127–8). For behind the debate on marriage is a further, no less important debate on which type of wisdom it is appropriate for January to emulate. January tends to rely on 'his owene auctoritee' (1597), a practice which Placebo encourages: '"I holde youre owene conseil is the beste"' (1490). Placebo here follows in letter, if not in spirit, the dictum of Solomon: '"Wirk alle thyng by conseil"' (1485). January, he suggests, is so full of '"sapience"' and '"heighe prudence"' that he has no need '"To weyven fro the word of Salomon"' (1481–3). Pluto is also an admirer of Solomon, calling him '"wys, and richest of richesse, / Fulfild of sapience and of worldly glorie"' (2242–3), and referring with approval to Solomon's views on women. Considering that Placebo 'reflects' January, and that he and Pluto have much in common, we may conclude that if January has a model for his 'sapience' it is Solomon. They are Solomon's words which he utters to May in the garden (2138–48).

Yet the words spoken in the garden are 'olde lewed wordes' (2149), hopelessly out of kilter with prevailing circumstances: January parodies, unwittingly, Christ's words to the church by reducing the Song of Songs to an exclusively erotic poem; the words assume a reciprocated love which is far from being the case; and the lines are loaded with visual images hardly appropriate to January's blindness. Thus the wisdom of Solomon, as a model for January's wisdom, is subjected to criticism, and nowhere more searchingly than in the debate between Pluto and Proserpina. She scorns Solomon and points out that, for all his vaunted wisdom, he was a fool who in old age forsook his God and almost lost his kingdom:

> 'Ey! for verray God that nys but oon,
> What make ye so muche of Salomon?
> What though he made a temple, Goddes hous?
> What though he were riche and glorious?
> So made he eek a temple of false goddis.
> How myghte he do a thyng that moore forbode is?
> Pardee, as faire as ye his name emplastre,
> He was a lecchour and an ydolastre,

And in his elde he verray God forsook;
And if God ne hadde, as seith the book,
Yspared him for his fadres sake, he sholde
Have lost his regne rather than he wolde.'
(2291–2302)

The links between this Solomon and old January, a lecher who
idolizes May, are not hard to see; for that matter, the connections
between Solomon and Edward III himself are not much further afield.

An alternative model of wisdom is indicated by Justinus, who refers
to Seneca (another adviser to princes) as providing, '"amonges othere
wordes wyse"' (1523), practical and down-to-earth advice about
inheritance. January is unimpressed: '"Straw for thy Senek, and for
thy proverbes!"' (1567). The name of Seneca carries for him the taint
of scholasticism: '"I counte nat a panyer ful of herbes / Of scole-
termes"' (1568–9). The commonsensical, realistic, and just variety of
wisdom is espoused by Proserpina in her rejoinder to Pluto. Pluto's
response to May's infidelity is traditionalist: she is to be seen as an
exemplar of that female vice on which the wise Solomon pronounced,
and is to be revealed in '"al hire harlotrye"' (2262). The analysis is
inadequate to Proserpina's way of thinking. Simply because Solomon
found no virtuous woman it does not follow that such women do not
exist. Solomon's words on virtue –

'"Amonges a thousand men yet foond I oon,
But of wommen alle foond I noon"'
(2247–8)

– are meant to indicate that true goodness is the preserve of only one
being, God himself, and that men and women are equally prone to
sin (2287–90). Applied to the court of January, or to the court of
Edward, such opinions, laced as they are with biblical references
(Besserman 1978: 25–7), are radical. They imply that the obvious,
traditional way of explaining the crisis at court – by blaming it on

the sinful, deceiving woman – will not do. The man is also culpable and must take his share of the blame.

It may be that the differentiation between two kinds of wisdom – that of Solomon and that of Seneca – and its presentation as a debate, was suggested to Chaucer from his reading of Robert Holcot's commentary on the Wisdom of Solomon. Holcot is by no means uncritical of Solomon, and he is prone to support his own observations with references to Seneca, and particularly his moral epistles, on which Chaucer draws elsewhere in his works (Ayres 1919). The careful, considered way in which Chaucer uses his sources is often as revealing as their content. In the Merchant's Tale he may be using Holcot's work to stimulate a debate which actually turns on the right selection of 'auctoritees'. Whether or not the ruler should seek to go the way of Solomon, or the way of Seneca, or neither, is quite crucial to the health of his 'governaunce'. This is the type of advice, or mirror, which a well-read writer such as Chaucer, involved in court life, is able to give to his ruler.

COMEDY

Technically, the Merchant's Tale is a comedy because it ends happily. May consummates her affair with Damian and conceals it from her husband; January leaves the garden in a state of contentment, perhaps believing that May will soon provide him with an heir:

> *This Januarie, who is glad but he?*
> *He kisseth hire, and clippeth hire ful ofte,*
> *And on hire wombe he stroketh hire ful softe,*
> *And to his palays hoom he hath hire lad.*
> *(2412–15)*

But it is a comedy of a particularly black variety, for January's happiness is dependent upon his own degeneration as ruler of his wife and, by extension, his dukedom. Old age, wilfulness, lust, jealousy, the deceptions of Damian and May, have combined to bring him to a worse state than ever. Nothing now seems capable of opening his eyes to the crisis in which he is enveloped, having ceded power and property to his wife.

If we laugh through clenched teeth at the outcome of the Merchant's Tale, it is but the culmination of a long and intensifying process of ridicule. Protagonists within the narrative themselves provide cues for treating January with mirth and derision. At the wedding-feast 'Venus laugheth upon every wight, / For Januarie was bicome hir knyght' (1723–4), and she and the other deities promote an atmosphere of mirth (1731 and 1739) because of the unlikely conjunction of youth and age. Justinus, hating January's 'folye', offers some observations in a jocular manner, 'Answerde anon right in his japerye' (1655–6), to the effect that May could become his lord's purgatory rather than his paradise.

The sardonic note hit by Justinus is characteristic of the tonal register in which the humour of the Merchant's Tale plays. The overall portrait of January is satirical in its ruthless determination to anatomize his faults. The keynote, introductory speech of the Merchant is choked with a biting irony – 'A wyf is Goddes yifte' (1311), 'womman is for mannes help ywroght' (1324) – which colours the entire tale, and which derives its force from being no more than an orthodox eulogy of marriage. It is just that, in the experience of both the Merchant and January, the practice falls so far short of the ideal. Occasionally, the irony becomes harsh enough to qualify as sarcasm: 'Lo, pitee renneth soone in gentil herte!' (1986). And the tendency of the wordplay is towards sexual suggestiveness. Thus the promptings for humour are all ambivalent, pointed, qualified. Laughter is released only to be held back. Sometimes, as in the passages on household betrayers and the scorpion, matters become too serious to admit of any kind of comic tone at all.

Looking beyond the verbal texture of the humour to the comedy of situation, it is possible to distinguish three devices which are deployed to intensify the contradictory pulls towards laughter and despair. First, Chaucer pushes to extremes the prevailing passions of January's psychology. He is an inveterate lecher, set in his ways, and as lubricious as ever in his married state; his method of making decisions is revealed as a stubborn wilfulness; and the jealousy which afflicts him is 'outrageous' (2087). Through accenting the less praiseworthy aspects of January's character, Chaucer makes of him a caricature of the moderate and prudent ruler. Second, Chaucer uses juxtaposition and incongruity to excite the sense that matters have become so farcical as to have reached breaking-point. January is not just an extremely old man, but one who is represented in close proximity to a fair and tender woman one-third his age; sexual experience is associated with religion, as when May expresses her yearning for the small green pears: '"Help, for hir love that is of hevene queene!"' (2334); a marriage set up in the context of high-falutin' debates gives way to adultery conducted out of pure self-interest; and January and May themselves, as months of the year, are opposite seasonal types.

Finally, Chaucer practises the familiar medieval technique of comic inversion, whereby individuals and situations become the opposite of what might be expected. It is a technique well suited to providing a critique of the subject matter, for it reveals the disparity between what is and what should be. Thus, the old man behaves as if he were green and young; the wise ruler behaves foolishly and against sound advice; the blind man whose sight is restored cannot trust the evidence of his own eyes, so affected is he by devotion to May; heavenly bliss becomes sexual bliss, which undergoes a further revolution into a kind of living hell; a romance is suddenly transformed into a fabliau. The cumulative impression created by these inversions is of an entire world turned upside-down. Of course the grotesqueries are created by the distortions of a fictional mirror. But if, as we have been suggesting, that mirror reflects accurately a real court world with living examples of excess, incongruity and inversion, then how much more pointed, sardonic and downright disturbing is the reign of January and May and the 'governaunce' which they promise.

THE MERCHANT'S COMPLAINT

The restless play of meanings and forms so far described does not convey a logical, linear system of metaphorical and allegorical description. If, however, it is fully recognized as an exploration of the significances of the political crises of the 1370s, the treatment of allegory, iconography, and genre, and the attention given to sexuality and faery, attain remarkable focus. What emerges is a deeply enriched envisaging of the nature of contemporary political problems written by a participant observer of unusual analytical power. If full resolution is not achieved it is with a self-conscious awareness of the active controversy which such matters continue to stimulate. More than any of his contemporaries, moreover, Chaucer provides a historical analysis in terms of mental structures which suggests the range of possible explanatory factors which comprise the understanding of political crisis in late fourteenth-century England.

The prologue to the Merchant's Tale presents a complaint against marriage. In many respects it is conventional and provides a simple introduction to the tale, enabling audience or reader to locate the story of January within the experience of the newly married Merchant, for whom the reality of marriage is utterly different from that of being married to a woman like patient Griselda of the Clerk's Tale. Perhaps it is only after reading the Merchant's Tale itself that the apparent conventionality of the prologue becomes questionable. The tale, indeed, invigorates that convention and the radical significance of the tale becomes located in the conventional complaint.

Close examination of the Merchant's Prologue reveals suggestive parallels with the tale. Like January, the Merchant was unmarried and has recently taken a wife. The Merchant's new wife is 'the worste that may be; / For thogh the feend to hire ycoupled were, / She wolde hym overmacche' (1218–20), just as May might be represented. The reference to coupling with the devil, moreover, gives a new dimension to May's relations with the demonic Damian (if such were needed). Finally, the observed contrast between Griselda and the Merchant's new wife provides a contrast or change in time which parallels the unmarried/married division and suggests that within the tale there may also be a Griselda/May contrast. Something happened to change critically the married status of Merchant and January profoundly for the worse.

Within the Merchant's Tale the marriage of January and May bears an obvious resemblance to descriptions by other contemporary writers whose central concern was political and moral criticism. Langland,

Brinton, Erghome, Gower and Walsingham all identified the relationship between Edward III and Alice Perrers as being of crucial and
damaging importance to the kingdom (Huppé 1939: 44–52; Bennett
1943: 566–7). The infatuation of the ageing king for his corrupt and
avaricious younger mistress was seen to be a major contributory cause
of the political, economic and religious malaise of the 1370s. The
depravity of the senile king became a powerful explanatory metaphor.

From the death of Queen Philippa in 1369 until his own death in
1376 Edward III progressively withdrew from personal involvement
in government and became increasingly obsessed with Alice Perrers,
who bore him a son later acknowledged at court as 'John Sotherey'.
In their analysis of the state of the kingdom in 1376 the commons, in
the subsequently named Good Parliament, looked back over the seven
years as ones in which the withdrawal of royal authority has permitted
the growth of corruption at court to the serious detriment of the
realm (Holmes 1975: 100–39). Central to their accusations were those
concerning the management of trade.

The Merchant, it appears, had something to complain about. In
the fourteenth century the activities of English merchants exporting
woollen cloth, and especially raw wool, were not only central to
English trade but were intimately involved with foreign policy, taxation, royal revenues and the development of parliament. The success
or failure of such merchants was a matter of the foremost political
concern. Before 1369, and perhaps particularly after 1363, English
merchants might have looked upon Edward III as their friend. But the
buoyancy of the English export trade in wool and cloth in the 1350s
and a reasonable subsequent prosperity came abruptly to an end at the
close of the 1360s. From 1369 until the end of Edward III's reign
England's export trade experienced a severe depression which seriously damaged English mercantile fortunes and played a key role in the
development of relations between the king, the court and parliament.

In the parliament of 1369 Edward III resumed the name of King of
England and of France and the two countries were once again at war.
The consequent disruption to trade was in part responsible for the
onset of depression. Plague and adverse weather conditions also
played their part, helping to produce sharply rising prices. But there
were other royal policies which, certainly to contemporaries, seemed

to be responsible for the sudden decline of their share of the market. The abolition of the Calais staple in 1369, six years after its creation as a quasi-monopoly for a company of English merchants, became identified as the single act most prejudicial to mercantile fortunes. At the same time the placing of a ban upon exports by denizen merchants allowed alien merchants to prosper at their expense. The restoration of the staple in August 1370 seems to have done little to enable English merchants to regain their control.

By February 1371, when parliament met, the wool trade had become a major subject of political concern. The commons sought to establish that 'no imposition or charge should be laid on wools, woolfells, or leathers, except the custom and subsidy granted to the King, in any manner *without the assent of Parliament*', and their request was conceded after the meeting of the Great Council at Winchester on 9 June. In an atmosphere of rumoured rebelliousness among merchants in London, Norwich and elsewhere, the Great Council (including some merchants) levied duty on wine and other merchandise with the exception of wool and hides. Anxious about the implementation of these decisions the government was concerned to secure the consent of local merchants in the ports.

From December 1371, however, it seemed that the government began to pursue policies which effectively undermined the restoration of the Calais staple. The issuing of licences for the export of wool to Middelburg or Dordrecht, first of all to alien merchants and then to denizens (though at the same extortionate rate as to aliens), though quite probably a response to growing tensions between England and France, created a system detrimental to the interests of many English merchants, encouraging the evasion of the Calais staple and making it once more of central importance in English politics.

In 1372, when wool exports to Calais were permitted until Michaelmas, conditions of war probably prevented the movement of shipping before 14 September. On 23 September, however, all exports were suspended in order to ensure the parliamentary grant of customs duties. Later, before the delayed meeting of parliament in November 1372, the export of wool was permitted provided that merchants would undertake to pay whatever duties might be granted by parliament; and licences allowing evasion of the Calais staple began to be issued on the same terms. The November parliament granted the wool duty and, after special deliberations by citizens and burgesses, they granted tunnage and poundage also. A petition by citizens and burgesses complained that export of wool to Middelburg was against the statute, and it went on to argue for the enstatement of a single, named staple. To this demand the king's reply was evasive, and licences for the avoidance of Calais continued to be issued throughout 1372–3, with denizens continuing to suffer financial disadvantage.

Further attacks upon this system were made in parliament in November 1373, when a commons petition claimed that the Calais staple had been established by the authority of parliament and demanded that it should now be restored and that licences of exemption should cease to be issued. The king said that he would be guided in this matter by 'son grant conseil', but licences continued to be granted until the assembly of the Good Parliament in April 1376.

At the beginning of the protracted debate in 1376 about the state of the kingdom, the commons were soon to voice complaint about the removal of the staple from Calais. The removal and the ejection of the merchants, it was alleged, had been carried out for the personal profit of the king's chamberlain, Lord Latimer, and the London merchant, Richard Lyons. Gradually a line of argument was developed in which it was asserted that parliament had created the staple by statute and only parliament, therefore, could undo that statute. Though it seems unlikely that the statutory origins were as the commons asserted, the political and constitutional significance of the claim was considerable.

Whatever the truth of the matter, in the minds of contemporaries, and perhaps especially in the minds of the majority of merchants, responsibility for the deterioration of merchant fortunes lay, in the absence of the direct involvement of the king, with Latimer and Lyons. The exclusion of denizens from the export trade, the levying of extra-parliamentary duties on wool, the issuing of licences, and the manipulation and exploitation of loans to the crown, were actions arguably damaging to crown, kingdom and merchants, while being designed for the profit of Latimer and Lyons. Even if the policies were not devised by Latimer the proceeds were paid into his department. Lyons admitted to involvement in the origins of the licencing scheme, although he claimed that he had acted on the personal authority of the king.

The corrupt mismanagement of trade, as well as the influence of Alice Perrers, seems to have played a crucial part in producing the political and constitutional crisis of 1376. In parliament, the influence of the merchants in the commons helped to produce a critical restlessness increasingly aimed at limiting the authority of the king and his ministers. The parliaments of 1371 and 1373, indeed, were exceptional in their demands. A petition of 1371 collected in *Rotuli Parliamentorum* argued 'that the government of the realm has for a long time been administered by people of Holy Church who are never amenable to justice in any case, whereby great harm and damage has resulted in times past and more may follow in time to come, in disinheritance of the Crown, and great prejudice of the realm' (ed. Strachey 1767–77: II. 304a), and went on to demand that laymen should be substituted for clerical ministers. Some lay lords, using two Austin friars to make their case in parliament, sought to establish the principle that in time of national emergency the property given to the church by the crown might be taken back into the hands of the king. As a result of the attack on the king's clerical ministers, Bishop Wykeham and Bishop Brantingham were removed from their offices as chancellor and treasurer, and the rift between lay and clerical leaders became surrounded by controversy. Pamphlet warfare, in which Wyclif took a leading role, continued the debate. In the Parliament of 1373 the Bishop of Hereford, William Courtenay, protested that the grievances of his clerics should be met before any more money was paid to the king. The commons, for their part, refused to grant a subsidy until they had consulted with a committee of peers. 'The King's chamberlain, Lord Latimer, was thought to be defrauding him, customs officers were said to be exceeding their powers, disreputable merchants to be enriching themselves at the expense of the nation' (McKisack 1959: 385).

In the light of these events the Merchant's complaint and the story of January and May become metaphors for the state of the realm (Zacher 1976: 107). That Chaucer had an interest in some of the key players is indicated by the fact that ten years earlier, his father –

evidently an associate of Lyons, also a vintner – gave security that Lyons 'would cause no harm to Alice Perrers or prevent her from going where she pleased and doing the business of the king as well as her own' (ed. Crow and Olson 1966: 5). Chaucer's own path crossed that of the king's mistress on a number of occasions, although there is no direct evidence that they were closely associated, in spite of Braddy's hypotheses and speculations (Braddy 1946 and 1977). The marriage of the Merchant may be seen as a reflection of the merchants' relations with king and government and, in running parallel to the king's own relationship with Alice Perrers, may suggest or permit connections between the state of the Merchant's marriage and the influence of the mistress. The marriage of January and May is above all a perversion of the true holy state of matrimony, one both caused by and aggravating the delusions of the king as they lead to his final humiliation. By extension his marriage may be applied metaphorically to the kingdom as a whole. Servile obsession has deprived the kingdom of royal authority; the creature that brought about the king's fall couples with the devil in the garden; and the mistress and the trusted servant betray the kingdom while continuing to exploit to their profit the favour of Edward III. Such an interpretation does not necessarily date composition of the poem earlier than is usual, for the case of Edward III's infatuation with Alice Perrers did not lose its topicality; Langland, for example, continued to use Lady Meed as a figure for Alice, with which to warn Richard II about the vices of his grand-father and their consequences for the government of the country (Baldwin 1981: 34).

For the merchants the treatment the Calais staple became emblem-atic of the political and constitutional crisis and its development. But the crisis was articulated in a wide variety of ways, and the metaphor of marriage is a fertile source of many possible meanings within this context. As already suggested, the 1370s saw conflict between secular and ecclesiastical authority and also between king, court and parlia-ment. Within the Merchant's Tale, those opening sections which deal with January's decision to marry consider the nature of marriage and the value of counsel in ways which suggest that a discussion of government is in progress. At the same time, they provide a deeply ironic anticipation of January's relationship with May and a bitterly critical commentary upon Edward III's relationship with Alice Perrers.

For January, marriage is a holy bond that provides an earthly paradise. Within that paradise the woman is to satisfy his appetites and cheerfully to serve his needs at all times:

> *Al that hire housbonde lust, hire liketh weel;*
> *She seith nat ones 'nay,' whan he seith 'ye.'*
> *'Do this,' seith he; 'Al redy, sire,' seith she.*
> *(1344–6)*

A wife should be 'humble' (1376), and although it might be necessary to listen to what she has to say, 'And yet she wole obeye of curteisye' (1379). In January's ideal world, within the state of matrimony, 'They moste nedes lyve in unitee' (1334). And he concludes:

> *I warne thee, if wisely thou wolt wirche,*
> *Love wel thy wyf, as Crist loved his chirche.*
> *If thou lovest thyself, thou lovest thy wyf;*
> *No man hateth his flessh, but in his lyf*
> *He fostreth it, and therfore bidde I thee*
> *Cherisse thy wyf, or thou shalt nevere thee.*
> *(1383–8)*

Between king and parliament such a relationship would seem to acknowledge the importance, within the constitution, of close ties, but to emphasize the ultimate authority of the king and the ultimate compliance of parliament. It might even appear that the king saw this 'marriage' as one vital to his self-interest, always provided that the partner understood her subservient condition.

In so stating the virtues of marriage, however, January was clearly opposed to clerical advice and determined to take a young bride: '"I wol no womman thritty yeer of age"' (1421). Pursuing the governmental metaphor it may be that Edward III was looking back to that earlier political and constitutional crisis of his reign, in 1340–1, when the commons, in the opening years of war with France, became involved in attempts to limit the control of the king over his servants, to curtail his freedom to exercise power, and to hold his ministers responsible to parliament. He wanted no relationship of that kind. As for the opposition to clerical advice this takes the form, in the tale, of the rejection of Theophrastus. Theophrastus declared it unwise to take a wife '"for housbondrye"', recommending rather '"A trewe servant"' and, in time of sickness, '"Thy verray freendes, or a trewe knave"' (1296–1306). January, however, decides to defy Theophrastus and his warnings of deceit and avarice. The importance of the advice of good friends and trusted servants in government is a theme to which the narrative returns and which is at the heart of the commons' complaints in 1376, while the rejection of the views of the clerks suggests the dismissal of Wykeham and Brantingham following the parliament of 1371 and the substitution of lay for clerical officers close to the crown.

When January finally calls his friends to him it is 'To tellen hem th'effect of his entente' (1398) and to '"prey yow to my wyl ye wole assente"' (1468). But his friends are divided, and especially his brothers, Placebo and Justinus. When Placebo speaks, in the first instance, he is concerned not with marriage but with counsel, though in the matter of government counsel and marriage are intimately involved with one another. The courtier Placebo, however, argues that January has little need '"Conseil to axe of any that is heere"' (1480), and argues that January should understand the words of Solomon, who recommended '"Wirk alle thyng by conseil"' (1485), to mean that he should rely upon his own counsel. It is suggested that January's relations with his advisers were such that he summoned them only to gain their consent to his intentions, and that Placebo provided him with the flattering subservience he sought. The position of friends, servants, and advisers, and the role of councils and committees in government, were essential elements of political and constitutional debate in the 1370s and perhaps especially in the parliaments of 1373 and 1376: the critical comments of the commons were directed against just that withdrawal from consultation and the dependence on sycophancy which the attitudes of January and Placebo suggest.

Justinus, for his part, advocates caution and repeatedly stresses the importance of advice. Citing the authority of Seneca he says '"that a man oghte hym right wel avyse / To whom he yeveth his lond or his catel"' (1524–5), and goes on to argue:

> '*And syn I oghte avyse me right wel*
> *To whom I yeve my good awey fro me,*
> *Wel muchel moore I oghte avysed be*
> *To whom I yeve my body for alwey.*'
> *(1526–9)*

Marriage is a serious business and '"no childes pley"' (1530), just as the relationship with Alice Perrers was fraught with danger. In other words, government needs the counsel of friends. In this the position of Justinus is akin to that of Theophrastus and the previously rejected clerical advice. As January disdains Justinus' warnings –

> '*Straw for thy Senek, and for thy proverbes!*
> *I counte nat a panyer ful of herbes*
> *Of scole-terms.*'
> *(1567–9)*

– it is tempting to see the division between the brothers of crown, lay courtiers and clergy which followed the actions of the parliament of 1371.

Once January has made his choice of wife he again sends for his friends, just as Edward III, perhaps, had called his Great Council in 1373 after that held in 1371. At the second council January's attitude has hardened:

> *...he bad hem alle a boone,*
> *That noon of hem none 'argumentes make*
> *Agayn the purpos which that he hath take ...*
> *(1618–20)*

Instead, he puts to his brothers Placebo and Justinus the deluded, selfish, and near-sacrilegious enquiry as to whether the heaven on earth of his perfect marital arrangements might in any way prevent him from coming ultimately '"to the blisse ther Crist eterne on lyve ys"' (1652). Only Justinus replies to this question, and he does so now more in the voice of the church, challenging January's view of the righteousness of his own decisions. Take such a wife in such a way, warns Justinus, and it will prove no impediment to entry into heaven, but

> 'Parauntre she may be youre purgatorie!
> She may be Goddes meene and Goddes whippe;
> Thanne shal youre soule up to hevene skippe ...'
> (1670–2)

Employing the teaching of contemporary canon law, Justinus' argument suggests an understanding of the crisis of the 1370s which sees Alice Perrers as a divine agent in a necessary process of punishment and purification. The decision to disregard the advice of friends, counsellors, church and commons, is to break the holy bonds of constitutional matrimony and to release a purgatory of self-destructive policies and conflict. Significantly Justinus, in conclusion, invokes the lessons of the Wife of Bath's Prologue and Tale '"If ye han understonde"' (1685–7). Only when the husband has submitted to the wife can he expect her obedience and can a holy and harmonious marriage develop.

January's refusal to countenance criticism, or to consider modifying his own views in response to traditionally accepted sources of advice, is followed by his marriage and wedding feast and the release of a powerful and lustful paganism in which Venus rules all judgement: 'For Januarie was bicome hir knyght' (1724). Confusing pleasure with happiness, the old man has adopted a hedonistic way of life; he 'Shoop hym to lyve ful deliciously' (2025):

His housynge, his array, as honestly
To his degree was maked as a kynges.
Amonges othere of his honeste thynges,
He made a gardyn, walled al with stoon ...
(2026–9)

Into that garden he withdraws, as he progressively withdraws psycho-
logically into his own world of deluded fantasies.

January's behaviour has striking parallels with the biography of
Edward III (Holmes 1975: 90–1; Given-Wilson 1986: 33–4). After
1369 and the death of his queen, Philippa, Edward was seen less and
less frequently at Westminster. The king was, moreover, known to the
Brut author as 'besy and corious in bildyng' (ed. Brie 1906: II.333). In
the 1350s and 1360s Edward had spent well in excess of £90,000
on building at Windsor, Queenborough, Eltham, Sheen, Hadleigh,
Leeds, Rotherhithe, Gravesend, Moor End, Henley-on-the-Heath,
four new hunting lodges in the New Forest, Kings's Langley, and
Rochester Castle – and in most of the work there seems to have been a
strong personal involvement in the direction of the projects (Colvin
et al. 1963: I. 236; Sherborne 1983: 10–17). Windsor, it seems, was
intended to become an expression of kingship, a centre of Edward
III's court and of chivalry, and he maintained a ring of satellite houses
and hunting lodges around the rebuilt castle.

Windsor Castle became his usual place of abode, with the manor-house
in the park as a private retreat, and Sheen, Havering, or Eltham as the
object of occasional excursions farther afield. After 1372 the chief
officers of the household remained almost permanently at Windsor or
Havering, while the King, accompanied by only his personal
attendants, sought a change of scene at one of his suburban residences.
(Colvin et al. 1963: I. 244–5)

At Windsor, Queenborough, King's Langley, Rotherhithe and Sheen
considerable sums must also have been spent on creating and

maintaining gardens. At Sheen, where Edward III was to die, expenditure on the garden was a constant feature of the accounts in the 1360s and 1370s. Intriguingly, between 1363 and 1366 large sums were spent on the provision of a great gate with a wicket within it .

The metaphors of the marriage and of the garden provide a language for the analysis of the declining years of Edward III seen in the aftermath of the parliamentary crisis of 1376, a time when Chaucer himself appears to have become detached from the inner circle of the court (ed. Crow and Olson 1966: 105). Skilfully incorporating fragments of biography, contemporary events and rumour, they make possible a range of criticism which extends from an indictment of personal moral behaviour to a savage attack upon a particular expression of kingship. At the close of the marriage feast for example, the tale describes how that

> ...this hastif Januarie
> Wolde go to bedde; he wolde no lenger tarye.
> He drynketh ypocras, clarree, and vernage
> Of spices hoote t'encreessen his corage;
> And many a letuarie hath he ful fyn,
> Swiche as the cursed monk, daun Constantyn,
> Hath writen in his Book De Coitu;
> To eten hem alle he nas no thyng eschu.
>
> (1805–12)

The passage works well to convey a picture of the disgusting old knight of Venus gobbling down as many aphrodisiacs as he can in the hope of improving his sexual performance. It also encourages condemnations of Edward III's personal relations with Alice Perrers, and all the more so since it was widely rumoured that she was in league with a magician who gave her various potions and herbs to stimulate Edward's sexual excitement and thereby further enslave him. By entering this relationship, rejecting advice, rejecting the church, confusing pleasure and happiness, and depending increasingly on a small circle of greedy sycophants, Edward III, with only old age as an excuse, was increasingly taking actions which would lead to his own humiliation, the degradation of kingship, and the destruction of the kingdom. The draughts he drank, believing that would increase his potency, could not disguise his fundamental weakness and progressive impotence. While rumour and the account of Walsingham might seem to provide Edwise III with an excuse for the actions of his later years (the black magic of Alice Perrers, preventing him from taking the course he would otherwise have chosen) the Merchant's Tale places more blame upon the king. In Chaucer's account, 'Alice Perrers' is much more the agent by means of which the deluded decisions of the king are carried to their logical and destructive conclusion, just as a *poirier* or pear tree is the means of January's humiliation.

In the garden there is also 'the feend' (1219), the creature that emerges at the marriage feast 'ravysshed on his lady May / ... So soore hath Venus hurt hym, with hire brond' (1774 and 1777). The very presence of such a woman in such a household is enough to set in motion the machinery of cuckoldry and Damian proceeds to seduce May into deceiving January. It is tempting to look for a Damian figure in the household and court of Edward III, to find someone who, with Alice Perrers, was at the corrupt centre of influence over the king in the later years of the reign. Certainly contemporaries were not slow to identify the guilty parties in their accusations of 1376 (Given-Wilson 1986: 142–54). John Neville, for example, was steward of the royal household from 1371 and was deeply involved in royal finances and in the conduct of war. The most obvious candidate, however, and the man who dominated the affairs of the court, especially after being appointed chamberlain in 1371, was William Latimer. Born in 1330 he became the most prominent English soldier and official in Brittany in the decade after 1359. Returning to England he rapidly established himself at court, being steward of the household from 1368 to October 1370 before becoming chamberlain. In the Good Parliament it was he who became the principal target for accusations of corruption and mismanagement. Within the Merchant's Tale it is this devil who activates the scourge of woman. In explaining the political crisis it would seem that by his own actions Edward III provides the means by which the devil can get to work in the kingdom and punishment may be inflicted.

The arrangement between Pluto and Proserpina, indeed, seems to be conducted in such terms. In a discussion reminiscent of the Wife of Bath's Prologue, Pluto attributes the betrayal of January to '"The tresons whiche that wommen doon to man"' (2239), citing Solomon in support of his arugument, and seeing January as an '"honurable"' (2254) and '"worthy"' (2259) knight now old and blind and, therefore, vulnerable. Proserpina, however, rejects Pluto's authority, in the passage quoted above, pp. 186–7 (lines 2292–302). She argues instead that January has brought cuckoldry upon himself. In condemning Solomon, moreover, Proserpina not only undermines Pluto's argument regarding the treacherous behaviour of women but obliquely issues a scathing attack upon Edward III from the vantage point of the gods.

The difference between Pluto and Proserpina provides an explanatory framework for the black and bitter comedy of the tale's conclusion. Pluto's decision to restore January's sight and reveal the coupling of May and Damian is met by the elaborate excuse which Proserpina provides for May. And January, pathetically, is persuaded by her explanation. Though the blindness of January has been healed, the true blindness of his self-delusion remains (P. Brown 1985). Seen from the days following the Hilary Parliament of 1377 the affairs of the realm may have seemed reduced to the same black comedy. The Good Parliament of 1376, with its revelations of corruption, greed and mismanagement, and its indictment of the guilty members of the court, should have opened the eyes of the king to the evil destroying the kingdom. By 23 February 1377, however, the Good Parliament had been declared no true parliament and its acts had been annulled. The nine new councillors had been dismissed, Latimer was restored to his seat on the council, and Alice Perrers was reinstated at court. The Hilary Parliament, in effect, returned political and constitutional relations to the conditions of the period between 1371 and 1373. The punishment and conflict of purgatory continued.

5

The Knight

One way in which contemporaries came to terms with their perceptions of the significance and unity of their experiences in late fourteenth-century England, moving from a series of crises to a general sense of crisis, was by reference to the explanatory system of astrology. In particular, astrologers and other writers looked to the governing influence of Saturn, the planet held to be responsible for such matters as plague, treason, revolt, violent death, bad weather and crop failure. The Knight's Tale offers a bleak view of Chaucer's times from this perspective.

Within the tale the experience of the protagonists is characterized by sudden turns of fortune, disagreement, violence and injustice. The death of Arcite sounds a profound note of pathos and despair at the inexplicability of human events. And the consolation offered by Theseus, with its stress upon order, patience and serenity, remains an assertion of faith which fails to satisfy the logic of experience within the tale. As an examination of values within a chivalric ideology the Knight's Tale proves a searching exercise in the self-analysis of its pilgrim teller while engaging in the long-term debate as to the nature of right order within chivalric society. More than this, however, it draws upon contemporary political experience and upon conflict in the courts of Edward III and Richard II, commenting implicitly upon government and kingship, suggesting the profound disappointment of hopes and expectation, and the unpredictable and regrettable nature of developments from the last years of the old king through to the coming of age of the new.

Such an examination tests the foundations of English society in the second half of the fourteenth century and Chaucer's own place within it. It is achieved, moreover, in poetic terms by means of conventional elements of the romance genre in the play of promises and obligations – promises, commitments and duties which lie at the heart of the chivalric ethic. But though the means are romantic, the tale, with its saga of broken promises, of obligations which cannot be met and of commitments which turn sour, does not serve to reinforce the literary genre or the social and political system which it articulates. With all its dire implications, in the end only Saturn is able to make and keep an unambiguous promise.

THE RETURN OF GAUNT

To appreciate what the Knight's Tale might have meant to Chaucer's contemporaries requires a knowledge of the date of the poem's completion, and this is unknown. Dating attempts, such as they are, are dependent upon stylistic and compositional judgements, upon the understanding of internal references, and upon the interpretation of the poem's thematic material and its intended application to events and developments during the poet's life. The summary of existing arguments in *The Riverside Chaucer* (ed Benson et al. 1987: 826–7), comes down conservatively on a date sometime in the 1380s, but acknowledges (though unfavourably) the implications of dismissions by Cook and Olson which suggest dates in the 1390s – a dating earlier advanced by Parr (1945), not without controversy (Weese 1948). Particularly interesting, perhaps, is Olson's view that the Knight's Tale is concerned with matter relevant to political attitudes in England and France in the 1390s, with Theseus characterized as 'the peacemaker to the peace movement of the early and mid 1390s' (ed. Benson et al. 1987: 826b). This hypothesis is helpful but incomplete in its predominant concentration on the conclusion of the tale. An examination of the whole framework of the Knight's Tale, while retaining the notion of the incorporation of the so-called peace movement into the narrative, may suggest a wider chronology and a more complex thematic treatment. It is proposed below that the Knight's Tale is principally concerned with issues touching the condition of England between 1386 and 1396–7, but that the strategy of the tale is not that of providing a simple allegorical description which may be read as a direct analysis of events between those dates. Rather, the Knight's Tale uses the Boccaccio narrative to activate in the mind of the reader themes and incidents which are judged crucial to or indicative of developments within this decade. What the Knight's Tale provides, it is argued, is more than a 'mirror for magistrates' (Reidy 1977: 406–8), more than a demonstration of 'the consequences of internecine war' (Cowgill 1975: 675–6). It is a reflective analysis from a critical position informed by later knowledge. And its analytical thrust, focusing on issues connected with Anglo-French relations, may have precedents in other Canterbury tales (Scattergood 1981).

The opening and closing of the Knight's Tale are important in determining the chronological framework of reference. Chaucer's decision to begin his tale with the return of Theseus, whom he calls duke, has an obvious parallel in the return of John of Gaunt, Duke of Lancaster, from Spain and Portugal in November 1389. Having left in July 1386, recognized by Richard II as King of Castile, to conquer Castile and force the French king to sue for peace, Gaunt returned with considerable personal profit, though little which directly benefited England. Notably, Gaunt's daughters, Philippa and Catalina, were married to the King of Portugal and the heir of Castile respectively, but Gaunt had renounced his claims to Castile and abandoned the cause of Pope Urban VI in Aragon, Navarre and Castile, providing no foundation for an alliance with Spain. Yet Gaunt's arrival was greeted enthusiastically by the king, the nobility, and the city of London, and the chroniclers recorded his reception as marking the opening of a new political era of reconciliation and harmony. But if Gaunt's return is signalled by Chaucer as decisive in the way he chooses to tell the Knight's Tale, it is clear that Theseus' return is at a critical time and one which calls on his prowess to deliver the oppressed from bloodshed and tyranny. While he has been engaged in conquest and marriage alliance in Femenye, Creon has taken Thebes and slaughtered the leading members of its nobility. It is striking, therefore, that Gaunt's three years abroad witnessed a similar slaughter among the English aristocracy.

While Gaunt was in Spain and Portugal, Thomas of Woodstock, Duke of Gloucester, younger brother of John of Gaunt and uncle to Richard II, began a series of political moves designed to destroy the power of the king's favourites at court, and the influence of de Vere in particular, while enhancing his own position. Eager to restore English policy to the traditional ways, as he saw them, of his father, Edward III, in the return to chivalric values – he was the author of 'The Ordenance and Fourme of Fightyng within Listes' (Lester 1982) – and aggression towards France, Gloucester considered England to be desolate and divided, undergoing a crisis produced by the corrupt and evil counsellors who surrounded Richard II. With Thomas Arundel, Bishop of Ely, he sought to rescue England and the crown from that crisis. Having secured the appointment of a Great and Continual Council to take charge of affairs of state for a year, which he intended should attack the entrenched position of royal favourites in government, he had, nevertheless, underestimated the extent to which Richard would continue to support his friends, and especially de Vere, now Duke of Ireland. In November 1387, however, Gloucester, Arundel and Warwick joined to petition the crown in London and, having successfully roused the citizens of London in their support, they presented the king's intermediaries with a formal appeal against Suffolk, de Vere, Tresilian, Brembre and the Archbishop of York, five of the king's most important friends. Fearing for his safety, Richard agreed to a proposal whereby the accused might be held until 2 February 1388, when they might face the charges against them in parliament.

Richard, however, failed to ensure the custody of the accused and the favourites escaped. The king withdrew to the safety of the Tower of London but the Appellants entered the Tower with a force of 500 men and confronted Richard. Warned and threatened, the king now agreed to be governed by these lords and when the so-called Merciless Parliament gathered in February 1388 the way was open for a full-scale attack upon the favourites of the crown. The accusations and the rhetoric were reminiscent of attacks upon Edward II and his supporters. On behalf of Gloucester, Arundel, Warwick, Denby and Nottingham, articles of appeal were read out for two hours, including revelations which profoundly disturbed the assembly, reducing many, so Favent recorded, to tears. The accused failed to appear but the charges against them were eventually judged in their absence by their peers in parliament in ten days of investigation which resulted in the condemnation to execution of Brembre, Tresilian, Usk, Blake, Burley, Beauchamp, Salisbury and Berners. Provision was made for the dismissal of Bohemians from the queen's household, the nomination of the King's Council, and for a review of the courts and offices of state. And on 3 June, in Westminster Abbey, lords and commons made ceremonial renewal of their oaths of allegiance and heard Richard promise his own future good behaviour.

Such executions and such purges, however, whatever promises might be made, could only provoke the most profound social and political consequences. 'The main consequence of the crisis of 1386–8', wrote Keen, 'was the venom that it instilled into the feuds of the aristocracy. Such feuds were bound to involve not the principals only, but also the whole train of friends, relatives and retainers that constituted the "affinities" of great noblemen.' Now the full potential of the conflict at court between the 'knights of Venus and the knights of Bellona' would be realized: 'a crop of vendettas that would not be easily forgotten had been baptized in blood' (Keen 1973: 285). This was the battlefield to which Gaunt returned in 1389 and over which Richard rode out from Reading two miles to meet him and give him the kiss of peace. It was also the battlefield from which were pulled Palamon and Arcite, destined to continue the internecine struggles of the kingdom.

Between 1386 and 1396, when Richard II's marriage to Isabella, daughter of Charles VI, secured international peace and greater domestic security, the consequences of the Merciless Parliament were to be worked out against a background of disorder and widespread social and economic disruption in which Gaunt struggled to achieve recociliation and stability. This is the matter with which the Knight's Tale is centrally concerned and to which Chaucer brings an astonishingly perceptive historical analysis.

ON SEEING EMELYE: LINES 1073–1186

If we accept that Palamon and Arcite are intended to arouse contemporary comparisons with Richard II and Thomas of Gloucester then
the interpretation of this episode acquires greater complexity. If
Palamon's eventual marriage to Emelye is seen as Richard's marriage
to Isabella and the achievement of peace between England and France,
then the first sight of Emelye and the conflict which breaks out between Palamon and Arcite may symbolize a conflict between Richard
and Thomas about relations with France. Gloucester was indeed an
opponent of the policy developed by Gaunt and Richard which aimed
at peace with France. The way in which the quarrel is expressed may
derive from this public conflict between royal kinsmen about foreign
policy. We first hear Palamon and Arcite speak in this episode and two
things are immediately remarkable: that they employ the intimate
vocabulary of kinship (in Boccaccio they are merely compatriots) and
that their feelings for Emelye are such that the relationships implied
by that vocabulary are threatened. For Palamon, to break the oaths
and bonds of kinship is to be a traitor and, further, to deny the
obligations of knighthood is to act without honour. Noticeably,
Palamon implies a net balance of obligation in which Arcite's is the
greater part. As '"cosyns"' and brothers they are mutually bound, but
being of Palamon's '"conseil"' Arcite is considered to have a special
obligation, and being '"ybounden as a knyght to helpen me"'
(1147–50) he is further obligated. It may be that this balance of obligation indicates the nature of he relationship between royal kinsmen
where one of them is a king, in which case the charges of treachery
carry greater significance, especially when linked to proceedings in
1388 and 1397 and the concern with accusations and definitions of
treason in Richard's reign. For Arcite, as for those opposing royal
authority in the reigns of Edward II, Edward III and Richard II, the
issues were not so simple. What mattered fundamentally was not so
much the system of obligation and obedience implied by kinship or
political structure but more the nature of the emotion experienced and
expressed.

'...Thou woost nat yet now
Wheither she be a womman or goddesse!
Thyn is affeccioun of hoolynesse,
Any myn is love as to creature...
....
'Love is a gretter lawe, by my pan,
Than may be yeve to any erthely man ...'
(1156–9 and 1165–6)

says Arcite, taking Palamon's earlier conceit and apostrophe to Venus at face value. The oppositions between woman and goddess, creature and holiness, love and 'affections', are critical here, seeming to imply a contrast between an emotion of flesh and blood reality (and perhaps genuineness) and a feeling of spiritual unreality (and perhaps even posturing or insincerity). Taken into the world of late fourteenth-century European politics Arcite's claims are those of a sincere, practical man of action and those of Palamon the insubstantial ideas of theorist or perhaps even of a poseur. Practical, indeed, almost to the point of cynicism, Arcite goes on to argue that given their present circumstances

'...at the kynges court, my brother,
Ech man for hymself, ther is noon oother.'
(1181–2)

Such a statement may serve as comment upon the state of Richard's court and government in the late 1380s and 1390s as well as reflecting upon Gloucester's ambition. The competition for Emily may be a competition for France, but if so it has far-reaching implications, domestic as well as international. Relations with France are one aspect of an international policy in the 1390s which embraces the healing the papal schism, the defeat of the Turks and the unification of Christendom, a policy which, in the manner of its pursuit, closely influences the government of England and the way that was perceived.

THE INFLUENCE OF SATURN

The imprisonment of Palamon and Arcite, their quarrel over Emelye, and its grim consequences, fall into a pattern: they are symptoms of the rule of Saturn. A number of critics have written about the importance of Saturn's role and function within the Knight's Tale. What follows is an attempt to pool their observations and findings, to add a few further gleanings, but above all to emphasize the extensiveness of Saturn's influence.

Until the end of Book III Saturn appears to be destined for a marginal existence in the world of Chaucer's narrative. He is mentioned twice before that point is reached, once by Arcite and once by Palamon. Each is struggling to find some explanation, some cause, for the miseries being endured. Arcite attributes their imprisonment first to Fortune, then to the '"wikke aspect or disposicioun"' (1087) of Saturn. Once Arcite has been released, Palamon continues to blame Saturn for his imprisonment (1328), but he gives much more emphasis to the malevolence of Juno, traditionally hostile to the house of Thebes, and to Venus.

The influence of Saturn, then, is but one possible explanation among several for the experiences of the two heroes. At line 2438 that impression changes as Saturn is revealed as the controlling force behind many of the events of the story on the human plane, as well as being the power-broker among the gods (Aers 1980: 179–80). The intimations of Palamon and Arcite that Saturn controls their lives are now revealed as giving a truth larger than they or anyone else imagined (Burrow 1984a: 43–8). Saturn says:

'My cours, that hath so wyde for to turne,
Hath more power than woot any man.'
(2454–5)

Before examining in more detail the nature of the power which Saturn claims it is important to recognize that the forty lines devoted to his effects are an innovation on Chaucer's part, the culmination of a process whereby he strengthened the significance and power of the gods as they were represented by Boccaccio (Salter 1983: 143–7 and 168–9). Saturn has no place in the *Teseida*: there Venus and Mars patch up their quarrel without Saturn's intervention, while the Fury which later unhorses Arcita obeys a summons from Venus, not Saturn. Nor is there precedent in the *Thebaid* of Statius, Boccaccio's own model and a work to which Chaucer independently refers (Wise 1911); in that work it is Jupiter who acts as cruel arbiter (Tinkle 1987: 302). In fact, Chaucer's source for the passage in question has not been pinpointed. One possibility, *De Universitate Mundi* by Bernardus Silvestris (which Chaucer did use elsewhere) identifies the tradition of a malevolent god, but provides few of the attributes given by Chaucer to his planetary deity (D. Loomis 1968). Again, although Chaucer did use a redaction of the *Ovidius Moralizatus* for his description of Venus in the Knight's Tale, that did not supply him with material for his account of Saturn (Wilkins 1957). In all probability his sources are to be found in astrological handbooks, or encyclopedias and illuminations (Curry 1923: 220–3; Minnis 1982: 110–11 and 140–1; Tinkle 1987). Be that as it may, the effect of introducing Saturn at such a strategic point in the narrative, with the gods in disarray and the outcome of the tournament between Palamon and Arcite as yet unknown, is to give him prominence among those who, whether human or divine, pretend to rule events in Athens. What has happened until this point in the narrative, as well as what will happen, is now put firmly under Saturn's sway (Blake 1973: 12–14).

In reading Saturn's speech one has he sense of entering another level of understanding, of being given a key to the mechanisms of the tale. When he says "'Myn is the prison in the derke cote [= cell]'" (2457), he confirms what Palamon and Arcite had suspected, namely that Saturn has been directing some of his malevolence at them, who have been imprisoned for the rest of their lives, without hope of ransom. But this is only the beginning. He is represented as "'pale Saturnus the colde'" (2443) and is therefore connected also with the deathly pallor and chilling emotions of the two knights (Windeatt 1979: 144–5). Palamon, for example, on seeing Emelye, is "'pale and deedly'" (1082), is then seized by a jealousy which consumes him to 'asshen dede and colde' (1302), and later by an anger likened to feeling through his heart 'a coold swerd sodeynliche glyde' (1575), an anger which turns his face 'deed and pale' (1578). Not to be outdone, Arcite in his love-sickness turns 'pale as asshen colde' (1364) which is ironic in view of his end, 'coold of deeth' (2800) on the funeral pyre, where he is 'brent to asshen colde' (2957). Saturn also claims responsibility for '"pryvee empoysonyng"' (2460), which recalls both the 'nercotikes and opie of Thebes fyn' (1472) with which Palamon drugs his gaoler to effect an escape, and the idea that Emelye is the cause of the 'venomous infection which causes Arcite's death' (Hallissy 1981: 33):

> 'Ye sleen me with youre eyen, Emelye!
> Ye been the cause wherfore I dye.'
> (1567–8)

Again, Saturn states that his province is the destruction of buildings and cities

> ... 'the ruyne of the hye halles,
> The fallynge of the toures and of the walles
> Upon the mynour or the carpenter.'
> (2463–5)

An early episode of the Knight's Tale recounts the sacking of Thebes by Theseus, who 'rente adoun bothe wall and sparre and rafter' (990). The ruined city of Thebes, whose '"waste walles wyde"' are recalled by Palamon (1331), is an image of desolation which haunts the narrative. It adds further to the conviction that Saturn is active from the beginning and throughout the tale.

Other effects of Saturn's rule have a more indirect bearing on the content of the Knight's Tale. Drowning at sea, strangling and hanging by the throat are his domain and, although these have no direct counterparts within the narrative, violent deaths of the sort described here recall those earlier attributed to Mars, indicating that beyond the influence of Mars lies that of Saturn. Saturn is also responsible for social discontent and discorder, '"The murmure and the cherles

rebellyng"' (2459), which cannot be paralleled in the tale except, perhaps, through the disorder brought about by the tyranny of Creon and
the quarrel of Palamon and Arcite, although these concern aristocratic, rather than plebeian, disturbance. Certainly the term 'cherles
rebellyng' would have established a link in the minds of Chaucer's
contemporaries between the social upheavals described in the story
and those with which they were more closely acquainted, such as the
peasants' uprising of 1381, even if no direct reference to a specific
event is intended (Parr 1954). Again it is not easy to see how 'derke
tresons, and the castes [=plots] olde' (2468), also Saturn's responsibility, fit the Knight's Tale, unless it be through Arcite's behaviour,
first in breaking his pact of mutual support with Palamon, for which
the latter twice accuses him of being a traitor (1130 and, at 1580, 'false
traytour wikke'), and, second, in the rather more technical matter of
Arcite's returning to Athens unlawfully once he has agreed as a condition of his release not to set foot there again.

What may help to explain the presence of details concerning
Saturn's effects which have a somewhat tenuous connection with the
narrative is the nature of Chaucer's source material at this point. As in
the case of the images which decorate the oratories of Mars, Venus
and Diana, he appears to be drawing on a tradition whereby, in both
literature and art, each planet was represented, together with an array
of human beings (the so-called 'children' of the planet), ordering
activities over which that deity had particular control. Chauncey
Wood (1970: 70–1), P. M. Kean (1972: 25–35) and, more recently,
V.A. Kolve (1984: 123–9) are among those critics who have drawn
attention to the importance of the 'children of the planet' tradition in
Chaucer's devising of Saturn and his effects. Attention to that tradition is indeed worthwhile because, as well as confirming some of the
details in Chaucer's portrait of Saturn, it also suggests other motifs
whose use by Chaucer has been hitherto unnoticed.

Pictorial images of Saturn and his children are by their nature
summaries of the more extended treatments of Saturn's power found
in written sources. The prisoner, either behind bars or in stocks, is
commonly shown as one over whom Saturn has dominion. Images of
mutilation (cripples, butchering) and of violent death (knifing, 'hanging by the throte') are much in line with what Chaucer also attributes

to Saturn (Plates 1, 2 and 4–7). Two other features of the 'children of Saturn' pictures are also remarkable for what they suggest about the influence of this tradition not just on Chaucer's set piece on Saturn but also on other areas of the Knight's Tale. Saturn's children are canny with money, and are shown carefully counting it (Plate 6). They also engage in arduous manual labour, such as ploughing, threshing, carrying water and cutting wood (Plates 2, 4 and 5–7). Both characteristics are found in Arcite, once he has returned in disguise to the court of Palamon. There, in order to be ever close to Emelye, he must suffer social degradation. He 'chaunged his array, / And cladde hym as a povre laborer' (1408–9). Arriving at Athens he offers menial service at court, 'To drugge and drawe' (1416), and is fortunate enough to find employment with a chamberlain dwelling with Emelye. He is made 'Page of the chambre of Emelye the brighte' (1427), an exceedingly lowly position, as has been emphasized (Green 1981), roughly on a level with kitchen-boy. There, he is engaged to 'hewen wode, and water bere' (1422). His experiences are explicable in terms of romance conventions (Green 1980: 39–42), but they also square with traditional Saturnine activities. Bearing water is, of course, a labour associated with Saturn since the zodiac sign of Aquarius is within his domain. A man bearing water, to indicate the zodiacal water bearer, is found in the manuscript illuminations (e.g. Frontispiece). Advancing after a year or two to being a squire in the service of Theseus, Arcite is given gold to maintain his new station in life. This he carefully and secretly supplements, like a true child of Saturn, with money of his own:

> ...*men broghte hym out of his contree,*
> *From yeer to yeer ful pryvely his rente;*
> *But honestly and slyly he it spente,*
> *That no man wondred how that he it hadde.*
> *(1442–5)*

In a written account of Saturn and his 'children', as found in John Trevisa's Middle English translation of the encyclopedia by

Bartholomaeus Anglicus, *De Proprietatibus Rerum* (ed. Seymour et al. 1975), there is corroboration of the pictorial detail, as well as further information with a bearing on the Knight's Tale. Trevisa writes 'Saturnus disposiþ to be erþe-teliers and bereres of hevy burþons' (VIII.13), that he is 'pale in colour oþir wan as leed' (VIII.12) and has 'tweye dedliche qualitees, cooldness and drynes' (VIII.12). Under the lordship of Saturn are Capricorn and Aquarius. Trevisa also says that under him 'is conteyned ... buldinge', which may suggest that Saturn is influential as much in the construction of buildings as in their destruction (Plate 8), in which case certain activities of Theseus who, like John of Gaunt, had an enthusiasm for building projects, being 'interested in nothing less than the best' (Sherborne 1983: 10), need to be brought into the orbit of Saturn's control. Saturn's colour, says Trevisa, is black: the funeral arrangements for Arcite, when the processional route, both street and buildings, 'sprad was al with blak' (2903), indicate the triumph of Saturn as well as the grief of the mourners. Similarly, Palamon may be seen in the same double light (Brooks and Fowler 1970: 138–9). He appears at the funeral unkempt, with 'flotery berd and ruggy, asshy heeres, / In clothes blake, ydropped al with teeres' (2883–4).

Ptolemy's *Tetrabiblos* (before AD 178), translated into Latin by 1138 (ed. and trans. Robbins 1956), lies behind much of what Bartholomaeus says concerning Saturn, and indeed behind what many other medieval writers stated (Braswell 1984: 339; North 1988: 410). Ptolemy is quite specific in making children of Saturn 'those who bury men, mourners, pipers at funerals ... who resort to wherever there are mysteries, laments, and bloody riots' (IV.4). Gold vessels full of blood are among those which the mourners at Arcite's funeral hurl into the blazing pyre (2907–8 and 2949–50). To Saturn, especially in association with Mars, Ptolemy also attributes 'intentional quarrels and schemings' (IV.7), so that the dispute over Emily, one which Arcite, a devotee of Mars, deliberately propagates, may also be seen as a symptom of Saturn's rule. The beginning of the love-story, no less than its end, is coloured by Saturn's influence.

An unpublished Middle English text (BL Sloane 1315) on the seven planets, which appears also to derive from the *Tetrabiblos*, provides a vignette of a person affected by Saturn which is quite close to

Chaucer's portrait of the sorrowing, dishevelled Palamon. The anonymous author writes that Saturn 'makethe men blacke fowle and slotty and slowe ... and hevy and sory of harte and of chere' (f.36). The particular intention of this astrological treatise is to identify characteristics which are likely to be found in those born under each of the seven planets. It is therefore particularly useful in providing a context for Arcite's remark in the first part of the tale when he and Palamon are attempting to account for their woes:

> 'Some wikke aspect or disposicioun
> Of Saturne, by som constellacioun,
> Hath yeven us this, although we hadde it sworn;
> So stood the hevene whan that we were born.'
>
> (1087–90)

There may be some truth in what Arcite says (Curry 1923: 214–15), which he later reinforces with the remarks: '"Allas ... that day that I was bore"' (1542), and '"shapen was my deeth erst than my sherte"' (1566). The author of the 'Seven Planets' writes of 'he þat ys bore under Saturnus he ys ... traytor' (as Palamon accuses Arcite of being), is 'envyse ... and covetyse of oþer mennys goodis' (as Palamon and Arcite are of each other once Emelye is sighted), 'whyll ly by hym selve alone to þyncke and to ymagen evell' (as Palamon does in prison and Arcite in exile, though neither with evil intention), and will 'be gyle oþer men', as Arcite does in returning to Athens in disguise where, as Palamon says, he '"byjaped ... duc Theseus, / And falsy chaunged [his] name"' (1585–6).

So Saturn controls certain activities and events, and those involved become his 'children'; and he affects the lives of those born under his influence. He, like the other planets, also governs personal appearance. The notable example in the Knight's Tale is Lygurgus, the champion of Palamon's cause. Here again Chaucer undertook a significant revision of this source material in the Teseida. There Boccaccio devotes his entire sixth book to a catalogue of valiant men invited to Athens by Theseus, from whom the two rivals choose their supporters. Lygurgus is one among many. Chaucer condenses, and epitomizes in twenty-seven lines, Palamon's one hundred followers in the person of this hero who is, as was recognized many years ago, the 'very form and fashion' of the Saturnalian man (Curry 1923: 225–9). From Greek and Arab sources, translated into Latin in the twelfth century, Curry demonstrated that the black beard of Lygurgus and his long hair black, 'As any ravenes fethere' (2144), the circles of his eyes, which 'gloweden bitwixen yelow and reed' (2132), his bushy overhanging eyebrows, described as 'kempe heeris on his browes stoute' (2134), and his strong stature and broad shoulders (2136), were all hallmarks of a man favoured by Saturn.

Some reservations about Curry's findings have been expressed (Tinkle 1987: 305–6), but they were confirmed by Books and Fowler (1970), who added further details. For example, Lygurgus' chariot is pulled by bulls (2139), the same animals which, in order to suggest the slowness of his orbit, traditionally pull the chariot of Saturn. And the chariot of Lygurgus, his dogs' muzzles, the wreath he wears on his head, the nails of his bearskin, are all made of gold, that metal which because of its heaviness was sometimes associated with Saturn. Thus Arcite faces a formidable adversary, and his worst fears about the mal-evolence of Saturn appear to be coming true.

Nor does Saturn's antagonism towards Arcite stop there (Salter 1983: 168–9); it reaches such a pitch that he has been identified as a tragic hero (Schmidt 1969: 112–16). Although Arcite goes on to defeat Palamon, Lygurgus and company, the tournament takes place at a time when Saturn's influence is paramount (Schweitzer 1981: 16–20). In the moment of victory, gazing at Emelye, Saturn strikes through the agency of a Fury sent at his request by Pluto. As earlier noted, Chaucer here again revises Boccaccio, who makes Venus the instigator of Arcite's downfall. The Fury causes Arcite's horse to shy for fear, leap aside, and founder, so throwing the rider forward on to his pommel, and causing a fatal heart wound (Donaldson 1983), appropriately enough for a heart-struck chivalric lover: 'His brest tobrosten with his sadel-bowe' (2691). He lies inert and, as if to emphasize the cause of the mishap, 'As blak ... as any cole or crowe' (2692). The colour and pageantry of the tournament scene is suddenly blighted by this ignominious fall of proud Arcite, but the celebrations go on unabated, with Theseus showing great hospitality towards both sides of the tournament. It is thought that Arcite's wound is *not* fatal (2705), and attempts are made to apply salves, charms and herbal remedies (2712).

But the patient does not respond to treatment. He is dying: 'Swelleth the brest of Arcite, and the soore / Encreeseth at his herte moore and moore' (2743–4). Chaucer spares few details in describing the horrendous and disgusting last moments of his hero. There is nothing of this in the *Teseida* (Boitani 1977: 139–41). Clotted blood is festering in his stomach, and neither blood-letting, nor cupping, nor herbal drink, is to any avail. Arcite's body has lost its natural ability to expel unwanted matter, here described as poison, 'venym', which he can neither 'voyden ne expelle' (2751). In this state the pipes of his lungs begin to swell and every muscle from his breast downwards is wasted, 'shent with venym and corrupcioun' (2754). He can neither vomit nor defecate because he has lost the ability to do either:

> *Hym gayneth neither, for to gete his lif,*
> *Vomyt upward, ne dounward laxatif.*
> *Al is tobrosten thilke regioun …*
> *(2755–7)*

There is no hope now for his cure: 'Nature hath now no dominacioun' (2758).

The power which does have domination is that of Saturn. Once again, it was Curry (1923: 236–8) who first indicated the crucial if invisible role played by Saturn during Arcite's last moments. Arcite's malady concerns the body's retention of substances which should have been voided. As is well known, medieval medical practitioners took a close interest in the effect of the stars on their patients' condition. Curry demonstrated that 'all astrologers interested in medicine affirm that the *retentive virtue belongs to and is ruled over by Saturn*'(his emphasis, p. 147), which is in any case but a more refined version of a claim Saturn makes for himself, one amply borne out by contemporary views of the cause of plague (Thorndike 1934: I.227, 244–5, 336–7 and 365; Biraben 1976: II. 9–10; Friedman 1985; Friedman 1986: 382), at the end of the third section of the Knight's Tale: '"myne be the maladyes colde ... / My lookyng is the fader of pestilence"' (2467 and 2469). Later scholars, notably Ciavolella (1979), Hallissy (1981), and Infusino and O'Neill (1985) have themselves refined Curry's claim, with which they have found no quarrel.

It is now possible to see within the Knight's Tale four types of evidence which may be taken as symptomatic of Saturn's influence: the nature of Arcite's death, the appearance of Lygurgus, Arcite's comments on the effect of Saturn at the birth of himself and Palamon, and Saturn's speech about his 'children'. It is clear that Saturn's influence spreads to all reaches of the narrative, and to all participants, and cannot be as easily discounted as some critics suggest (Gaylord 1973). It is also apparent that, increasingly as the tale progresses, Arcite, not Palamon (Holtz 1977), is singled out as Saturn's victim. Why should this be so? It is because, long before his gruesome death, Arcite succumbs to a disease which is Saturn's particular province, that of melancholy, which had attracted Chaucer's attention on another occasion (Heffernan 1986) and which is indicated in some pictures by Saturn's dark, brooding appearance (Frontispiece). Arcite's melancholy is, then, the fifth type of evidence which manifests Saturn's influence within the Knight's Tale. In many ways it is the most important, partly because of its extensiveness, partly because of its interrelations with the other types of evidence.

The classic account of Saturn's association with melancholy is that by Klibansky, Panofsky and Saxl (1964). What follows is a paraphrase of some of their remarks concerning the causes and symptoms of the malady, which may now be supplemented with a more recent study (Jackson 1986: 46–64). The bodily humour generating a melancholic disposition was known as black bile. This substance, together with the other humours, was thought to exist to a greater or lesser degree within all human beings. When black bile predominated, then a person's constitution was called melancholic. Such a temperament, like the others (choleric, sanguine, phlegmatic) was predisposed to certain illnesses. Thus melancholy could be either constitutional or pathological. As an illness, melancholy was one 'mainly characterised by symptoms of mental change, ranging from fear, misanthropy and depression to madness in its most frightful forms' and anxiety (Klibansky et al. 1964: 14–15). It also brought about bodily changes, including emaciation (p. 35). Black bile was therefore accepted as the source of insanity, and (since the great figures of classical legend showed traits of madness) melancholy was from an early period known as a disease or disposition of heroes.

Black bile was considered a volatile substance, responding quickly to heat and cold, and producing in the melancholic person either ecstasy or torpor. Thus the melancholic temperament was itself variable, unpredictable, and could manifest itself in swings between sudden fits of anger or desire, and violent terrors; or between over-confidence and irrational despondency. The melancholic by nature was also particularly susceptible to visual images, memory producing in him strong and compelling pictures. This sensitive, imaginative faculty was prone to produce hallucinations and prophetic dreams. The normal individual, possessing a reasonable balance among the humours, was liable to melancholic disorders, but they had no lasting effect. The constitutional melancholic, on the other hand, was likely to be permanently and qualitatively altered if he contracted a melancholic disease such as epilepsy, paralysis, depression or phobias.

Both Palamon and Arcite are affected by melancholy, as they are affected in other ways by Saturn's influence. Palamon's reaction to the sight of Emelye, whom his suggestible imagination makes into Venus herself, his angry retort to Arcite when the latter also falls in love at first sight, and his despondency and suffering in prison, where 'wood out of his wit he goth for wo' (1456), is sufficient indication that he is undergoing a melancholic disorder. Similar symptoms may be observed in the case of Arcite, but there are also in his case others, which point to a basic difference in complexion between the two cousins, namely that whereas Palamon's melancholy has no lasting effect, in Arcite the disease brings about a fundamental change in his constitution. To couch their difference in the terms used by Klibansky et al., one would say that Palamon is normal but is temporarily suffering Saturn's disease, whereas Arcite is a congenital melancholic.

So much is clear as a result of what happens when Arcite returns to Thebes. Having been heated up by what he later calls the '"firy dart"' of love (1564), Arcite is now banished, as Saturn was (Tinkle 1987: 296), and plunges into the chilly depths of a serious disease, one that makes him 'lene … and drye as is a shaft … His hewe falow and pale as asshen colde' (1362–4). He cannot eat, sleep or drink, his eyes turn hollow 'and grisly to biholde' (1363). He is unduly sensitive to music, which triggers sorrowful recollections: 'And if he herde song or instrument, / Thanne wolde he wepe, he myghte nat be stent' (1367–8). His 'spiritz' are so feeble, low and 'chaunged' that his speech, voice and appearance have become unrecognizable (1369–71). Later gazing into a mirror, Arcite sees the transformation for himself: he

> ...saugh that chaunged was al his colour,
> And saugh his visage, al in another kynde.
> ....
> ...his face was so disfigured
> Of maladye the whiche he hadde endured ...
> (1400–1404)

As Chaucer elsewhere puts it, Arcite has undergone a physical inversion (one that is soon to be matched by social inversion):

> ...turned was al up so doun
> Bothe habit and eek disposicioun
> Of hym, this woful lovere daun Arcite.
> (1377–9)

What has caused the utter alteration in Arcite's physical and psychological state? Not only 'the loveris maladye / Of Hereos', an erotic species of melancholy (Lowes 1914), but also the 'manye [= mania or madness], / Engendered of humour malencolik' (1373–6) operating in the faculty by means of which objective reality is apprehended, his 'celle fantastik' (Neaman 1975: 22–4; Schweitzer 1981: 21–3). And it is a dream, of course, which prompts Arcite's return to Athens. He thinks he sees Mercury standing before him and bidding him cheer up. He is told to go back to the city of Emelye and Theseus, '"Ther is thee shapen of thy wo an ende"' (1392) – an ambiguous promise if ever there was one. Long before his grisly death, Saturn has taken control of Arcite's life.

THE SPEECH OF SATURN: LINES 2453–2469

When Saturn intervenes to settle the struggle between Venus and Mars, and thereby to settle the issue between Palamon and Arcite, deciding and anticipating the direction of the narrative, the implied astrological determinism corresponds with contemporary scientific thought regarding Saturn's influence as well as recalling the passage in *Troilus* (*TC* III.625) where the unusual conjunction between Saturn and Jupiter is referred to. Chaucer's contemporaries were, indeed, in no doubt about the influence of Saturn (e.g. Langland, Walsingham). Saturn's speech, therefore, takes on a significance which at once goes beyond the narrative of the fiction and transforms it. The characteristic influence which Saturn describes as in his power is especially well known to Chaucer's audience and the description invites that audience to discover contemporary correspondences, to further invest the fiction with their own experience and to discover in it a greater metaphorical, allegorical and satirical depth.

Certain correspondences are immediately apparent. As already noted, '"The murmure and the cherles rebellyng"' (2459) brings to mind the rising of 1381 and the reference to '"pestilence"' (2469) suggests the Black Death of 1348–9. Such simple correspondences are no doubt intended, or were unavoidable, but just as pestilence had become endemic within late fourteenth-century English society so peasant rebellion had become a pervasive social contagion. Saturn's speech has the potential to activate the general and the particular. And given the overarching structure of the narrative and its chronological and thematic context in the period between 1386 and 1396–7 the reference to pestilence may well have special application to the early 1390s when heavy rainfall and pestilence combined to such effect that they aroused general comment and were possibly commemorated further in Chaucer's 'Scogan'. 'The cherles rebellyng' may also have had an immediate context in the so-called Cheshire Rising of 1393, especially since many of the issues raised by the rebels were directly relevant to the central political struggles of the years between 1386 and 1397 and, therefore, arguably, to the conflict between Palamon and Arcite. Thomas Walsingham reported that the manifesto of the rebels, which was pinned to church doors, attacked the alleged intention to surrender the king's title to the throne of France and abolish the ancient liberties of Cheshire. Furthermore, the rebel leaders announced their intention to kill the Earl of Denby, the Duke of Lancaster, the Duke of Gloucester, and other kinsmen of the king whom they saw as responsible for disastrous foreign policies. However complex the issues at the root of the unrest, and however confused the analysis indicated in the manifesto, the rising did identify the critical conflict over Richard II's overtures of peace towards France – overtures which, it seems probable, were strongly opposed by the Duke of Gloucester and the Earl of Arundel. Though it seems unlikely, Arundel was widely believed to have encouraged the rising and in the Hilary Parliament of 1394 Gaunt angrily accused him of complicity, only to be attacked in return for his own self-seeking policies and his over-familiarity with Richard. Whatever the truth of the matter, Saturn's reference to rebellion had contemporary implications which went to the heart of a narrative transformed by its increasingly obvious correspondences with the experiences of its audience.

If references to pestilence and rebellion provide particular as well as general indications of a specific context for the Knight's Tale, then Saturn's other claims arouse in the audience further expectations of contemporary parallels. It would not have been difficult to find a general context for remarks about strangling, hanging, poisoning and imprisonment and Richard II's reign. What becomes an interesting possibility, however, if a date of final composition of c.1398 is acceptable for the Knight's Tale, is that Saturn's remarks contain suggestions of the rumours which surrounded the death of the Duke of Gloucester in 1397. A prisoner in Calais castle, it seems he was strangled, murdered by Richard's instruction. If Saturn's speech does make reference to this then not only does it have important consequences for the consideration of the composition of Chaucer's narrative; it also acts as a device in the narrative which enables the audience to anticipate the course of the story and to become acutely aware of its direction, swiftly and relentlessly aimed at the heart of their immediate concerns. They know, indeed, the story of their own lives as Chaucer depicts them before they know the course of the novel narrative which he is using.

Notably, however, Chaucer's depiction challenges the orthodox analysis. If the struggle for peace and good government is the way in which Theseus/Gaunt might represent these years, Chaucer's view is much more bleak. Theseus' final speech must seem platitudinous rhetoric to an audience already alive to the force of Saturn in their own lives, which have extended beyond the illusion of peaceful marriage at the close of the tale. Venus can only succeed, at this time, in defeating Mars, Palamon can only win Emelye and defeat Arcite, Richard can only defeat Gloucester, by enlisting the help not of her father, but of Saturn, and this is a bitter commentary on the state of the kingdom.

As always, the relationship between Chaucer and his patron Gaunt becomes a critical matter in the Knight's Tale. Chaucer, not for the first time, appears to attack what he regards as the dangerous delusions of Gaunt's policies. In this connection it is tempting to link the reference to Sampson (2466) in Saturn's speech with the previously discussed references in the Pardoner's Tale (PardT 554–5 and 572), where a warning is issued not to become drunk with power achieved in foreign lands. Perhaps Saturn's remarks serve as a chastening reminder of a previous defeat when Gaunt's ambitions overreached him.

THE JUSTICE OF JUPITER

The preceding account of Saturn's activities within the Knight's Tale may have given the impression that he is exclusively an arbitrary and disruptive force, causing misery among the undeserving and confounding the best of human intentions. That would be to confuse his effects with the principles on which he operates. In fact the speech in which he lays claim to murder, devastation and disease is carefully framed with statements concerning his more beneficent qualities. Traditionally associated with wisdom (Tinkle 1987: 300–1), he is in practice a peacemaker between Mars and Venus, and the only god with sufficient power to quell their disagreement.

Saturn is effective as an arbitrator both because of his power and because of his experience. Chaucer lays considerable stress on the

wisdom and skill that come with age. Jupiter is unable to remedy the
heavenly 'strif' (2438)

> *Til that the pale Saturnus the colde,*
> *That knew so manye of aventures olde,*
> *Foond in his olde experience an art*
> *That he ful soone hath plesed every part.*
> *As sooth is seyd, elde hath greet avantage;*
> *In elde is bothe wysdom and usage;*
> *Men may the olde atrenne and noght atrede.*
> *(2443–9)*

To some extent, Saturn is acting out of character, for 'to stynten strif
and drede ... is agayn his kynde' (2450–1), but nevertheness he finds a
'remedie' (2452) for the strife such that Palamon will have his lady and
Mars will be able to help Arcite. The result will be a temporary (and
exceptional) lull in the perennial hostilities of Mars and Venus:

> *'Betwixe yow ther moot be som tyme pees,*
> *Al be ye noght of a compleccioun,*
> *That causeth al day swich divisioun.'*
> *(2474–6)*

To be the recipient of Saturn's justice may entail human suffering,
but it is justice nevertheless. The perception of Saturn in a judicial role
is a privileged one, available to the gods and to the audience of the
Knight's Tale, but not to the protagonists. As earlier indicated,
Palamon and Arcite have some inkling that Saturn is controlling their
lives, but at best they see only his baleful effects, not the judicial
principles according to which he operates. Even less does any participant in the tale perceive the extensiveness of Saturn's power and in
particular his systematic influence over Arcite's experiences. What is
more, Saturn's representative, Egeus, the 'olde fader' of Theseus
(2838), is unable to offer an explanatory perspective on Arcite's death

(Aers 1980: 186–7). His mind-numbing 'wisdom' is based on the life-long observation of change.

> ... *this worldes transmutacioun,*
> *As he hadde seyn it chaunge both up and down,*
> *Jo after wo, and wo after gladness ...*
> *(1839–41)*

The 'up and down' process here described is the movement of Fortune's wheel: that is as far as Egeus can see. Consequently the consolation he offers Theseus, if such it can be called, is bleak in its banality. Just as no man died who did not at some time live, so no man ever lived who did not at some time die (2843–6). He concludes with a platitude which, shorn of its Christian context as it is within Athenian society, seems forlorn in its view both of life and of death:

> *This world nys but a thurghfare ful of wo,*
> *And we been pilgrymes, passynge to and fro.*
> *Deeth is an ende of every worldly soore.*
> *(2847–9)*

At best, Egeus provides a Saturnine account of human experience which, while true to the blacker features of the god's rule, does not allow for the idea of there being a pattern of justice in what Saturn does.

The audience's awareness of the extent of Saturn's influence within the tale, and of the justice according to which he operates, create an impression of distance between the protagonists and what, did they but know it, is patterning their lives. From the gap between knowing audience and blind participants proceed many bitter ironies, and not least a sense of the inadequacy of alternative explanations for what befalls Arcite. In particular the double ending of the tale accentuates the disparity between a comprehensive Saturnine explanation and the limited explanation of Theseus, who sees justice as being in the control of Jupiter.

A number of factors contribute to the feeling that the final speech of Theseus is makeshift, covering over issues rather than facing them, 'a statement which will attempt to transcend difficulties, rather than to analyse and solve them' (Salter 1983: 169), that it is a speech rooted not in the contention and suffering which the tale has exposed, but in a preconceived ideal of harmonious peace (Spearing 1966: 75–8; Burlin 1977: 105–6). There is, first, the sudden prominence given to Jupiter, now introduced as '"The Firste Moevere of the cause above"' (2987). Yet, as earlier noticed, Jupiter was impotent when it came to quelling the strife between Mars and Venus (2442). Later, the dying Arcite mentions the god – '"And Juppiter so wys my soule gye"' (2786) – but not in any way which suggests that his power is to be seen as re-placing that of Saturn, the causer of Arcite's death (Boitani 1977: 152).

Second, there is a disjunction of mood between the 'first ending' of the tale at Arcite's funeral and the 'second ending' at the marriage of Palamon and Emelye. With the death of Arcite, Chaucer hits a note of chilling, piteous despair (McCall 1979: 78–9). He has won Emelye according to the rules of the tournament, according to the best form of chivalric justice that Theseus can devise, and yet he has suffered a fatal accident (caused by Saturn, unknown to the Athenians). Confronted by the inexplicability of his death, grief is extreme:

> Shrighte Emelye, and howleth Palamon,
> And Theseus his suster took anon
> Swownynge, and baar hire fro the corps away.
> *(2817–19)*

The entire city is in mourning:

> Infinite been the sorwers and the teeres
> Of olde folk and folk of tendre yeeres
> In al the toun for deeth of this Theban.
> For hym ther wepeth bothe child and man ...
> ....

> ... *Allas, the pitee that was ther,*
> *Cracchynge of chekes, rentynge eek of heer.*
> *(2827–30 and 2833–4)*

The sorrowing women express their sense of fate's inscrutability: ' "Why woldestow be deed ... | And haddest gold ynough, and Emelye?" ' (2835–6). Egeus' consolation, which follows, only sounds the more empty by the side of such passionate, deeply felt outbursts. True, the communal grief is to some extent sluiced through the funeral ceremonies and formal processions, but even here there is a sense of unanswered, unmollified emotion. In preparation for the ceremonies the

> ... *grove, swoote and grene,*
> *Ther as he hadde his amorouse desires,*
> *His compleynte, and for his love his hoote fires ...*
> *(2860–1)*

is now to become the source of another fire – that of Arcite's pyre. Theseus commands the grove's destruction, 'to hakke and hewe | The okes olde' (2865–6) as if in frustrated revenge for events which have escaped his control. Felling the grove is an act of desecration, a gesture of defiance against those powers which have thwarted Arcite's enjoyment of his just reward:

> ... *the goddes ronnen up and doun,*
> *Disherited of hire habitacioun,*
> *In which they woneden in reste and pees ...*
> *(2925–7)*

The lasting impression is of bewilderment, bitterness and anger. The funeral is a ceremonial articulation of these feelings rather than a salve. Yet when Theseus delivers his speech the perspective is entirely different, the mood optimistic, or so he would have his listeners believe. It seems consolatory, but is actually un-Boethian in its final effects (Schweitzer 1981: 40–5). Arcite's death, he claims, is a matter for rejoicing, for he died at the very pitch of honour, in his prime, and at the height of his renown. Better this abiding fame than the ignominy of old age:

> *'And certeinly a man hath moost honour*
> *To dyen in his excellence and flour,*
> *Whan he is siker of his goode name;*
> *Thanne hath he doon his friend, ne hym, no shame.*
> *And gladder oghte his freend been of his deeth,*
> *Whan with honour up yolden is his breeth,*
> *Than whan his name appalled is for age,*
> *For al forgeten is his vassellage.*
> *Thanne is it best, as for a worthy fame,*
> *To dyen whan that he is best of name.'*
>
> *(3047–56)*

It does not take much imagination to remember the gruesome actuality of Arcite's death, so unlike its glorification here, with the 'clothered blood' (2745) and 'venym and corrupcioun' (2754). One is left trying to reconcile the two versions of Arcite's death and the opposite feelings which they each evoke. As a consequence, it is difficult not to believe that Theseus' account is a fabrication, an attempt to mythologize the dead knight. It is significant that in doing so he uses terms central to the idea of chivalry: 'honour', contrasted with 'shame'; and 'goode name', 'worthy fame' and 'best of name'. So what is put in question is not merely Theseus' version of Arcite's death, but the very ethic according to which Arcite, Theseus, and indeed the narrator, operate. It is also clear from the terms used that chivalry is founded on public values: it is the perception of a knight by others that bestows on him the heroic qualities of honour and reputation. Here then is another limitation of the ethic and of Theseus' point of view: they exclude those private experiences and emotions with which much of the tale has been concerned and which characterize the reader's own response to the narrative.

It may be objected that the retrospective account of Arcite's death is persuasive precisely because it is taking place after the event, at a distance of some years, when passions have cooled and when the wise counsels of Theseus can prevail:

> By processe and by lengthe of certeyn yeres,
> Al stynted is the moornynge and the teres
> Of Grekes, by oon general assent.
> *(2967–9)*

Time may have had a placating effect, but it has not answered the fundamental issue of by what scheme of justice Arcite should have been allowed to die at the moment of victory. The Athenian women's anguished cry continues to be heard:

> 'Why woldestow be deed,' thise wommen crye,
> 'And haddest gold ynough, and Emelye?'
> *(2835–6)*

Nor is the persuasiveness of Theseus' case actually helped by the passage of time: what he says seems disjointed from the story proper, said in a manner half-forgetful of the misery endured, not stemming organically from the body of the tale. Such discontinuities have a curious effect on the audience or reader, who is not returning to the text after an absence of several years, and who recalls all too vividly the contention, violence, jealousy, suffering and prison-like atmosphere of the tale proper. The ideology of Theseus, based as it is on faith in the ultimate benevolence of ruling powers and on the virtue of resignation towards what those powers intend, seems an inadequate and deficient attempt to explain the complexities of what has happened, most of all because a satisfactory, and comprehensive, if nevertheless worrying, explanation has already been provided: Athenian society is, or was, in the grip of Saturn's power. As a reminder of that, Palamon appears, when summoned, 'in his blake clothes sorwefully' (2978). He, at least, has not forgotten past woe.

The ideology of Theseus is an instrument of political control (Neuse 1962: 305–6). For a ruler to persuade his populace that the justice of the universe is in the hands of a benevolent (if inscrutable) power who requires resignation in the face of apparently arbitrary and unjust events, is to ensure personal and political power, and social stability and acquiesence – these as long as the earthly ruler is perceived by his subjects as being in an elevated part of the hierarchy which has the benevolent deity at its apogee. That Theseus is using the speech, and the way in which he delivers it, in a politically calculated way, is clear from the way in which it is framed. The presentation of the speech, and its after-effects, add further to the conviction that what Theseus says is an expedient and cannot be taken as absolute truth (Aers 1980: 187–95). Thus the occasion for the speech is the need for an alliance with Thebes such that the submission of the city will be assured:

> ...ther was a parlement
> At Atthenes, upon certain pointz and caas;
> Among the whiche pointz yspoken was,
> To have with certain contrees alliaunce,
> And have fully of Thebans obseisaunce.
> *(2970–4)*

Before beginning his speech, the duke makes sure that his words will have the right effect. His rhetorical manipulations include the strategic deployment of silence, glance, facial expression and sighing:

> When they were set, and hust was al the place,
> And Theseus abiden hadde a space
> Er any word cam fram his wise brest,
> His eyen sette to ther as was his lest.
> And with a sad visage to siked stille,
> And after that right this he sayde his wille ...
> *(2981–6)*

What follows might therefore be read at one level as a skilfully contrived act of political persuasion, designed to secure certain diplomatic objectives. In this it is successful. It culminates in a brilliantly stage-managed public betrothal of Palamon and Emelye, one in which future man and wife are mute, if acquiescent, and in which Theseus is compère-cum-master-of-ceremonies, wielding a power and enacting a policy which derive from parliamentary debate. Palamon and Emelye are to be married and '"this is my fulle assent, / With al th'avys heere of my parlement"' (3075–6). There is no time and no opportunity for refusal. Theseus goes on to characterize the match in utterly conventional terms, ones which ignore the extent to which the pursuit of Emelye has, in the past, brought misery and death. Thus Palamon '"serveth you with wille, herte, and myght"' (3078) and Emelye is enjoined '"That ye shul of youre grace upon hym rewe ... / Lat se now of youre wommanly pitee"' (3080 and 3083). Social status is not left out as an important consideration: '"He is a kynges brother sone, pardee"' (3084), although such is the ideal nature of the romance fiction that Theseus is weaving that he is sure Emelye would consider Palamon, in view of the length and adversity of his service, even though he were a '"povre bachelor"' (3085), '"For gentil mercy oghte to passen right"' (3089). Having taken Emelye's hand (3082) he now joins it with Palamon's in an act of public and irreversible bond-making. It is an alliance at once matrimonial and political, a matter of public policy with profound consequences for the future personal lives of Palamon and Emelye:

> Bitwixen hem was maad anon the bond
> That highte matrimoigne or mariage,
> By al the conseil and the baronage.
> (3093–5)

Although the culmination of the story is seen as a happy outcome for Palamon's long desire for Emelye – 'God ... / Sende hym his love that hath it deere aboghte' (3099–100) – it is ironic that he should finally win Emelye's love (3103) not through his own efforts but because, from a political point of view, it has become convenient that he should do so.

The persuasiveness of Theseus' speech is also undermined by weaknesses and contradictions in the logic of the argument. He maintains, for example, that the First Mover or '"Prince"' (2994) has established for human beings certain durations of time '"Over the whiche day they may not pace, / Al mowe they yet tho dayes wel abregge"' (2998–9). This is to have one's cake and eat it. How would anyone know, on the point of death, if they had run their allotted time, or curtailed it? The process of annihilation which Theseus describes and the actual ignorance of when a lifetime is at its limit is taken as '"preeved by experience"' (3001), an '"ordre"' indicating that the '"Moevere stable is and eterne"' (3003–4), yet what is being appealed to here is not so much experience as faith. There is in fact no way of knowing whether what Theseus says is true or not, and on the basis of the evidence which he himself cities there are grounds for thinking that *dis*order is the governing principle of human experience.

Another 'proof' of the stability and benevolence of the First Mover is '"That every part dirryveth from his hool"' (3006). Nature is changeable, '"corrumpable"' (3010), but cannot begin from nothing. *Ergo* the whole from which it derives '"parfit is and stable"' (3009). Not much room is allowed for opposition to this argument – '"Wel may men knowe, but it be a fool"' (3005) – and yet it is not clear why the whole from which corruptible nature descends is necessarily perfect. For the second time, Theseus posits the existence of supreme perfection on evidence that might equally well indicate its absence. He goes on to provide examples of the natural process of atrophy, but in doing so he undermines his own position because the tale itself has provided instances of how man, not nature, or the First Mover, is responsible for death and destruction. Thus Theseus observes that the oak, which enjoys such a long life, '"at the laste wasted is"' (3020), yet Theseus himself had earlier '"leet comande anon to hakke and hewe / The okes olde"' (2865–6). Again, he observes that even hard stones are subject to natural wastage, dissolution: '"grete tounes se we wane and wende"' (3025). It is difficult not to remember Thebes, destroyed, once more, by Theseus, the unwitting agent of Saturn (Scheps 1977: 25–30). As on other occasions, the evidence of the tale is at odds with what Theseus here claims to be the truth: man-made ordinances (of the lists, of the funeral ceremony, of revenge) not the '"ordinaunce"' of a supposed deity (3012) are the cause of the ruination of existence, whether vegetable, inanimate or human.

In referring to the demise of 'grete touns' and, in what follows, to death in youth and age of king or page – '"Som in his bed, some in the depe see, / Som in the large feld"' (3031–2) – it is hard to see how Jupiter's effects are to be distinguished from Saturn's, who also claims that sudden death and '"The fallynge of the toures and of the walles"' (2464) are his province. It is as if the reality of Saturn is being glimpsed behind the fiction of Jupiter. In other respects Jupiter's rule, if we are to believe in it, is sharply differentiated from Saturn's. In spite of its similar effects it is supposedly benevolent, and therefore the human response should be acceptance. Why strive against a deity whose destructiveness is all for the best? Rebellion is pointless: '"no creature on lyve, / Of no degree, availleth for to stryve"' (3039–40). Wisdom therefore lies in accepting Jupiter's scheme of things, in making '"vertu of necessite"' (3042) (a politician's motto if ever there was one) and in taking in good part what cannot be avoided and what is everybody's due. There is, apparently, no room for alternatives: anyone who complains, '"gruccheth"', is committing folly, a '"rebel ... to hym that al may gye"' (3045–6). Jupiter's rule, theoretically so just, in practice is repressive. Better the vaunted injustices of Saturn, who does encourage dissension and revolt, '"The murmure and the cherles rebellyng"' (2459). Jupiter, of course, knows what the dire consequences of revolt can be: according to the legend, and as Chaucer would have known from the *Romance of the Rose* (6270–5), it was he who rebelled against his father, Saturn, and castrated him (Plate 9) (Tinkle 1987: 291–3).

THE CLOSE OF THE KNIGHT'S TALE

But shortly to the point thanne will I wende
And maken of my longe tale an ende.
(2965–6)

The conclusion of the Knight's Tale is the marriage of Palamon and Emelye made possible by the death of Arcite. Lydgate's interpretation of the marriage in his *Siege of Thebes*, as representing a settlement of peace between England and France (ed. Erdmann 1911: I.8–9), is a persuasive one, and it seems probable that the marriage of Richard II and Isabella of France, daughter of Charles VI, is the marriage which symbolized the peace in 1396 (Olson 1986: 50–2). This marriage is, of course, as much of Gaunt's making as Richard's, and was the outcome of a foreign policy in which the marriage of Gaunt's daughter in Spain and Gaunt's acquisition of the duchy of Aquitaine put great pressure upon France, especially when it was proposed that Richard should enter into a marriage alliance with the kingdom of Aragon by marrying Yolande, daughter of King John of Aragon. The grand design of this policy may have been to enforce an Anglo-French peace, to end the papal schism by uniting Christendom, and to turn to the destruction of the Turks in expelling the infidel from Europe, but to France there was a clear short- and long-term threat to her national security, especially if, as seemed possible, Richard should succeed to the Spanish throne. The offer of Isabella's hand and with it a peace treaty was a means by which Charles VI might recover for France a more favourable balance of power, and in the event it proved a practical alternative for Richard.

The marriage, then, was the product of a skilful and ambitious foreign policy which may have incorporated the aspiration on Richard's part to be crowned Emperor, King of the Romans. The fictional narrative, however, places a different emphasis, essentially English in its understanding and not European. The peaceful marriage 'alle blisse and melodye' (3097), 'Lyvynge in blisse, in richnesse, and in heele' (3102), free 'Of jalousie or any oother teene' (3106) is seen as only possible when the conflict between Palamon and Arcite is brought to an end. If the struggle between Arcite and Palamon represents the struggle between the knights of Bellona and the knights of Venus personified by Thomas of Woodstock, Duke of Gloucester and Richard II himself, then only with the destruction or defeat of Woodstock can Richard succeed. In so far as the fictional narrative corresponds with the historical narrative it is at a psychological and explanatory level. Only with the murder of Gloucester does the peaceful settlement with France become possible.

The close of the Knight's Tale begins at lines 2965–6 and it is particularly interesting to see at lines 2970–4 the reference to a

> ...*parlement*
> *At Atthenes, upon certain pointʒ and caas;*
> *Among the whiche pointʒ yspoken was,*
> *To have with certain contrees alliaunce,*
> *And have fully of Thebans obeisaunce.*

It may well be that the reference here is to the 1397 parliament in which, according to *Rotuli Parliamentorum*, Richard spoke of the need for peace between England and France (ed. Strachey 1767–77: III. 338b); and, indeed, Theseus' speech may well be seen as some kind of parliamentary sermon in this context not far from a serious parody of the Bishop of Exeter's sermon at the opening of the Hilary Parliament of 1397 in which he took as his text these words from Ezekiel: 'Rex unus erit omnibus'; and proceeded to expound upon the power of the king and its source and the need for obedience. In a parliament in which the king took violent revenge for the violence and intimidation of the Merciless Parliament of 1388 the bishop's sermon carried considerable menace. The gap between the theory and rhetoric of kingship and the practical application of power was as wide as the gap between Theseus' philosophical explanations and the death of Arcite. What is more, it is striking that Theseus uses words which appear to give a fourteenth-century constitutional blessing to the marriage:

> *'Suster,' quod he, 'this is my fulle assent,*
> *With al th'avys heere of my parlement'* ...
> *(3075–6)*

And the final bond was made

That highte matrimoigne or mariage,
By al the conseil and the baronage.
(3095–6)

Everything suggests that the close of the Knight's Tale is to be seen in a fourteenth-century parliamentary and constitutional context in which peace is achieved with the full support of the political nation and the overall control of Theseus/Gaunt. The misgivings which Theseus' speech arouses in the context of the fictional narrative are mirrored in the profound misgivings which contemporaries had about the achievements of the 1397 parliaments. The beheading of Arundel was followed by the announcement of Gloucester's death and Warwick's banishment as well as action taken against Sir Thomas Mortimer and John Lord Cobham. Peace was being bought with blood and justified in parliamentary terms by accusations of treason and impeachments of the kind which had characterized the parliament of 1388. This was to be Richard's last use of parliament, and Chaucer's audience, if this analysis is correct, was awaiting its outcome with anxiety. Their awareness of the hollowness of *domestic* peace since 1396 can only have made their view of Theseus' speech one sceptical of its banal rhetoric, just as their view of the foreign policy of Gaunt and Richard must have doubted its ability to solve problems in England. For Chaucer's audience the power of Saturn was more convincing than that of Jupiter. The destruction of Woodstock was not the answer, only part of the problem. Richard's marriage to Isabella, whatever its underlying motives, is a marriage which is mistrusted and is the product of a continuing internecine conflict. For these reasons the close of the Knight's Tale is bleakly ironic for Chaucer's audience.

6

Conclusions

The Age of Saturn is a study in *mentalité* and *conjoncture*. It seeks to examine the interaction between the structures of collective psychology and the dynamic concatenation of circumstances in late fourteenth-century England, during the lifetime of Geoffrey Chaucer. In choosing Chaucer's poetry as the locus for such an investigation, and in selecting no more than a handful of his *Canterbury Tales*, we have placed clear restrictions on the scope of our enquiry. We believe, however, that those restrictions are not as confining as might at first be imagined. A close reading and inter-reading of text and context provide a rich and thick texture of description whose interpretation simultaneously manifests both aesthetic and social structures and processes. So profound and so pervasive was Chaucer's aesthetic engagement with all levels of political life, moreover, that even so limited an investigation reveals a system of perception and analysis of remarkable complexity and range developed self-consciously in response to crisis. To understand this system and its development is to enlarge conceptions of the literature and history of the period but, more than this, it is to penetrate to the centre of the nature of change in late fourteenth-century England and Christendom.

As Le Goff has observed, 'the term *"mentality"* is still a novelty and already devalued by excessive use'. At its best the history of *mentalités* may be imagined as forging links with a variety of other disciplines in the human sciences and establishing areas of research beyond the reach of traditional historiography. Furthermore, 'it is also a meeting point for opposing forces which are being brought into contact by the dynamics of contemporary historical research: the individual and the collective, the long-term and the everyday, the unconscious and the intentional, the structural and the conjunctural, the marginal and the general'. The programme is excitingly vertiginous but its achievements so far are slight, especially among English historians, many of whom remain suspicious of both its methods and its claims. And its use of literary materials has been a matter for only cautious enthusiasm despite the pioneering work of Lucien Febvre (Febvre 1942; Le Goff 1974: 166–80).

The preceding chapters, however, have been centrally concerned with the identification and discussion of aspects of *mentalité* in our selection of Canterbury tales. And this concern has been encouraged by Chaucer's own clear awareness of the structure of perception in fourteenth-century society. In part this is an aspect of an awareness of genre, diction, rhetoric, iconography and varieties of modes of discourse and, indeed, it is important to recognize, as Chaucer does, the contribution which these make to *mentalité* – and not only the *mentalité* of the audience for his poetry. More remarkable than this, however, is Chaucer's searching examination of a range of interpretive structures of thought by means of which he sought to explore meaning in and understanding of the world around him.

Most simply expressed these structures resolve themselves into general systems such as the beliefs and values of chivalry and aristocracy, Christianity and the medieval Church, economy and commerce, astrology, magic, faery, gender relations, individual and social identity, folk tradition, and nature. Within such general systems the various component parts possess both collective and independent existence: codes of honour and shame; ideas of court, kingdom and kingship; models of Arthurian society; oaths and bonds; the nature of government; *gentillesse*; blood and inheritance; the authority of theology and the Bible; ceremony and ritual; cults of saints, relics and pilgrimage; calendar; order, disorder and apocalypse; Christendom; chance, fortune and grace; work, money, trade and market; the influence of the planets and their 'children'; the role of illusion, fantasy and occult power; marriage and sexuality; family, kinship and estate; humour and emotion; audience, reader and poet; experience and gossip; seasonal and cosmic forces; the visual, the spoken word, the image and the text. Each component possesses its own sub-system and each element possesses the necessary power of interaction with any other element. The sum of these systems and their interactions is what constitutes *mentalité*. And even as limited an investigation as ours shows that this is no narrow literary construct. The tales we have discussed are clearly parts of a literature which has extensively, if not entirely, incorporated the constituent elements of contemporary modes of thought. It has done this, moreover, with a high degree of self-consciousness which makes a critical awareness of *mentalité* doubly imperative. A crucial aspect of our argument is that this characteristic of Chaucer's work in these tales is essentially a response to social and political crisis as generally perceived in late fourteenth-century England and as more widely and variously understood throughout Christendom. For this reason, it is important to appreciate that our foregoing analysis of *mentalité* has been conducted, in so far as it is derived from Chaucer's *Canterbury Tales*, from within Chaucer's critically represented system of contemporary thought, a representation which is frequently radically subversive and reformist, deliberately deconstructing, dismantling and laying bare established orthodoxy and tradition to reveal perceived inadequacy and contradiction.

Our study of the Wife of Bath's Prologue and Tale illustrates the value of this approach to *mentalité* as well as the dynamics of Chaucer's treatment. If we consider the discussion to be fundamentally concerned with conflict and harmony in gender relations it is soon clear that the range of that discussion extends literally and metaphorically to the nature and significance of power relations for the whole of society from the individual to the kingdom. The traditional power and authority of church and crown in chivalric and aristocratic society are at issue, as are the alternative power structures of the female world represented by the Wife of Bath in, for example, experience, gossip and the values of the market. The interaction of these power structures provides a description of contemporary *mentalité*. But Chaucer's consideration goes further. Previously gender relations have generated conflict and a system of constraint and subordination in which mutual exploitation degrades both men and women. The traditional power and authority of church and crown is exposed as

divisive and internally self-contradictory. Alternative power structures developed within the overall structure of constraint (and
subordination), though expressing real and neglected social forces, can
do no more than reproduce the prevailing conditions. Chivalric,
aristocratic and ecclesiastical values are insufficient to produce social
and political harmony between ruler and subject. By recourse to the
expressive worlds of Arthurian and faery fantasy and magic, and by
isolating the chivalric ideal of *gentillesse* and giving it both individual
and collective significance, it becomes possible to envisage the necessary conditions for personal, social and political reciprocity and harmony, and for the resolution of conflict and contradiction. What is
now being described through the person of the poet is contemporary
mentalité in the process of change.

Equally significant, therefore, is Chaucer's self-conscious aesthetic
response. As we have argued, the literary techniques employed by
Chaucer in the Wife of Bath's Prologue and Tale are deliberately
designed to confront and subvert audience expectation. The construction of the character of the Wife of Bath from texts prejudicial to her
own argument, the play of genres, the variously unreliable nature of
the Wife of Bath as narrator, and the heightened sensitivity to the
social and political construction of modes of discourse, all dissolve any
sense of stable relationship between poet and audience. Here too
power relations are in question. They extend, moreover, to the position of the poet within the society of the royal court and to his
relations with his patron, and they touch upon the very essence of his
relationship with his art. This examination by Chaucer of *mentalité* in
relation to structures of power inevitably includes, if it does not start
from, his own life and his own social and political position.

It seems likely that the matter of personal biography also informs
his treatment of the Squire's Tale and the Franklin's Tale. Though
these tales are structured around the importance of honour in chivalric
and aristocratic society, they are designed so that this issue is explored
through relationships within the estate structure of feudal society. In
the course of this exploration, the roles of astrology, magic, religion
and the church in sustaining and maintaining aristocratic society and
its values are also examined. Once again gender relations, and especially
marriage, extend the argument in terms of the right exercise of power,

and in identifying concepts of 'maistrye', 'love', 'friendship', 'freedom', 'patience', 'governaunce', 'constraint', 'sovereignty' and 'temperaunce' it permits the development of the discussion in terms of government and the exercise of political power. The discussion of rhetoric elevates one aspect of previously considered poetics to the body of the narrative. As in the Wife of Bath's Tale, however, each element of *mentalité* is subjected to criticism. The conflicting rhetoric of Squire and Franklin emphasizes social and political conflict and disorder. Aristocratic value systems are found wanting. The estate structure of feudal society, with its demarcations of blood and inheritance, is found to be inadequate to personal and social realities. Astrology, magic, religion and the church can do no more than provide temporary solutions. Only the force of *gentillesse*, redefined to embody a quality of aristocracy which transcends blood and inheritance and the sharp lines of social division in traditional feudal society, is able to restore honour and avoid social and political disaster.

Aesthetically, Chaucer's intentions are equally radical. The discussion of rhetoric and estate touched his own condition, and the solution advanced implied a change in self-perception, just as it implied a radical realignment among his narrator's fellow pilgrims, and just as it implied a change in his relationship with his audience and his social superiors. Acutely aware of the social distinctions of genre, Chaucer also sought within these tales to subvert, by satire and parody, aristocratic literary forms. Effectively, in both the Squire's Tale and the Franklin's Tale, he reinforced, in this way, the argument of the narrative which exposed the sterile inadequacy of traditional aristocratic values and asserted the virtue and vigour of those social orders who spoke simply, directly and sincerely. To argue in such a way was, of course, once more to confront his own role as poet. The implication of such an analysis was the need to revitalize the form and content of poetic fiction.

An awareness of structure and change, and the place of himself and his art in relation to both, similarly characterizes Chaucer's treatment of the Pardoner's Prologue and Tale and the Merchant's Prologue and Tale. There is, however, we argue, a different dimension to these works. Whereas in the Wife of Bath's Tale, the Squire's Tale and the Franklin's Tale there is a concern to express, in general terms, the discontinuity of *mentalités* perceived as part of a general social and political crisis, Pardoner and Merchant are intent upon addressing that crisis by reference to specific circumstances. Nevertheless, the same analysis of discontinuity invests the narrative.

Ostensibly, The Pardoner's Prologue and Tale are concerned with Christian values and practice in contemporary society. Expressed by a papal representative of the church in Christendom, in the self-conscious rhetoric of a preacher employing the language and imagery of the Bible and contemporary theological doctrine, they seem intended to embody the attitudes of both the papacy and the late four-teenth-century church. Central to the discussion is an exploration of the significance of a variety of sins but also of contemporary cults of saints and relics and, especially, the sacrament of the eucharist. Inextricably implicated with the secular world, this religious matter has relevance too for the policies of princes and government. The symbolism of Christ's body and blood in contemporary political philosophy extended to the description of social and political harmony in community and realm.

So much would not be out of place in a conventional contemporary sermon. By raising the Pardoner's rhetorical technique and his manipulative skills to the surface of the fiction, however, and to the attention of his fellow pilgrims and the poem's audience, and by revealing the Pardoner's cynicism, Chaucer once more undermines the conventionality of the matter in question. By demonstrating the Pardoner's hypocrisy, furthermore, he makes the Pardoner a focal point within his own narrative, destabilizing expectations of the role of the church and the value of contemporary Christian practice. The Pardoner's own position and that of the authority of the church are also challenged by the admission of Lollard criticism, though Chaucer's parody of Lollard rhetoric (unconsciously mimicked by the undiscriminating Pardoner) and the implied criticism of Lollard views on transubstantiation (ironically reflecting upon the Pardoner's own wilful lack of spirituality) subtly modify a simple view of a divided church. The Pardoner's tale, no less than his sermon, recoils upon himself. Not only is he guilty of the sins which he condemns in others for his own material benefit but his actions, like those of the tavern revellers, suggest inevitably his own irredeemable self-destruction. In so far as the Pardoner represents the church it would seem to suffer the same condemnation.

The implications of the Pardoner's Tale, however, do not stop there. The Pardoner's rhetorical technique of thematic elision, and his almost unbearable extension of the metaphorical significance of the eucharist, permit the introduction of subjects of immediate concern. The present urgency of the prologue and tale is, to a greater extent than even the Merchant's Tale, taken to the point at which the boundary is traversed between the fictional and the real. Once again this involves the assimilation of the contingent made emblematic. The Treaty of Bruges of 1375 assumes a significance within the narrative of the tale which greatly enhances the metaphorical resonance of the Pardoner. The Pardoner's sermon and tale damn not only himself and the church but also those ecclesiastical and secular princes, their agents and counsellors, who have betrayed the kingdom of England for the satisfaction of their own pride, ambition and greed. Christian values and Christian practice at all levels within church and government have been abandoned, and a profound dislocation of traditional expectations has resulted in a perceived discontinuity in *mentalité*.

Dislocation and discontinuity are again manifested in the aesthetic process. It is easy to see a cruel equivalence between the Pardoner, as preacher, mocking fool, and cynical apologist, and Chaucer himself. The Pardoner's relationship with his fellow pilgrims is paralleled in the poet's relationship with his audience. Chaucer seems to invite condemnation and rejection as his arrogant Pardoner implies the spiritual emptiness of the very activity in which they are all engaged. Once again his relationship with the court and his patron, John of Gaunt, is threatened by his scathing criticism of the parts they have played in the events to which he alludes. But better, perhaps, to be a rejected Seneca than a 'Stilboun' Wyclif or a Pardoner. If the *Canterbury Tales* are not to have a redemptive purpose, and are not to be capable of offering resistance to the perceived corruption and some capacity for social and political regeneration, then they are themselves without value. The Pardoner's Tale must be terminated by his fellow pilgrims. Proceeding by parody and travesty, the Pardoner's fabliau sermon is deeply unsettling to its audience, demanding of that audience that it should examine its own received values (as the poet has examined his) and reassert them in the light of contemporary experience.

Marriage and gender relations within Christian society are again at the centre of the enquiry in the Merchant's Tale, juxtaposed with considerations of kingship, government and counsel, and with the significance of merchant influence. Such themes are pursued through the traditional language and iconography of the seasons, astrology and the Bible. But throughout the tale traditional Christian values are travestied, kingship and government are corrupt and deluded, only the counsel of sycophants and deceivers is heeded, and traditional iconography and language are imbued with a degrading ambiguity. Central to this examination of gender relations is a consideration of sexuality, cruelly describing the pitifully deluded potency of the senile January. And at every stage of the narrative there is the thinly veiled presence of the relationship between Edward III and Alice Perrers, a relationship whose contemporary meaning had become so emblematic of social and political crisis that it might be incorporated within the *mentalité* of late fourteenth-century England. For Chaucer such a narrative demanded new forms of expression in a hybrid genre of romance and fabliau in which the expressive capacity of faery was employed to allow the ultimate degradation of January in a parody of the fall of man in which, by implication, the English king was mercilessly ridiculed. A despairingly blasphemous derision was turned upon English government and political life at court. There was no suggestion here of the possibility of reform. Chaucer, like Seneca, was an unheard counsellor. His tale implicitly challenged his relationship with his audience and his patron as his sense of the urgency of the crisis demanded the inclusion of a symbolism derived from contemporary experience. In using such matter he was not alone. What distinguishes his contribution in this is the novelty and variety of the techniques whereby he extended the meanings of traditional *mentalité*.

In the analysis of *mentalité*, the Knight's Tale has a special part to play in the *Canterbury Tales*. As our limited analysis suggests, the dominant themes of the Knight's Tale recur pervasively at different levels within other tales. The nature of order and governance in chivalric and aristocratic society is an entirely appropriate subject for the Knight to consider and, indeed, is an entirely appropriate subject for a representative company of pilgrims to consider, according to their degree. More significantly, however, the Knight's treatment of his subject also becomes influential. And Chaucer's own perception of that treatment engages the critical evaluation of the audience.

Central to the explorations of the Knight's Tale are the beliefs and values of chivalric and aristocratic society, astrology, gender relations, individual and collective identity, and nature. Once more, codes of honour and shame; ideas of court, kingdom, and kingship; oaths and bonds; the nature of government – from tyranny to parliament, conseil, and baronage; *gentillesse*; blood and inheritance; ceremony and ritual; order and disorder; chance, fortune, and destiny; the influence of the planets and their 'children'; family, kinship, and degree; humour and emotion; and seasonal and cosmic forces, constitute the declared agenda of the tale. And, pursued within a pagan, classical world, the story incorporates a rich and diverse symbolism of the natural world as well as that of the chivalric institutions of heraldry, feasting, hunting and tournament.

Told by the Knight, by these means, the story is of a prince who, by the assertion of traditional values, tempered by *gentillesse*, returns from conquest overseas to restore peace and order to a society torn by conflict. The Knight, however, is an unreliable narrator. The outward forms of a chivalric, aristocratic society barely disguise the repeated transgressions of the beliefs and values they supposedly manifest: oaths and bonds and codes of honour are violated; '"at the kynges court, my brother, / Ech man for hymself, ther is noon oother"' (1181–2); ties of aristocratic blood are no guarantee of *gentil* behaviour; ceremony and tournament are inadequate to achieve their purposes; the power of *gentillesse* cannot prevent violent conflict and bloodshed.

Both the Knight and his protagonists seem equally deluded, unable to see the destructive contradictions within the social and political system they advocate. The theatre built by Theseus as the place where right order will be restored is a theatre of false consciousness. The poem's audience, however, is differently informed. The system of planetary influence and control is seen to be ultimately in conflict with chivalric and aristocratic values and beliefs. It follows, therefore, that the idea of a divided society brought to peace and harmony by the princely assertion of traditional values is a misapprehension and, as the audience is led to understand, what appears to be the restoration of order is no more than a passing phase within the malign and destructive progress of Saturn's rule. The structure of the Knight's narrative, framed as a kind of epic romance, is equally misleading, an embodiment of its narrator's failure of perception, and part of the problem with which Chaucer confronts his audience.

For while the chronological structure of the narrative is the product of the Knight's false analysis, it is drawn from a chronology familiar to its audience 'Were it in Engelond' (2113). As in the Merchant's Tale and the Pardoner's Tale, Chaucer invests contemporary experience with symbolic significance, choosing the return of John of Gaunt from Spain and Portugal, in 1389, and the marriage of Richard II and Isabella, daughter of Charles VI of France, in 1396, to frame the tale. The implication would seem to be that the events of the intervening years are misunderstood and must be reinterpreted. Chaucer's Knight's Tale provides the means by which his audience may discover the extent of their own and their contemporaries' false consciousness, being confronted with an alternative, melancholy and pessimistic explanation of events which draws metaphorically upon contemporary views of astrological influence. Saturn, indeed, speaks directly to the poem's audience not merely by being a recognized element in a contemporary system of explanation but by his pointed reference to events within its recent memory.

The Knight's ideologically conservative version of these years will not do. The profound crisis in contemporary society is far from being resolved and traditional values, as currently perceived, are far from adequate to address the problem. In the absence of satisfactory explanations, therefore, and from within the inevitable structures of false consciousness, the Knight's fellow pilgrims are free to explore these issues from different social positions. Their audience may self-consciously assess each contribution with an awareness of a greater causal complexity which in the light of contemporary experience seems distinctly inauspicious, though they might travel with the pilgrims in forlorn hope.

Chaucer's use of the notion of Saturn's determining influence seems to owe more to the explanatory concept of astrological conjunction than the twentieth-century concept of *conjoncture*. Yet there is a sense in which Saturn is Chaucer as historian identifying the laws of motion of a distinctive historical period. The idea of an autonomous general crisis becomes a means of understanding contemporary social and political developments. But for Chaucer the influence of Saturn is essentially a metaphor whose application is at the level of description. His own critical analysis, after all, indicating different levels of perception, is apparently exempt from the false consciousness he associates with his contemporaries. When Chaucer uses the influence of Saturn as an explanatory mechanism it is to argue that it is of the nature of the *conjoncture* which he has identified that human action leads, among other dire eventualities, to treachery, murder and rebellion. For Chaucer, however, the *conjoncture* is also characterized by a profound moral and spiritual malaise. His concern is not to identify its origins but to provide a description which will enable reform and regeneration to take place. His ambition is no less than the restoration within the existing structures of Christian, chivalric and feudal society of those values and beliefs which will maintain harmony and prosperity. Such a restoration implies radical change at all levels of society and for the individual as much as for the collective.

This perception of *conjoncture* in English society in the second half of the fourteenth century is clearly different from that of twentieth-century historians. The task is to understand the relationship between the two. In examining the critical interaction between long-, medium- and short-term dynamics today's historians place great emphasis upon the agency of profound demographic change in this period. The impact of high death rates from plague upon a population at the end of a long cycle of expansion undoubtedly had profound consequences for social, economic and political relations. Changes in birth rates, age and sex structures, courtship, marriage, and remarriage, mobility, and the size of communities, had considerable impact upon family, kinship and inheritance, as well as personal relations. The reduction in the size of the labour force, rising wages and a generally improved standard of living, the contraction and restructuring of demand with all its consequences for production and consumption, rising landlord costs and falling revenues with resultant changes in agricultural policies, and an increased social mobility, all significantly altered the relationship between those who work, those who pray, and those who fight. Subsequent changes in political relations throughout society were experienced, most dramatically following landlord retrenchment and restrictive government legislation, in widespread discontent and rebellion in the ranks of those below the aristocracy in town and countryside. In time of papal schism challenges to the authority of the church and religious orthodoxy, with its origins, perhaps, in the late thirteenth century, stimulated further repression and conflict. Failure in warfare and international relations was exacerbated by an often violent dissension among the aristocracy and an exercise of royal power which, despite the deliberate elaboration of the cult of kingship and chivalric ethos, swung from the dangerously ineffectual in the last years of Edward III through the minority and early years of Richard II to his later autocracy. The intersection of these and other forces is what determines the nature of *conjoncture* in England in the second half of the fourteenth century.

In his use of the metaphor of Saturn's influence Chaucer does not seek the complex, layered and interlocking structure of causation implicit in the analysis of a twentieth-century historian, though his descriptive model of perception has its own undoubted sophistication. What is more, though Chaucer may not isolate the same variables, it is clear that, in the *Canterbury Tales*, he responds to the same stimuli, articulating his response through the structures of contemporary *mentalité*. Thus, it is perhaps not surprising to find him expressing his central moral and spiritual concerns by means of metaphors drawn from gender relations, marriage, sexuality and family at a time when such issues are of such critical concern. The demographic has become especially charged with moral, spiritual and political significance. Similarly, under the impact of rapid economic and social change, the meaning and consequence of social mobility become questions intimately related to the perceived crisis of late fourteenth-century society. The contemporary debate over the nature of the eucharist becomes the obvious way to tackle the challenge to the authority of the church, and its moral, spiritual and political ambivalence is embodied in the creation of the Pardoner. In the Merchant's Tale, the Pardoner's Tale and the Knight's Tale, moreover, the behaviour of

Edward III and his court, the management of international relations between England, France, Castile and the papacy in the 1370s, and the conflict among the aristocracy in the 1380s, all find fictional correlatives in the reworking of traditional forms and images of immediate relevance at the level of change. The tales acquire their substance at the point of intersection between *mentalité* and *conjoncture* through the imagination of a poet whose literary techniques, including irony, have been developed for the purpose of engagement with his own society and its problems.

In advancing these arguments, we have had no intention of suggesting that the tales are some kind of linked series of allegorical tracts but rather that they seek an exploration of meanings, in the spirit of moral and political reform, which essentially and deliberately incorporates matter of contemporary debate and concern. The order in which we have chosen to consider our selection of tales is intended, in part, to demonstrate progressively the ways in which this incorporation is achieved – though it is not intended to imply that Chaucer necessarily worked progressively to achieve these ends. We do suggest, however, that the embodiment of the circumstances of the 1390s in the Knight's Tale necessarily has consequences for the reading of the rest of the *Canterbury Tales*.

We would also argue, as we have done earlier in respect of the Pardoner's Tale, that the identification of contemporary matter within the tales has implications for their composition and dating. Our intention, as we have indicated, is not to claim that the inclusion of such material provides evidence for a precise date of composition, though it is clear that the tales, as we now possess them, could not have been written before the occurrence of the events which they employ. The progress of composition, however, is likely to have been lengthy and the thematic resonances such that the relevance of this contemporary material would not have been narrowly restricted in time. We suggest, indeed, that such was its symbolic energy, and so receptive to its inclusion was contemporary *mentalité*, that its application would have been recognized, whenever its origins, late into Chaucer's lifetime and, indeed, beyond. Nevertheless, in the Merchant's Tale, the Pardoner's Tale and the Knight's Tale, there is the incorporation of a degree of detail (and probably more than we have been able to identify) which seems unlikely to have been appreciated except fairly close in time to the events in question and by a particularly knowledgeable audience. Such a manner of composition may have been essentially for Chaucer's own satisfaction but it may signal special intentions with regard to audience. If the audience was intended to respond to detail and nuance of this kind then it would seem that these tales or versions of them were composed with the intention of rapid consumption – not that this would prevent their later reworking into the project of the *Canterbury Tales*.

These conclusions, in the spirit of the whole book, are intended not to be prescriptive but polemical. The dialectical nature of our own method of composition has been revealing enough of the dangers of closure. To be engaged with Chaucer's work, moreover, as we have suggested, is to become self-consciously part of a process of deconstruction and reform which, though not that of the fourteenth-century reader, is none the less revealing of the limitations of perception. Influenced perhaps, if such influence were necessary, by Chaucerian radicalism, we do, however, hope that this study, in contributing to the established enterprise of the reintegration of Chaucer's writings with the social and political history of the fourteenth century, extends the range of meanings of those writings and those of other contemporary authors. At the same time, we believe that this study has many implications for the examination of the social and political history of England in the second half of the fourteenth century. In this period, as in many others, a non-positivist reconsideration of the abundant chronicle literature, for example, is long overdue.

References

Aarsleff, Hans 1985: Scholarship and Ideology: Joseph Bédier's Critique of Romantic Medievalism. In McGann 1985b: 93–113.

Adams, John F. 1974: The Janus Symbolism in *The Merchant's Tale*. *Studies in Medieval Culture*, 4, 446–51.

Aers, David 1980: *Chaucer, Langland and the Creative Imagination*. London: Routledge and Kegan Paul.

——1983: Representations of the 'Third Estate': Social Conflict and Its Milieu around 1381. *Southern Review*, 16, 335–49.

——(ed.) 1986: *Medieval Literature: Criticism, Ideology and History*, Brighton: Harvester.

——1988: *Community, Gender, and Individual Identity: English Writing 1360–1430*. London: Routledge.

Alford, John A. 1984: Richard Rolle and Related Works. In Edwards: 35–60.

Amyot, Thomas 1829: Transcript of a Chronicle in the Harleian Library of MSS. No. 6217, entitled 'An Historicall Relation of certain passages about the end of King Edward the Third, and of his Death'. *Archaeologia*, 22, 204–84.

Anderson, J. J. (ed.) 1974: *Chaucer: The Canterbury Tales*. Casebook series. London: Macmillan.

Askins, William 1985: The Historical Setting of *The Manciple's Tale*. *Studies in the Age of Chaucer*, 7, 87–105.

Aston, Margaret 1984: *Lollards and Reformers: Images and Literacy in Late Medieval Religion*. History series, 22. London: Hambledon Press.

Aston, T. H., Coss, P. R., Dyer, C., and Thirsk, J. 1983: *Social Relations and*

Ideas: Essays in Honour of R. H. Hilton. Cambridge: Cambridge University Press.

Ayres, Harry Morgan 1919: Chaucer and Seneca. *Romanic Review,* 10, 1–15.

Babington, C., and Lumby J. R. (eds) 1865–86: *Polychronicon Ranulphi Higden monachi Cestrensis; together with the English translations of John Trevisa and of an unknown writer of the fifteenth century,* 9 vols. Rerum Britannicarum medii aevii scriptores. London: HMSO.

Bachman, W. Bryant, Jr, 1977: 'To Maken Illusioun': The Philosophy of Magic and the Magic of Philosophy in the *Franklin's Tale. Chaucer Review,* 12, 55–67.

Baker, Donald C. 1961: A Crux in Chaucer's *Franklin's Tale*: Dorigen's Complaint. *Journal of English and Germanic Philology,* 60, 56–64.

Bakhtin, M. M. 1981: *The Dialogic Imagination,* ed. Michael Holquist, trans. Caryl Emerson and Michael Holquist. University of Texas Press Slavic series, 1. Austin: University of Texas Press.

Baldwin, Anna P. 1981: *The Theme of Government in Piers Plowman.* Piers Plowman Studies, 1. Woodbridge: Boydell and Brewer.

Barthes, Roland 1967: *Writing Degree Zero,* trans. Annette Lavers and Colin Smith. London: Cape.

——1972: *Mythologies,* trans. Annette Lavers. London: Cape.

Beidler, Peter G. 1981: Noah and the Old Man in the *Pardoner's Tale. Chaucer Review,* 15, 250–4.

Bennett, J. A. W. 1943: The Date of the A-Text of *Piers Plowman. PMLA,* 58, 566–72.

Benskin, Michael, and Samuels, M. L. (eds) 1981: *So meny people longages and tonges: Philological Essays in Scots and Mediaeval English Presented to Angus McIntosh.* Edinburgh: Benskin and Samuels.

Benson, Larry D. (ed.) 1974: *The Learned and the Lewed: Studies in Chaucer and Medieval Literature.* Harvard English Studies, 5. Cambridge MA: Harvard University Press.

——et al., (eds) 1987: *The Riverside Chaucer: Based on the Works of Geoffrey Chaucer Edited by F. N. Robinson.* Boston: Houghton Mifflin.

Benson, Larry D., and Wenzel, Siegfried (eds) 1982: *The Wisdom of Poetry: Essays in Early English Literature in Honor of Morton W. Bloomfield.* Kalamazoo: Medieval Institute Publications, Western Michigan University.

Benson, Robert G. 1980: *Medieval Body Language: A Study of the Use of Gesture in Chaucer's Poetry.* Anglistica, 21. Copenhagen: Rosenkilde and Bagger.

Besserman, L. L. 1978: Chaucer and the Bible: The Case of the *Merchant's Tale. Hebrew University Studies in Literature,* 6, 10–31.

Besserman, Lawrence, and Storm, Melvin 1983: Chaucer's Pardoner. *PMLA*, 98, 405–6.

Beston, John B. 1974: How Much Was Known of the Breton Lai in Fourteenth-Century England? In L. Benson: 319–36.

Billington, Sandra 1979: 'Suffer Fools Gladly': The Fool in Medieval England and the Play *Mankind*. In P. Williams: 36–54.

——1984: *A Social History of the Fool*. Brighton: Harvester; and New York: St Martin's Press.

Biraben, Jean Nöel 1976: *Les hommes et la peste en France et dans les pays européens et méditerranéens*, vol. 2. Ecole des Hautes Etudes en Sciences Sociales, Centre de Recherche Historique, Civilisations et Sociétés, 36. Paris: Mouton.

Blake, Kathleen A. 1973: Order and the Noble Life in Chaucer's *Knight's Tale*. *Modern Language Quarterly*, 34, 3–19.

Blake, N. F. (ed.) 1980: *The Canterbury Tales by Geoffrey Chaucer Edited from the Hengwrt Manuscript*. London: Arnold.

Blanch, Robert J. 1985: 'Al was this land fulfild of fayerye': The Thematic Employment of Force, Willfulness, and Legal Conventions in Chaucer's *Wife of Bath's Tale*. *Studia Neophilologica*, 57, 41–51.

Bleeth, Kenneth A. 1974: The Image of Paradise in the *Merchant's Tale*. In L. Benson: 45–60.

Blenner-Hassett, Roland 1953: Autobiographical Aspects of Chaucer's Franklin. *Speculum*, 28, 791–800.

Bloomfield, Morton W. 1978: *The Merchant's Tale*: A Tragicomedy of the Neglect of Counsel – The Limits of Art. In Wenzel: 37–50.

——1981: Contemporary Literary Theory and Chaucer. In Rose: 23–36.

Boitani, Piero 1977: *Chaucer and Bocaccio*. Medium Aevum Monographs, NS 8. Oxford: Society for the Study of Mediaeval Languages and Literature.

——(ed.) 1983: *Chaucer and the Italian Trecento*. Cambridge: Cambridge University Press.

Boitani, Piero, and Torti, Anna (eds) 1983: *Literature in Fourteenth-Century England*. The J. A. W. Bennett Memorial Lectures: Perugia 1981–1982. Tübingen: Gunter Narr; and Cambridge: Brewer.

Bornstein, Diane 1983: *The Lady in the Tower: Medieval Courtesy Literature for Women*. Hamden CT: Archon.

Braddy, Haldeen 1946: Chaucer and Dame Alice Perrers. *Speculum*, 21, 222–8.

——1977: Chaucer, Alice Perrers, and Cecily Chaumpaigne. *Speculum*, 52, 906–11.

Bramley, H. R. (ed.) 1884: *The Psalter or Psalms of David and Certain Articles with a Translation and Exposition in English by Richard Rolle of Hampole.* Oxford: Clarendon Press.

Braswell, Laurel 1984: Utilitarian and Scientific Prose. In Edwards: 337–87.

Brewer, D. S. 1968: Class Distinction in Chaucer. *Speculum*, 43, 290–305.

Brie, F. W. D. (ed.) 1906: *The Brut: or, The Chronicles of England.* EETS os 131 (1906).

Brooks, Douglas, and Fowler, Alastair 1970: The Meaning of Chaucer's *Knight's Tale. Medium Aevum*, 39, 123–46.

Brown, Carleton 1940: *Essays and Studies in Honor of Carleton Brown.* New York: New York University Press; and London: Oxford University Press.

Brown, Emerson, Jr. 1970: *Hortus Inconclusus*: The Significance of Priapus and Piramus and Thisbe in the Merchant's Tale. *Chaucer Review*, 4, 31–40.

——1978: Chaucer, the Merchant, and Their Tale: Getting beyond Old Controversies, Part II. *Chaucer Review*, 13, 141–56.

——1979: Chaucer, the Merchant, and Their Tale: Getting beyond Old Controversies, Part II. *Chaucer Review*, 13, 247–62.

——1983: Chaucer and a Proper Name: January in *The Merchant's Tale. Names*, 31, 79–87.

Brown, Peter 1985: An Optical Theme in *The Merchant's Tale*. In Strohm and Heffernan: 231–43.

Brown, Peter, and Butcher, Andrew 1987: Teaching 'Crisis, Text and Image'. *Literature and History*, 13, 3–13.

Bryan, W. F., and Dempster, Germaine (eds) 1941: *Sources and Analogues of Chaucer's Canterbury Tales*. Rpt. New York: Humanities Press, 1958.

Bugge, John 1973: Damyan's Wanton *Clyket* and an Ironic New *Twiste* to the *Merchant's Tale. Annuale Medievale*, 14, 53–62.

Burgess, Glyn S. (ed.) 1981: *Court and Poet.* Selected Proceedings of the Third Congress of the International Courtly Literature Society (Liverpool 1980). ARCA: Classical and Medieval Texts, Papers and Monographs, 5. Liverpool: Cairns.

——1987: *The Lais of Marie de France: Text and Context.* Athens GA: University of Georgia Press.

Burlin, Robert B. 1974: The Art of Chaucer's Franklin. In Anderson: 183–208.

——1977: *Chaucerian Fiction.* Princeton: Princeton University Press.

Burnley, J. D. 1976: The Morality of The Merchant's Tale. *Year's Work in English Studies*, 6, 16–25.

——1979: *Chaucer's Language and the Philosophers' Tradition.* Chaucer Studies,

2. Cambridge: Brewer; and Totowa NJ: Rowman and Littlefield.

Burrow, J. A. 1957: Irony in the Merchant's Tale. *Anglia*, 75, 199–208. Rpt. in Burrow 1984b: 49–59.

——(ed.) 1969: *Geoffrey Chaucer: A Critical Anthology*. Harmondsworth: Penguin.

——1982: *Medieval Writers and Their Work: Middle English Literature and Its Background 1100–1500*. Opus Book. Oxford: Oxford University Press.

——1984a: Chaucer's *Knight's Tale* and the Three Ages of Man. In Burrow 1984b: 27–48.

——1984b: *Essays on Medieval Literature*. Oxford: Clarendon Press.

Bushnell, Nelson S. 1931: The Wandering Jew and the Pardoner's Tale. *Studies in Philology*, 28, 450–60.

Butler, Marilyn 1985: Against Tradition: The Case for a Particularized Historical Method. In McGann 1985b: 25–47.

Carruthers, Mary 1979: The Wife of Bath and the Painting of Lions. *PMLA*, 94, 209–22.

——1981: The Gentilesse of Chaucer's Franklin. *Criticism*, 23, 283–300.

Childs, Wendy R. 1978: *Anglo-Castilian Trade in the Later Middle Ages*. Manchester: Manchester University Press.

Ciavolella, M. 1979: Medieval Medicine and Arcite's Love Sickness. *Florilegium*, 9, 222–41.

Clifford, Paula 1982: *Marie de France: Lais*. Critical Guides to French Texts, No. 16. London: Grant and Cutler.

Coffman, George R. 1934: Old Age from Horace to Chaucer: Some Literary Affinities and Adventures of an Idea. *Speculum*, 9, 249–77.

Coleman, Janet 1981: *English Literature in History 1350–1400: Medieval Readers and Writers*. London: Hutchinson.

——1983: English Culture in the Fourteenth Century. In Boitani: 33–63.

Colvin, H. M., Brown, R. Allen, and Taylor, A. J. 1963: *The History of the King's Works*, vol. 1: *The Middle Ages*. London: HMSO.

Coss, P. R. 1983: Literature and Social Terminology: The Vavasour in England. In Aston et al.: 109–50.

Cowgill, Bruce Kent 1975: The *Knight's Tale* and the Hundred Year's War. *Philological Quarterly*, 54, 670–9.

Crow, Martin M., and Olson, Clair C. (eds) 1966: *Chaucer Life-Records ... from Materials Compiled by John M. Manly and Edith Rickert with the Assistance of Lilian J. Redstone and Others*. Oxford: Clarendon Press.

Culler, Jonathan 1975: *Structuralist Poetics: Structuralism, Linguistics and the Study of Literature*. London: Routledge and Kegan Paul.

——1983: *On Deconstruction: Theory and Criticism after Structuralism*. London: Routledge and Kegan Paul.

Curry, Walter Clyde 1923: Astrologizing the Gods. *Anglia*, 47, 213–43.

Dahlberg, Charles, trans. 1971: *The Romance of the Rose by Guillaume de Lorris and Jean de Meun*. Princeton, NJ: Princeton University Press.

Daiches, David 1938: *Literature and Society*. London: Gollancz.

Dalbey, Marcia A. 1974: The Devil in the Garden: Pluto and Proserpine in Chaucer's Merchant's Tale. *Neuphilologische Mitteilungen*, 75, 408–15.

Daly, L. J. 1962: *The Political Theory of John Wyclif*. Jesuit Studies. Chicago: Loyola University Press.

Davenport, W. A. 1988: *Chaucer: Complaint and Narrative*. Chaucer Studies, 14. Cambridge: Brewer.

David, Alfred 1965: Criticism and the Old Man in Chaucer's Pardoner's Tale. *College English*, 27, 39–44.

——1976: *The Strumpet Muse: Art and Morals in Chaucer's Poetry*. Bloomington and London: Indiana University Press.

Davis, Norman, et al., (compilers) 1979: *A Chaucer Glossary*. Oxford: Clarendon Press.

Dean, Christopher 1968: Salvation, Damnation and the Role of the Old Man in the Pardoner's Tale. *Chaucer Review*, 3, 44–9.

Deanesly, Margaret 1920: *The Lollard Bible and Other Medieval Biblical Versions*. Cambridge Studies in Medieval Life and Thought. Cambridge: Cambridge University Press.

Delany, Sheila 1975: Sexual Economics, Chaucer's Wife of Bath, and *The Book of Margery Kempe*. *Minnesota Review*, NS 5, 104–15. Rpt. in Delany 1983: 76–92.

——1983: *Writing Woman: Women Writers and Women in Literature, Medieval to Modern*. New York: Schocken Books.

Delasanta, Rodney 1973: Sacrament and Sacrifice in the *Pardoner's Tale*. *Annuale Medievale*, 14, 43–52.

Dempster, Germaine 1937: Chaucer at Work on the Complaint in the *Franklin's Tale*. *Modern Language Notes*, 52, 16–23.

Dollimore, Jonathan 1985: Introduction: Shakespeare, Cultural Materialism and the New Historicism. In Jonathan Dollimore and Alan Sinfield (eds), *Political Shakespeare: New Essays in Cultural Materialism*. Manchester: Manchester University Press, 2–17.

Donaldson, E. Talbot 1954: Chaucer the Pilgrim. *PMLA*, 69, 928–36. Rpt. in Donaldson 1970: 1–12.

——1970: *Speaking of Chaucer*. London: University of London/Athlone Press.

——1983: Arcite's Injury. In Gray and Stanley: 65–7.

Donovan, Mortimer J. 1957: The Image of Pluto and Proserpine in the *Merchant's Tale*. *Philological Quarterly*, 36, 49–60.

——1969: *The Breton Lay: A Guide to Varieties*. Notre Dame IN, and London: University of Notre Dame Press.

Douay Bible 1609: *The Holy Bible: Douay Version*. Translated from the Latin Vulgate (Douay, A.D. 1609; Rheims, A.D. 1582). London: Catholic Truth Society, 1956.

Drakakis, John 1985: Introduction. In his *Alternative Shakespeares*. New Accents. London and New York: Methuen, 1–25.

Dupaquier, J. et al. (eds) 1981: *Marriage and Remarriage in Populations of the Past*. London: Academic Press.

Eade, J. C. 1982: 'We ben to lewed or to slowe': Chaucer's Astronomy and Audience Participation. *Studies in the Age of Chaucer*, 4, 53–85.

Eagleton, Terry 1976: *Marxism and Literary Criticism*. London: Methuen.

——1978: *Criticism and Ideology*: A Study in Marxist Literary Theory. London: Verso.

——1985: Ideology and Scholarship. In McGann 1985b: 114–25.

Edwards, A. S. G. (ed.) 1984: *Middle English Prose: A Critical Guide to Major Authors and Genres*. New Brunswick NJ: Rutgers University Press.

Eisner, Sigmund 1937: *A Tale of Wonder: A Source Study of The Wife of Bath's Tale*. Rpt. Folcroft PA: Folcroft Press, 1970.

Emmerson, Richard Kenneth, and Herzman, Ronald B. 1987: The Apocalyptic Age of Hypocrisy: Faus Semblant and Amant in the *Roman de la Rose*. *Speculum*, 62, 612–34.

Empson, William 1961: *Seven Types of Ambiguity* (2nd edn). Harmondsworth: Penguin.

Erdmann, A. (ed.) 1911: *John Lydgate: Siege of Thebes*. EETS, es 108.

Esch, Arno (ed.) 1968: *Chaucer und seine Zeit: Symposion für Walter F. Schirmer*. Buchreihe der Anglia Zeitschrift für Englische Philologie, vol. 14. Tübingen: Niemeyer.

Everett, Dorothy 1922: The Middle English Prose Psalter of Richard Rolle of Hampole. *Modern Language Review*, 17, 217–27 and 337–50. Continued in Everett 1923.

——1923: The Middle English Prose Psalter of Richard Rolle of Hampole. *Modern Language Review*, 18, 381–93.

——1929: A Characterization of the English Medieval Romance. *Essays and Studies*, 15, 98–121.

Febvre, Lucien 1942: *Le Problème de l'incroyance au xvie siècle: la religion de Rabelais*. Paris: Michel. Trans. Beatrice Gottlieb as *The Problem of Unbelief in the Sixteenth Century: The Religion of Rabelais* (Cambridge, MA: Harvard University, Press, 1982).

Ferguson, Arthur B. 1965: *The Articulate Citizen and the English Renaissance.* Durham NC: Duke University Press.

Ferster, Judith 1986: Interpretation and Imitation in Chaucer's Franklin's Tale. In Aers: 148–68.

Fisher, John H. 1988: Animadversions on the Text of Chaucer, 1988. *Speculum*, 63, 779–93.

Ford, Boris (ed.) 1982: *Medieval Literature: Chaucer and the Alliterative Tradition ... with an Anthology of Medieval Poems and Drama.* The New Pelican Guide to English Literature, vol. 1, pt. 1. Harmondsworth: Penguin.

Fradenburg, Louise O. 1986: The Wife of Bath's Passing Fancy. *Studies in the Age of Chaucer*, 8, 31–58.

Frank, Luanne (ed.) 1977: *Literature and the Occult: Essays in Comparative Literature.* UTA Publications in Literature. Arlington TX: University of Texas at Arlington.

Fremantle, W. H. (trans.) 1893: *The Principal Works of St Jerome.* A Select Library of Nicene and Post-Nicene Fathers of the Christian Church, vol. 6. Oxford: Parker; and New York: Christian Literature Co.

Friedman, John B. 1985: Henryson's *Testament of Cresseid* and the *Judicio Solis in Conviviis Saturni* of Simon of Couvin. *Modern Philology*, 83, 12–21.

——1986: 'He hath a thousand slayn this pestilence': The Iconography of the Plague in the Late Middle Ages. In Newman: 75–112.

Frow, John 1986: *Marxism and Literary History.* Oxford: Blackwell.

Frye, Northrop 1976: *The Secular Scripture: A Study of the Structure of Romance.* Cambridge MA: Harvard University Press.

Fyler, John M. 1987: Love and Degree in the Franklin's Tale. *Chaucer Review*, 21, 321–37.

Galbraith, V. H. (ed.) 1927: *The Anonimalle Chronicle, 1333 to 1381, from a MS Written at St Mary's Abbey, York.* Publications of the University of Manchester, No. 175; Historical series, No. 45. Manchester: Manchester University Press.

Gaylord, Alan T. 1973: The Role of Saturn in the *Knight's Tale. Chaucer Review*, 8, 172–90.

Gerould, G. H. 1926: The Social Status of Chaucer's Franklin. *PMLA*, 41, 262–79.

Gifford, D. J. 1974: Iconographical Notes towards a Definition of the Medieval Fool. *Journal of the Warburg and Courtauld Institutes*, 37, 336–42. Rpt. in P. Williams 1979: 18–35.

Given-Wilson, C. 1986: *The Royal Household and the King's Affinity: Politics and*

261

Finance in England 1360–1413. New Haven and London: Yale University Press.

Goldberg, Jonathan 1982: The Politics of Renaissance Literature: A Review Essay. *English Literary History,* 49, 514–42.

Gray, Douglas, and Stanley, E. G. (eds) 1983: *Middle English Studies Presented to Norman Davis in Honour of His Seventieth Birthday.* Oxford: Clarendon Press.

Green, Richard Firth 1980: *Poets and Princepleasers: Literature and the English Court in the Late Middle Ages.* Toronto: University of Toronto Press.

——1981: Arcite at Court. *English Language Notes,* 18, 251–7.

Greenblatt, Stephen 1982: *The Power of Forms in the English Renaissance.* Norman OK: Pilgrim Books.

Gummere, Richard M. (ed. and trans.) 1920: *Seneca: Ad Lucilium Epistolae Morales,* vol. 2. Loeb Classical Library. London: Heinemann.

Haller, Robert S. 1965: Chaucer's Squire's Tale and the Uses of Rhetoric. *Modern Philology,* 62, 285–95.

Hallissy, Margaret 1981: Poison and Infection in Chaucer's Knight's and Canon's Yeoman's Tales. *Essays in Arts and Science,* 10, 31–9.

Halverson, John 1960: Aspects of Order in the Knight's Tale. *Studies in Philology,* 57, 606–21.

Hamilton, Marie Padgett 1939: Death and Old Age in *The Pardoner's Tale. Studies in Philology,* 36, 571–6.

Hamlin, B. F. 1974: Astrology and the Wife of Bath: A Reinterpretation. *Chaucer Review,* 9, 153–65.

Hanning, R. W. 1985: Roasting a Friar, Mis-taking a Wife, and Other Acts of Textual Harassment in Chaucer's *Canterbury Tales. Studies in the Age of Chaucer,* 7, 3–21.

Hanning, Robert, and Ferrante, Joan (trans.) 1978: *The Lais of Marie de France.* New York: Dutton.

Harrison, Benjamin S. 1935: The Rhetorical Inconsistency of Chaucer's Franklin. *Studies in Philology,* 32, 55–61.

Hartung, Albert E. 1967: The Non-Comic *Merchant's Tale,* Maximianus, and the Sources. *Mediaeval Studies,* 29, 1–25.

Hatcher, Elizabeth R. 1975: Life without Death: The Old Man in Chaucer's *Pardoner's Tale. Chaucer Review,* 9, 246–52.

Heffernan, Carol Falvo 1986: That Dog Again: Melancholia Canina and Chaucer's Book of the Duchess. *Modern Philology,* 84, 185–90.

Hermann, John P., and Burke, John J. (eds) 1981: *Signs and Symbols in Chaucer's Poetry.* Fourth Alabama Symposium on English and American

Literature (University of Alabama 1977). University ALA: Alabama University Press.

Hieatt, A. Kent 1975: *Chaucer Spenser Milton: Mythopoeic Continuities and Transformations*. Montreal and London: McGill–Queen's University Press.

Hilton, Rodney Howard 1975: *The English Peasantry in the Later Middle Ages: The Ford Lectures for 1973 and Related Studies*. Oxford: Clarendon Press.

Hoepffner, Ernest 1959: The Breton Lays. In R. Loomis: 112–21.

Holmes, George 1975: *The Good Parliament*. Oxford: Clarendon Press.

Holtz, Nancy Ann 1977: The Triumph of Saturn in the *Knight's Tale*: A Clue to Chaucer's Stance against the Stars. In Frank: 159–73.

Howard, Donald R. 1972: Medieval Poems and Medieval Society, *Medievalia et Humanistica*, NS 3, 99–115.

——1976: *The Idea of the Canterbury Tales*. Berkeley: University of California Press.

Howard, Jean E. 1986: The New Historicism in Renaissance Studies. *English Literary Renaissance*, 16, 13–43.

Howell, Martha C. 1986: *Women, Production, and Partriarchy in Late Medieval Cities*. Women in Culture and Society. Chicago and London: University of Chicago Press.

Hudson, Anne (ed.) 1978: *Selections from English Wycliffite Writings*. Cambridge: Cambridge University Press.

——1981: A Lollard Sect Vocabulary? In Benskin and Samuels: 15–30. Rpt. in Hudson 1985: 165–80.

——(ed.) 1983: *English Wycliffite Sermons*, vol. 1. Oxford: Clarendon Press.

——1984: Wycliffite Prose. In Edwards: 249–70.

——1985: *Lollards and Their Books*. London and Ronceverte: Hambledon Press.

——1988: *The Premature Reformation: Wycliffite Texts and Lollard History*. Oxford: Clarendon Press.

Hulbert, James R. 1912: *Chaucer's Official Life*. Rpt. New York: Phaeton, 1970.

Hume, Kathryn 1972a: Why Chaucer Calls the Franklin's Tale a Breton Lai. *Philological Quarterly*, 51, 365–79.

——1972b: The Pagan Setting of the *Franklin's Tale* and the Sources of Dorigen's Cosmology. *Studia Neophilologica*, 44, 289–94.

Huppé, Bernard F. 1939: The A-Text of *Piers Plowman* and the Norman Wars. *PMLA*, 54, 37–64.

Infusino, Mark H., and O'Neill, Ynez Violé 1985: Arcite's Death and the New Surgery in *The Knight's Tale*. In Strohm and Heffernan: 221–30.

REFERENCES

Jackson, Stanley W. 1986: *Melancholia and Depression: From Hippocratic Times to Modern Times*. New Haven and London: Yale University Press.

Jacobs, Kathryn 1985: The Marriage Contract of the *Franklin's Tale*: The Remaking of Society. *Chaucer Review*, 20, 132–43.

Jameson, Frederic 1972: *The Prison-House of Language: A Critical Account of Structuralism and Russian Formalism*. Princeton: Princeton University Press.

——1981: *The Political Unconscious: Narrative as a Socially Symbolic Act*. London: Methuen.

Jauss, Hans Robert 1979: The Alterity and Modernity of Medieval Literature. *New Literary History*, 10, 181–229.

——1982: Literary History as a Challenge to Literary Theory. In his *Toward an Aesthetic of Reception*, trans. Timothy Bahti. Brighton: Harvester, 3–45.

Jeffrey, David Lyle 1984: Chaucer and Wyclif: Biblical Hermeneutic and Literary Theory in the XIVth Century. In Jeffrey (ed.), *Chaucer and Scriptural Tradition*, Ottawa: University of Ottawa Press, 109–40.

Johnston, Grahame 1972: Chaucer and the Breton Lays. In Maslen: 230–41.

——1974: The Breton Lays in Middle English. In Turville-Petre and Martin: 151–61.

Jones, W. R. 1972: Lollards and Images. *Journal of the History of Ideas*, 34, 27–50.

Jordan, Robert M. 1963: The Non-Dramatic Disunity of the *Merchant's Tale*. *PMLA*, 78, 293–9. Rpt. in Jordan 1967: 132–51.

——1967: *Chaucer and the Shape of Creation: The Aesthetic Possibilities of Inorganic Structure*. Cambridge MA: Harvard University Press.

Kahrl, Stanley J. 1973: Chaucer's Squire's Tale and the Decline of Chivalry. *Chaucer Review*, 7, 194–209.

Kean, P. M. 1972: *Chaucer and the Making of English Poetry*, vol. 2: *The Art of Narrative*. London and Boston: Routledge and Kegan Paul.

Kee, Kenneth 1975: Illusion and Reality in Chaucer's Franklin's Tale. *English Studies in Canada*, 1, 1–12.

Keen, Maurice 1973: *England in the Later Middle Ages: A Political History*. London: Methuen.

——(ed.) 1986: Wyclif, the Bible, and Transubstantiation. In Kenny: 1–16.

Kenny, Anthony 1985: *Wyclif*. Past Masters. Oxford: Oxford University Press.

——1986: *Wyclif in His Times*. Oxford: Clarendon Press.

Kittredge, George Lyman 1915: *Chaucer and His Poetry*. 55th Anniversary Edition with an Introduction by B. J. Whiting. Cambridge MA: Harvard University Press, 1970.

Klibansky, Raymond, Panofsky, Erwin, and Saxl, Fritz 1964: *Saturn and Melancholy*. New York: Basic Books.

Knight, Stephen 1969: Rhetoric and Poetry in the *Franklin's Tale*. *Chaucer Review*, 4, 14–30.

——1977: Politics and Chaucer's Poetry. In Knight and Wilding: 169–92.

——1980a: Chaucer and the Sociology of Literature. *Studies in the Age of Chaucer*, 2, 15–51.

——1980b: Ideology in 'The Franklin's Tale'. *Parergon*, 28, 3–35.

Knight, Stephen, and Wilding, Michael (eds) 1977: *The Radical Reader*. Sydney: Wild and Woolley.

Kolve, V. A. 1984: *Chaucer and the Imagery of Narrative: The First Five Canterbury Tales*. London: Arnold.

Kurath, H., Kuhn, S. M., et al. (eds) 1954–: *Middle English Dictionary*. 8 vols published. Ann Arbor: Michigan University Press.

Lawler, Traugott 1985: The Chaucer Library 'Jankyn's Book of Wikked Wives.' *Chaucer Newsletter*, 7: 1, 1–4.

Lawton, David 1977: English Poetry and English Society 1370–1400. In Knight and Wilding: 145–68.

——1985: *Chaucer's Narrators*. Chaucer Studies, 13. Cambridge: Brewer.

——1987: Chaucer's Two Ways. *Studies in the Age of Chaucer*, 9, 3–40.

Leach, MacEdward (ed.) 1961: *Studies in Medieval Literature in Honor of Professor Albert Croll Baugh*. Philadelphia: University of Philadelphia Press; and London: Oxford University Press.

Leff, Gordon 1967: *Heresy in the Later Middle Ages: The Relation of Heterodoxy to Dissent c.1250–c.1450*. 2 vols. Manchester: Manchester University Press; and New York: Barnes and Noble.

Le Goff, Jacques. 1974: Mentalities: A History of Ambiguities. Trans. David Denby in Le Goff and Nora: 166–80.

Le Goff, Jacques, and Nora, Pierre (eds) 1985: *Constructing the Past: Essays in Historical Methodology*. Cambridge: Cambridge University, Press; and Paris: Editions de la Maison des Sciences de l'Homme. Originally published in French as *Faire de l'histoire* (Paris: Gallimard, 1976), vol. 3: *Nouveaux objets*.

Leitch, Vincent B. 1983: *Deconstructive Criticism: An Advanced Introduction*. London: Hutchinson.

Lester, G. A. 1982: Chaucer's Knight and the Medieval Tournament. *Neophilologus*, 66, 460–8.

Lewis, C. S. 1936: *The Allegory of Love: A Study in Medieval Tradition*. London: Oxford University Press.

Lewis, Robert E. (ed. and trans.) 1978: *Lotario dei Sengi (Pope Innocent III): De Miseria Condicionis Humane*. The Chaucer Library. Athens GA: Georgia University Press.

Longhurst, Derek 1982: 'Not for all time, but for an Age': An Approach to Shakespeare Studies. In Widdowson: 150–63.

Loomis, Dorothy Bethurum 1968: Saturn in Chaucer's 'Knight's Tale'. In Esch: 149–61.

Loomis, Laura Hibbard 1941: Chaucer and the Breton Lays of the Auchinleck Ms. *Studies in Philology*, 38, 14–33.

Loomis, Roger S. 1940: Was Chaucer a Laodicean? In C. Brown: 129–48.

——(ed.) 1959: *Arthurian Literature in the Middle Ages: A Collaborative History*. Oxford: Clarendon Press.

Lowes, John Livingston 1914: The Loveres Maladye of Hereos. *Modern Philology*, 11, 491–546.

Luengo, Anthony E. 1978: Magic and Illusion in *The Franklin's Tale*. *Journal of English and Germanic Philogy*, 77, 1–16.

Lumiansky, R. M. 1955: *Of Sondry Folk: The Dramatic Principle in the Canterbury Tales*. Austin TX: University of Texas Press.

McCall, John P. 1979: *Chaucer among the Gods: The Poetics of Classical Myth*. University Park and London: Pennsylvania University Press.

McFarlane, K. B. 1952: *John Wycliffe and the Beginnings of English Nonconformity*. London: English Universities Press.

——1972: *Lancastrian Kings and Lollard Knights*. Oxford: Oxford University Press.

McGann, Jerome J. 1985a: *The Beauty of Inflections: Literary Investigations in Historical Method and Theory*. Oxford: Clarendon Press.

——(ed.) 1985b: *Historical Studies and Literary Criticism*. Madison WI and London: University of Wisconsin Press.

McKisack, May 1959: *The Fourteenth Century, 1307–1399*. Oxford History of England, vol. 5. Oxford: Clarendon Press.

Manly, John Matthews 1926: *Some New Light on Chaucer: Lectures Delivered at the Lowell Institute*. London: Bell.

Manly, John Matthews, and Rickert, Edith 1940: *The Text of the Canterbury Tales: Studied on the Basis of All Known Manuscripts*. 8 vols. Chicago and London: University of Chicago Press.

Mann, Jill 1973: *Chaucer and Medieval Estates Satire: The Literature of Social Classes and the General Prologue to the Canterbury Tales*. London: Cambridge University Press.

——1982: Chaucerian Themes and Style in the *Franklin's Tale*. In Ford: 133–53.

——1983: Parents and Children in the 'Canterbury Tales'. In Boitani and Torti: 165–83.

Martin, Wallace 1986: *Recent Theories of Narrative*. Ithaca and London: Cornell University Press.

Martines, Lauro 1985: *Society and History in English Renaissance Verse*. Oxford: Blackwell.

Maslen, K. I. D. (ed.) 1972: *Proceedings and Papers of the Fourteenth Congress of the Australasian Universities' Language and Literature Association*. University of Otago (1972). Dunedin, New Zealand: AULLA.

Matthews, William 1956: Eustache Deschamps and Chaucer's 'Merchant's Tale'. *Modern Language Review*, 51, 217–20.

——1974: The Wife of Bath and All Her Sect. *Viator*, 5, 413–43.

Middleton, Anne 1978: The Idea of Public Poetry in the Reign of Richard II. *Speculum*, 53, 94–114.

——1980: Chaucer's 'New Men' and the Good of Literature in the Canterbury Tales. In Said: 15–56.

Miller, Clarence H., and Bosse, Roberta Bux 1971: Chaucer's Pardoner and the Mass. *Chaucer Review*, 6, 171–84.

Miller, Robert P. (ed.) 1977: *Chaucer: Sources and Backgrounds*. New York: Oxford University Press.

Millichap, Joseph R. 1974: Transubstantiation in the *Pardoner's Tale*. *Bulletin of the Rocky Mountain Modern Language Association*, 28, 102–8.

Minnis, A. J. 1982: *Chaucer and Pagan Antiquity*. Chaucer Studies, 8. Cambridge: Brewer; and Totowa NJ: Rowman and Littlefield.

Mitchell, Jerome, and Provost, William (eds) 1973: *Chaucer the Love Poet*. Athens GA: University of Georgia Press.

Montrose, Louis 1986: Renaissance Literary Studies and the Subject of History. *English Literary Renaissance*, 16, 5–12.

Morgan, Gerald 1977: A Defence of Dorigen's Complaint. *Medium Aevum*, 46, 77–97.

Movshovitz, Howard P. 1977: The Trickster Myth and Chaucer's Pardoner. Dissertation, University of Colorado.

Muscatine, Charles 1957: *Chaucer and the French Tradition: A Study in Style and Meaning*. Berkeley and Los Angeles: University of California Press.

——1972: *Poetry and Crisis in the Age of Chaucer*. University of Notre Dame Ward-Phillips Lectures in English Language and Literature, vol. 4. Notre Dame IN and London: University of Notre Dame Press.

Neaman, Judith S. 1975: *Suggestion of the Devil: The Origins of Madness*. New York: Anchor Press/Doubleday.

Neuse, Richard 1962: The Knight: The First Mover in Chaucer's Human

Comedy. *University of Toronto Quarterly*, 31, 299–315. Rpt. in Burrow 1969: 242–63.

Newman, Francis X. (ed.) 1986: *Social Unrest in the Late Middle Ages*. Papers of the Fifteenth Annual Conference of the Center for Medieval and Early Renaissance Studies. Medieval and Renaissance Texts and Studies, vol. 39. Binghamton, New York: Center for Medieval and Early Renaissance Studies.

Newton, Stella Mary 1980: *Fashion in the Age of the Black Prince: A Study of the Years 1340–1365*. Woodbridge: Boydell and Brewer; and Totowa NJ: Rowman and Littlefield.

Nichols, Robert E., Jr. 1967: The Pardoner's Ale and Cake. *PMLA*, 82, 498–504.

Norbrook, David 1984: *Poetry and Politics in the English Renaissance*. London: Routledge and Kegan Paul.

Norris, Dorothy Macbride 1933: Chaucer's *Pardoner's Tale* and Flanders. *PMLA*, 48, 636–41.

North, J. D. 1988: *Chaucer's Universe*. Oxford: Clarendon Press.

Olson, Paul A. 1986: *The Canterbury Tales and the Good Society*. Princeton: Princeton University Press.

Owen, Charles A. 1953: The Crucial Passages in Five of the Canterbury Tales: A Study in Irony and Symbol. *Journal of English and Germanic Philology*, 52, 294–311.

Owst, G. R. 1961: *Literature and Pulpit in Medieval England: A Neglected Chapter in the History of English Letters and of the English People* (2nd edn). Oxford: Blackwell.

Pace, George B. 1965: The Scorpion of Chaucer's *Merchant's Tale*. *Modern Language Quarterly*, 26, 369–74.

Parr, Johnstone 1945: The Date and Revision of Chaucer's *Knight's Tale*. *PMLA*, 60, 307–14.

——1954: Chaucer's *Cherles Rebellyng*. *Modern Language Notes*, 69, 393–4.

Parry, Adam (ed.) 1971: *The Making of Homeric Verse: The Collected Papers of Milman Parry*. Oxford: Clarendon Press.

Parry, Milman 1936: The Historical Method in Literary Criticism. In A. Parry 1971: 408–13.

Patterson, Lee 1983: 'For the Wyves love of Bathe': Feminine Rhetoric and Poetic Resolution in the *Roman de la Rose* and the *Canterbury Tales*. *Speculum*, 58, 656–95.

——1987: *Negotiating the Past: The Historical Understanding of Medieval Literature*. Madison WI: University of Wisconsin Press.

Pearcy, Roy J. 1973: Chaucer's Franklin and the Literary Vavasour. *Chaucer Review*, 8, 33–59.

Pearsall, Derek A. 1964: The Squire as Story-Teller, *University of Toronto Quarterly*, 34, 89–92.

——1985: *The Canterbury Tales*. Unwin Critical Library. London: Allen and Unwin.

——1986: Chaucer's Poetry and Its Modern Commentators: The Necessity of History. In Aers: 123–47.

Peck, Russell 1967: Sovereignty and the Two Worlds of the Franklin's Tale. *Chaucer Review*, 1, 253–71.

——1986: Social Conscience and the Poets. In Newman: 113–48.

Perroy, Edouard (ed.) 1952: *The Anglo-French Negotiations at Bruges 1374 –1377*. Camden Miscellany, vol. 19. Camden Third Series, vol. 80. London: Royal Historical Society.

Pollard, Alfred W. (ed.) 1903: *Fifteenth Century Prose and Verse: An English Garner*. London: Constable.

Postan, M. M. 1942: Some Social Consequences of the Hundred Years' War. *English Historical Review*, 12, 1–12.

Pratt, Robert A. 1961: The Development of the Wife of Bath. In Leach: 45–79.

——1962: Jankyn's Book of Wikked Wyves: Medieval Antimatrimonial Propaganda in the Universities. *Annuale Medievale*, 3, 5–27.

——1966: Chaucer and the Hand That Fed Him. *Speculum*, 41, 619–42.

Reidy, John 1977: The Education of Chaucer's Duke Theseus. In Scholler: 391–408.

Richardson, Janette 1970: *Blameth Nat Me: A Study of Imagery in Chaucer's Fabliaux*. Studies in English Literature, vol. 58. The Hague and Paris: Mouton.

Riley, H. T. (ed.) 1863–4: *Thomae Walsingham, quondam monachi S. Albani, Historia Anglicana*, 2 vols. Rerum Britannicarum medii aevi scriptores. London: HMSO.

Robbins, F. E. (ed. and trans.) 1956: Ptolemy, *Tetrabiblos*. Loeb Classical Library. Cambridge MA: Harvard University Press; and London: Heinemann.

Robertson, D. W., Jr 1951: Historical Criticism. In Alan S. Downer (ed.) *English Institute Essays 1950*. New York: Columbia University Press, 3–31. Rpt. in Robertson 1980c: 1–20.

——1962: *A Preface to Chaucer: Studies in Medieval Perspectives*. Princeton: Princeton University Press.

——1974: Chaucer's Franklin and His Tale. *Costerus*, NS 1, 1–26; rpt. in Robertson 1980c: 273–90.

——1980a: 'And For My Land Thus Hastow Mordred Me?': Land Tenure, the Cloth Industry, and the Wife of Bath. *Chaucer Review*, 14, 403–20.

——1980b: Author's Introduction. In Robertson 1980c: xi–xx.

——1980c: *Essays in Medieval Culture*. Princeton: Princeton University Press.

——1981: Simple Signs from Everyday Life in Chaucer. In Hermann and Burke: 12–26.

——1986: Chaucer and the Economic and Social Consequences of the Plague. In Newman: 49–74.

Rose, Donald M. (ed.) 1981: *New Perspectives in Chaucer Criticism*. Essays presented at the Second International Congress of the New Chaucer Society (New Orleans) 1980, with one new essay. Norman OK: Pilgrim Books.

Rosenburg, Bruce A. 1971: The 'Cherry-Tree Carol' and the *Merchant's Tale*. *Chaucer Review*, 5, 264–76.

Rowland, Beryl 1979: Chaucer's Idea of the Pardoner. *Chaucer Review*, 14, 140–54.

Ruggiers, Paul G., and Baker, Donald C. (eds) 1979–: *A Variorum Edition of the Works of Geoffrey Chaucer*. Norman OK: University of Oklahoma Press.

Russell, P. E. 1955: *The English Intervention in Spain and Portugal in the Time of Edward III and Richard II*. Oxford: Clarendon Press.

Said, Edward (ed.) 1980: *Literature and Society: Selected Papers from the English Institute*. NS 3 (1978). Baltimore and London: Johns Hopkins University Press.

Salter, Elizabeth 1983: *Fourteenth-Century English Poetry: Contexts and Readings*. Oxford: Clarendon Press.

Sands, Donald B (ed.) 1966: *Middle English Verse Romances*. New York: Holt, Rinehart and Winston.

Saul, Nigel 1983: The Social Status of Chaucer's Franklin: A Reconsideration. *Medium Aevum* 52, 10–26.

Scattergood, V. J. 1981: Chaucer and the French War: Sir Thopas and Melibee. In Burgess: 287–96.

Scattergood, V. J., and Sherborne, J. W. (eds) 1983: *English Court Culture in the Later Middle Ages*. London: Duckworth.

Scheps, Walter 1977: Chaucer's Theseus and the *Knight's Tale*. *Leeds Studies in English*, NS 9, 19–34.

Schiff, Hilda (ed.) 1977: *Contemporary Approaches to English Studies*. London: Heinemann Educational Books for the English Association; and New

York: Barnes and Noble.

Schlauch, Margaret 1956: *English Medieval Literature and Its Social Foundations.* Polska Akademia Nauk Komitet Neofilologiczny. Warsaw: Panstwowe Wydawnictwo Naukowe.

Schmidt, A. V. C. 1969: The Tragedy of Arcite: A Reconsideration of the *Knight's Tale. Essays in Criticism,* 19, 107–17.

Scholler, Harald 1977: *The Epic in Medieval Society: Aesthetic and Moral Values.* Tübingen: Niemeyer.

Schweitzer, Edward C. 1981: Fate and Freedom in the Knight's Tale. *Studies in the Age of Chaucer,* 3, 13–45.

Seaman, David M. 1986: 'The Wordes of the Frankeleyn to the Squier': An Interruption. *English Language Notes,* 24, 12–18.

Seymour, M. C. et al. (eds) 1975: *On the Properties of Things: John Trevisa's Translation of Bartholomaeus Anglicus De Proprietatibus Rerum.* 2 vols. Oxford: Clarendon Press.

Sherborne, J. W. 1983: Aspects of English Court Culture in the Later Fourteenth Century. In Scattergood and Sherborne: 1–27.

Shumaker, Wayne 1951: Alisoun in Wander-Land: A Study in Chaucer's Mind and Literary Method. *English Literary History,* 18, 77–89.

Silverman, Albert H. 1953: Sex and Money in Chaucer's Shipman's Tale. *Philological Quarterly,* 32, 329–36.

Sledd, James 1947: Dorigen's Complaint. *Modern Philology,* 45, 36–45.

Smithers, G. V. 1953: Story-Patterns in Some Breton Lays. *Medium Aevum,* 22, 61–92.

Spearing, A. C. (ed.) 1966: *The Knight's Tale from the Canterbury Tales by Geoffrey Chaucer.* Cambridge: Cambridge University Press.

Specht, Henrik 1981: *Chaucer's Franklin in the Canterbury Tales: The Social and Literary Background of a Chaucerian Character.* Publications of the Department of English, University of Copenhagen, vol. 10. Copenhagen: Akademisk Forlag.

Stevens, John 1961: *Music and Poetry in the Early Tudor Court.* London: Methuen.

Stevens, Martin, and Falvey, Kathleen 1982: Substance, Accident and Transformations: A Reading of the *Pardoner's Tale. Chaucer Review,* 17, 142–58.

Stillwell, Gardiner 1948: John Gower and the Last Years of Edward III. *Studies in Philology,* 45, 454–71.

Stockton, Eric W. 1961: The Deadliest Sin in *The Pardoner's Tale. Tennessee Studies in Literature,* 6, 47–59.

Stockton, John (trans.) 1962: *The Major Latin Works of John Gower: The Voice of One Crying and the Tripartite Chronicle*. Seattle: University of Washington Press.

Storm, Melvin 1984: Chaucer's Franklin and Distraint of Knighthood. *Chaucer Review*, 19, 162–8.

Strachey, J. (ed.) 1767–77: *Rotuli Parliamentorum: ut et petitiones, et placita in Parliamento...* (collected and arranged by R. Blyke et al.) 6 vols. London: printed in accordance with an order of the House of Lords.

Strohm, Paul 1977: Chaucer's Audience. *Literature and History*, 5, 26–41.

——1979: Form and Social Statement in *Confessio Amantis* and *The Canterbury Tales*. *Studies in the Age of Chaucer*, 1, 17–40.

Strohm, Paul, and Heffernan, Thomas J. (eds) 1985: *Reconstructing Chaucer*. *Studies in the Age of Chaucer* Proceedings, No. 1 (York 1984). Knoxville: New Chaucer Society / University of Tennessee.

Tatlock, John S. P. 1916: Chaucer and Wyclif. *Modern Philology*, 14, 257–68.

Tatlock, John S. P., and Kennedy, Arthur G. 1927: *A Concordance to the Complete Works of Geoffrey Chaucer and to the Romaunt of the Rose*. Washington: Carnegie Institution. Rpt. Gloucester MA: Peter Smith, 1963.

Thomas, Keith Vivian 1971: *Religion and the Decline of Magic: Studies in Popular Beliefs in Sixteenth and Seventeenth Century England*. London: Weidenfeld and Nicolson.

Thompson, E. P. 1978: The Poverty of Theory: Or, an Orrery of Errors. In his *The Poverty of Theory and Other Essays*. London: Merlin Press, 193–397.

Thorndike, Lynn 1934: *A History of Magic and Experimental Science*. Vol. 3: *Fourteenth and Fifteenth Centuries*. History of Science Society Publications, NS 4. New York: Columbia University Press.

Tinkle, Theresa 1987: Saturn of the Several Faces: A Survey of the Medieval Mythographic Traditions. *Viator*, 18, 289–307.

Tupper, Frederick 1914: The Pardoner's Tavern. *Journal of English and Germanic Philology*, 13, 553–65.

——1941: The Pardoner's Tale. In Bryan and Dempster: 415–38.

Turville-Petre, Gabriel, and Martin, John Stanley (eds) 1974: *Iceland and the Mediaeval World: Studies in Honor of Ian Maxwell*. Victoria, Australia, Organising Committee for Publishing a Volume in Honour of Professor Maxwell.

Turville-Petre, Thorlac 1982: The Lament for Sir John Berkeley. *Speculum*, 57, 332–9.

Urry, William 1988: *Christopher Marlowe and Canterbury*. With an introduction by Andrew Butcher. London: Faber.

Utley, Francis Lee 1965: Robertsonianism Redivivus. *Romance Philology*, 19, 250–60.

Wallace, David 1983: Chaucer and Boccaccio's Early Writings. In Boitani 1983: 141–62.

Weese, Walter E. 1948: 'Vengeance and Pleyn Correccioun'. *Modern Language Notes*, 63, 331–3.

Welsford, Enid 1935: *The Fool: His Social and Literary History*. London; Faber.

Wenzel, Siegfried (ed.) 1978: *Medieval and Renaissance Studies, Number 7*. Proceedings of the Southeastern Institute of Medieval and Renaissance Studies (1975). Chapel Hill: University of North Carolina Press.

——1982: The Wisdom of the Fool. In Benson and Wenzel: 225–40.

White, Gertrude M. 1965: 'Hoolynesse or Dotage': The Merchant's January. Philological Quarterly, 44, 397–404.

White, Hayden 1973: *Metahistory: The Historical Imagination in Nineteenth-Century Europe*. Baltimore and London: Johns Hopkins University Press.

——1978: *Tropics of Discourse: Essays in Cultural Criticism*. Baltimore and London: Johns Hopkins University Press.

Whiting, Bartlett Jere 1934: *Chaucer's Use of Proverbs*. Harvard Studies in Comparative Literature, vol. 11. Cambridge MA: Harvard University Press.

——1941: The Wife of Bath's Prologue. In Bryan and Dempster: 207–22.

Whiting, Bartlett Jere, with Whiting, Helen Wescott 1968: *Proverbs, Sentences, and Proverbial Phrases from English Writings Mainly before 1500*. Cambridge MA: Belknap Press of Harvard University Press; and London: Oxford University Press.

Widdowson, Peter (ed.) 1982: *Re-Reading English*. London: Methuen.

Wilkins, Ernest H. 1957: Descriptions of Pagan Divinities from Petrarch to Chaucer. *Speculum*, 32, 511–22.

Willeford, William 1969: *The Fool and His Sceptre: A Study in Clowns and Jesters and Their Audience*. London: Arnold.

Williams, George 1965: *A New View of Chaucer*. Durham NC: Duke University Press.

Williams, Paul V. A. (ed.) 1979: *The Fool and the Trickster: Studies in Honour of Enid Welsford*. Cambridge: Brewer; and Totowa NJ: Rowman and Littlefield.

Williams, Raymond 1960: *Culture and Society 1780–1950*. London: Chatto and Windus.

——1977: Literature *in* Society. In Schiff: 24–37.

Wimsatt, James I. 1973: Chaucer and the Canticle of Canticles. In Mitchell and Provost: 66–90.

Windeatt, Barry 1979: Gesture in Chaucer. *Medievalia et Humanistica*, NS 9, 143–61.

Wise, Boyd Ashby 1911: *The Influence of Statius upon Chaucer*. Dissertation, Johns Hopkins University, 1905. Baltimore: Furst.

Wood, Chauncey 1970: *Chaucer and the Country of the Stars: Poetic Uses of Astrological Imagery*. Princeton: Princeton University Press.

Wood–Legh, K. L. 1928: The Franklin. *Review of English Studies*, 4, 145–51.

Wurtele, Douglas 1977: The Figure of Solomon in Chaucer's *Merchant's Tale*. *Revue de l'Université d'Ottawa/University of Ottawa Quarterly*, 47, 478–87.

Yeager, R. F. 1984: Aspects of Gluttony in Chaucer and Gower. *Studies in Philology*, 81, 42–55.

Yoder, Emily K. 1977: Chaucer and the 'Breton' Lay. *Chaucer Review*, 12, 74–7.

Zacher, Christian K. 1976: *Curiosity and Pilgrimage: The Literature of Discovery in Fourteenth-Century England*. Baltimore and London: Johns Hopkins University Press.

Index

audience 4, 7, 21–2, 106, 175, 241, 246–7, 253; benefactors 19; biography 243; *Canterbury Tales* 207; Christian radical 14, 20–1, 65; Christian values 60; circle 61; composition 148, 196, 206, 225, 252–3, as clerk 146; as compiler 146; as preacher 146; method of 4, 8, 146; condemnation of 246; contemporaries 205–6; counsellor 247; court 246; court poet 156; descriptive habits 9; detachment 6; engagement 19, 252; esquire, armigerous 62; false consciousness 250; father of and Lyons 196; General Prologue and 60; genius of 146; historian 250; historical analysis 209; historical moment 20; historical situation 26; imagination 19–20; 252; indirection 19; intellectual biography 19; irony 5, 252; jester 156; life 243; career 60–5; literary techniques 243, 252; methods of composition 4, 6; moral concerns 251; narrative art 58; narrator 5; novelty 20; patron 246–7; patronage 156; patrons 19; perception 250–1; place in society 206; poet 244; poetic transformation 8; political life 240; political position 243; profession 6; psychological imbalance 18–19; radical reform 158; realism 22;

reflexivity 20; rejection of 246; relativism 6; satire 140, 141; Saturn as metaphor 250–1; Scogan 224; self 244; Seneca 247; social position 243; social standing 61; spiritual concerns 251; techniques, novelty 247, variety 247; *The Riverside* 206; vintner's family 117; wine merchant's son 61, 62; works, dating of 146–51; world 7; *Wreched Engendrynge of Mankynde* 147

Chaucer, his patron, John of Gaunt 226

Chaucer as Pardoner 246

Cher 118

Cheshire 225

Cheshire Rising of 1393 224

chivalry 13, 55, 59–61, 63–4, 70, 73–4, 205–6, 229, 231, 241–3, 247–8, 250–1

Christ, body and blood 128–30, 150, 153, 245

Christendom 237, 241–2, 245; unification of 211

Christian: glosses 6; practice 177, 245–6; society 250; values 60, 106, 114, 245–7

Christianity 14, 20–1, 65, 241

chroniclers 207

chronicles 253

Chronique des quatre premiers Valois 122

Church 18, 26, 36–7, 115, 120–3, 145, 157, 195, 200, 241–6; authority 245, 251; crisis 120; English 119; moral, spiritual and

INDEX

190; Ymeneus 179; youth
160, 180
merchants 158, 194–5; English
193; Italian 119
Merciless Parliament 208–9, 238
Meun, Jean de, *Romance of the Rose*
24
Miller's Tale 53, 91, 181–2
ministers, clerical 195
mobility 250
money viii, 216, 241
Montague 118
Montlucon 118
Moor End, building at 201
Mortimer, Sir Thomas 239
murder 226, 250
Muscatine 7, 11, 14
mutilation viii, 215

narrative 15–16, 58, 77, 183,
207, 224–5, 238, 244, 249
narrator 5, 23, 156, 164, 170,
231, 243–4, 249
nationalism 2
nature 34–6, 235, 241, 248
Navarre 207; king of 122
Neville, John, chamberlain 118,
203; steward of royal household
203
New Critics 5–6, 8, 14
New Forest, building at 201
New Historicism 16
nobility, English 207–8
Normandy 117
Nottingham 209

oaths 128, 138, 145, 151, 241,
248; allegiance 209
obedience 102, 210, 238
occult 241

offices of state 209
old age 177–8, 188, 202, 231
order 205, 241, 247–8
orthodoxy 242
Ovid 24, 30; *Metamorphoses* 54
Ovidius Moralizatus 213

pagan world 179, 248
Papacy 18, 114, 119–22, 138,
245, 252; Garnier, representative
119; provisions 119;
representative 245;
reservations 119; schism 211,
237, 251
Papal taxation 148
paradise 19
paradox 5, 105
Pardoner 18–19, 32, 245–6, 251;
cynical apologist 246; fool
Plate 3, 137, 143; fool, psalters
131; fools, mystery plays
131–2; General Prologue 131,
136; hypocrite 143; mocking
fool 246; preacher 246;
spiritual emptiness 246;
trickster 131
Pardoner's Prologue: audience
246; avarice 156; cake and ale
127; parody 246; pilgrims
144; preaching 144; rhetoric
136; sermon 246; travesty
246
Pardoner's Prologue and Tale
114–56 *passim*, 244–6; aesthetics
246; ambition 246; audience
131, 144, 154–5, 245; avarice
115, 119, 124, 137, 148, 155–6;
betrayal 246; Bible 124,
Proverbs 125; biblical glosses
156; blasphemy 141; blood

288